VINCENT O'BRIEN

The Master of Ballydoyle

Other books by Raymond Smith include:

Under The Blue Flag (1980)
The Poker Kings of Las Vegas (1982)
Charles J. Haughey: The Survivor (1983)
Garret: The Enigma (1985)
Haughey and O'Malley: The Quest for Power (1986)

VINCENT O'BRIEN

The Master of Ballydoyle

RAYMOND SMITH

First published in Great Britain in 1990 by
Virgin Books
A division of W. H. Allen & Co Ltd
26 Grand Union Centre
338 Ladbroke Grove
London W10 5AH

Cataloguing in Publication Data available from the British Library

ISBN 1 85227 143 4

Set in Linotron Palatino by
Input Typesetting Ltd, London

Printed and bound by
Mackays of Chatham Ltd, Chatham, Kent.

Contents

Author's Note xi
Foreword by Lester Piggott xv
Acknowledgements xvii

PART ONE – THE HINGE OF DESTINY
1. 'IT HAS GOT TO BE VINCENT' 3
2. LESTER ON THE MASTER 10
3. A 'CRAZY' MOMENT AT KEENELAND 21
4. 'WHAT IS TO BE, WILL BE' 30
5. THE FIFTH OF SEVEN SONS 39
6. 'A THOROUGH GENTLEMAN' 52
7. A LEGACY FROM AMERICA 61
8. A DISEASE CALLED 'CHELTENHAMITIS' 74
9. THE RAKE'S PROGRESS TO TRIPLE TRIUMPH 87
10. NO ONE TOLD MARTIN NOT TO TRY 103
11. NIGHTS AT THE ADELPHI WITH
    'MINCEMEAT' JOE 119
12. 'A MASTER OF HIS ART' 127
13. WHEN VINCENT FIRST LOST HIS LICENCE 134
14. VINCENT OFFERS NATIONAL WINNER FOR
    £2500 149

PART TWO – IN THE SHADOW OF SLIEVENAMON
15. THE MOVE TO BALLYDOYLE 161
16. THE CHEMISTRY OF LOVE 170
17. DAYS OF GLADNESS AND BALLYMOSS 177

18. THE DAY IT ALL TURNED SOUR 189
19. CURRAGH CROWDS CHANT 'WE WANT
    VINCENT' 200
20. PICKING UP THE THREADS 205
21. 'I PUT SIR IVOR BEFORE NIJINSKY' 212
22. PIGGOTT ON NIJINSKY'S ARC FAILURE 220
23. 'LET THE PILOT DO THE FLYING' 236
24. THE FLOATING COCKTAIL PARTY 250
25. EDDERY ON EL GRAN SENOR'S EPSOM
    DEFEAT 259
26. DAVID WALKS AWAY FROM IT ALL 272
27. A WONDERFUL FATHER 286

EPILOGUE 294

APPENDICES:
1. *Big Race Successes at Home* 298
2. *Big Race Successes Abroad*
        England 303
        France 307
        USA 307
3. *Year-by-Year Irish Record* 308
4. *Memorable Seasons in Britain* 310

BIBLIOGRAPHY 311

INDEX 312

Illustrations

Between pages 44 and 45

Vincent O'Brien's parents, Dan and Kathleen
Vincent's first school, in Churchtown
The school register showing Vincent's name
The class of 1923
Dinny Fisher, one of Vincent's schoolmates, in 1988
Vincent's only sister, Pauline Fogarty
Clashganniff House, Vincent's childhood home, as it is today
Vincent aged 17, with his brother Dermot
On an Alpine holiday: Vincent with Martin Molony and the late Jim Blake
Dan O'Brien chatting with Jimmy Canty, father of Curragh trainer Phil Canty
Dan O'Brien leading in Hallowment on 7 November 1940 after the horse had won the November Plate at Limerick
Aubrey Brabazon leading over the last hurdle on Hatton's Grace to win the Champion Hurdle for the first time in 1949
Martin Molony shows his style as a jump jockey
Martin Molony powering Hatton's Grace home to beat Knock Hard in the 1949 Irish Cesarewitch
Molony winning the race again in 1950 for Vincent O'Brien

Between pages 108 and 109

Vincent at the Ballsbridge Sales in 1950
Vincent with his brothers Dermot and Phonsie at
     Limerick in 1950
Jackie O'Brien with his point-to-point winner, China
     Cottage
Dr 'Otto' Vaughan with Cottage Rake after winning at
     Leopardstown
Noel O'Brien at The Galloping Field at Churchtown
The Galloping Field, now used for cattle grazing
Hatton's Grace coming at the last to beat National Spirit
     in the 1950 Champion Hurdle: Martin Molony
     challenges on Harlech
Mrs Moya Keogh leads in Hatton's Grace with Aubrey
     Brabazon up
Martin Molony in 1989
Michael O'Hehir, the famous commentator
Vincent and Jacqueline on their wedding day
Vincent the family man
Vincent displaying the catch of the day
Vincent at home with Jacqueline and four of the five
     children
'Mincemeat Joe' Griffin
Miss Dorothy Paget, who bought Solford from Vincent
     O'Brien's father

Between pages 172 and 173

T. B. Burns
Tim Molony
Lester Piggott taking the 1970 Epsom Derby on Nijinsky
Lester on Nijinsky with Gyr immediately behind
Lester being led in on The Minstrel after winning the
     1977 Irish Derby
Lester's triumph on Alleged over Balmarino in the 1977
     Prix de l'Arc de Triomphe
Golden Fleece (Pat Eddery up) wins the 1982 Epsom
     Derby with consummate ease
The 'wonder colt', El Gran Senor, cuts down Chief Singer
     and Lear Fan in the 1984 English 2,000 Guineas

Secreto wins by a short head over El Gran Senor in the
    Epsom Derby
Ballydoyle House, home of Vincent and Jacqueline
    O'Brien
The stables area and gallops at Ballydoyle
Australian Scobie Breasley, who scored memorable
    victories on Ballymoss in the 1958 season
Pat Eddery, who succeeded Lester Piggott as first jockey
    to the Ballydoyle stable
Vincent O'Brien and Robert Sangster
The Keeneland sales auditorium
Sheikh Mohammed pictured in the desert with his pet
    falcon
American trainer, D. Wayne Lukas

Between pages 268 and 269

Law Society (Pat Eddery up) winning the 1985 Irish
    Derby
Caerleon, the 1983 French Derby winner, with Bob
    Lanigan
John Magnier, the Coolmore boss
Be My Guest
Vincent O'Brien and his son Charles look at a yearling
    in the barn area at Keeneland
Vincent displays his total attention to detail
David O'Brien and his Australian-born wife, Catherine,
    on their wedding day
One of David's outstanding triumphs as a trainer, the
    victory of the filly Triptych over the colts in the 1985
    Irish 2,000 Guineas
Vincent O'Brien and his brother Phonsie chatting with
    President Hillery at Punchestown
Vincent with the Australian Prime Minister Bob Hawke
    in October 1987
Vincent with Irish Racing Board Chairman, Dr Michael
    Smurfit
Vincent with actor John Forsythe at the Curragh on
    Budweiser Irish Derby Day 1989
Charles O'Brien after receiving the Bollinger 'Irish

Trainer of the Year' Award on behalf of his father in December 1988

Father and son in a tactical discussion with stable jockey John Reid at the Phoenix Park

Vincent and daughter Susan Magnier chatting with Jimmy Fitzgerald

Vincent with the American Cash Asmussen, who had a controversial season in Ireland

Margaret O'Brien with Pauline and Mark in the yard of Clashganniff House

Vincent out hunting with Lord Waterford and his daughter Liz

Vincent on the day he received the Kaliber Award in Dublin, with Bryan Marshall and Pat Taaffe

Jacqueline O'Brien's classic picture of 1955 Aintree Grand National winner, Quare Times

Grandson Sean McClory with Storm Bird

Vincent and Jacqueline's thirteen grandchildren at Ballydoyle House, Christmas 1988

Vincent with his first grandchild, Andrew

Jacqueline and Alleged

Author's Note

The inspiration to write this book first came to me when I stood on the gallops at Ballydoyle with Vincent O'Brien on Monday, 30 March 1987 – four days before he celebrated his 70th birthday.

The research carried me to places as far apart as Cashel of the Kings to Lexington in the Bluegrass country of Kentucky and Barbados in the West Indies, while the immense task of completing the manuscript by the publisher's deadline was pursued in settings as diverse as the Caribbean, the West of Ireland, Cyprus and Spain's Costa del Sol.

Of the twenty books I have written, none has been more demanding and yet as rewarding as this one – rewarding most of all in the way it brought me into the homes of a quartet of jockeys I had always deeply admired: Lester Piggott, Scobie Breasley, Martin Molony and Aubrey Brabazon. Each in his own way provided absorbing data.

I shall always cherish the memory of meeting Lester in his Newmarket home twice in the spring of 1989 and the two interview sessions I had with Scobie Breasley, sitting on the lovely patio of his Barbados home looking out over the sun-drenched Caribbean.

There were others that I spent fascinating times with – from the American trainers I met at the Keeneland Sales to the people in the Churchtown-Buttevant area of County

Cork and, likewise, those in the Cashel district of County Tipperary; to the members of the O'Brien family, Vincent's brothers, Dermot and Phonsie, and his sister, Pauline, and son-in-law, John Magnier; Noel O'Brien and his wife, Margaret, on the family homestead in Churchtown and, of course, the co-operation I received from Vincent and Jacqueline and their children.

This does not profess to be the official, authorised biography of the Master of Ballydoyle. That was understood and agreed between Dr O'Brien and Jacqueline and myself from the outset.

My approach has been to pinpoint the destiny that directed Vincent O'Brien to full involvement in the life he had already shared with his father, Dan – working with horses. Pinpointed, too, is the amazing story of how he sold a greyhound for £8 but had to settle for £4 and with this money landed his first gamble on a horse called White Squirrel in the Sportsman's Plate, an amateur flat race (1 mile 5 furlongs) at Clonmel on 8 May 1941. White Squirrel, ridden by Vincent himself, won in a field of 27 and Vincent had £4 on at 10–1.

We follow his rise from the time when, as he confessed to me, 'we had to bet to survive', to the era when, switching totally to training horses on the Flat, he acquired wealthy American owners and no longer had to gamble to make ends meet.

He helped create a breeding empire through the establishment of Coolmore Stud and its American arm, the Ashford Stud Farm in Kentucky. In 1975 he formed, with John Magnier and Robert Sangster, 'The Syndicate', which changed the face of things at the Keeneland July Sales. By spotting the potential of Northern Dancer blood, Vincent O'Brien produced a string of brilliant Epsom Derby and other big race winners. The triumvirate he created with Robert Sangster and Lester Piggott made a lasting imprint not alone on the racing scene but also in the rich syndication of these colts as stallions.

The world of stocks and shares meant nothing to Vincent O'Brien when he was starting out as a trainer in Churchtown. He had reached the point towards the close of the 'eighties when he would become one of the central figures in the launching of Classic Thoroughbreds, which was quoted on the Stock Exchange. The wheel had turned full circle for the man who confessed in 1943 that he was 'unknown outside of a very small circle'.

There are few success stories comparable with that of Vincent O'Brien.

It has been a labour of love writing this book about a man who is a genius where horses are concerned – as great composers like Mozart, Beethoven, Verdi and Wagner were with the body of music they left us.

'What is the stars, Joxer, what is the stars?' From the very outset Michael Vincent O'Brien's star was set for greatness. The teacher in Churchtown National School had predicted it correctly when he said prophetically: 'This lad is something different.'

Yes, something different entirely . . .

RAYMOND SMITH

Foreword

My first association with Vincent O'Brien goes back to the early 'fifties when I was riding over hurdles in addition to the Flat and I met him during the Cheltenham Festival. I recall quite well what he said to me: 'If you ever want to ride in a Grand National, come to me.'

I rode Gladness to victory in the Ascot Gold Cup for the Ballydoyle stable. Over a span of more than 30 years, my friendship with Vincent has never waned, though there came a day when I no longer rode for the stable.

The great years were in the 'sixties and 'seventies – the years of Sir Ivor, Nijinsky, Roberto, The Minstrel and Alleged. I came to admire very deeply Vincent's qualities as a trainer. It was not just ambition that set him apart. Every top-class trainer displays that quality. What struck me most forcibly was his total dedication. For every minute of the day, he put his mind into the responsibilities of his profession.

The greatest tribute I can pay him is this – if the horses that passed through his hands were good, he got the very best out of them. He was uncanny in the skill he showed in bringing a Classic or big-race contender to its peak on the day that mattered.

I welcome this full-length biography on the man who helped in providing me with some of my greatest moments in the saddle. I realise the extent of the world-wide research that this book entailed for Raymond Smith.

I am glad that Vincent's unparalleled record of achievement, both in the National Hunt and Flat spheres, has been chronicled in a manner that I am sure will give immense pleasure to racing followers everywhere.

LESTER PIGGOTT

'Florizel',
Hamilton Road,
Newmarket

At the suggestion of Lester Piggott, the publishers have agreed to make separate contributions to the Injured Jockeys' Fund in Britain and Ireland from the proceeds of this book. Lester rode over the jumps and on the Flat in the early part of his career and, having had some narrow escapes from serious injury himself, he realises what permanent incapacitation can mean to a jockey. Everyone in racing in Britain and Ireland will applaud Lester for his kind thought.

Acknowledgements

I am pleased to acknowledge the assistance I received from a great many people in the course of the wide and intensive research for this book and the completion of the manuscript.

I thank in particular the Keeneland Association, Inc., and Jim Williams, Director of Publicity, for all the facilities provided to me during my research in Kentucky.

I deeply appreciate the ready co-operation and assistance and generous hospitality that was forthcoming from Wes Hall, Minister for Tourism and Sports in the Barbados Government, also from the Board of Tourism itself and individual officers like Hugh Foster; BWIA International Airline and Roger Perkins, Director of Hanschell Innis Ltd (sponsors of the Cockspur Gold Cup Day at the Garrison Savannah racecourse) and the Barbados Turf Club when I went to the Caribbean in the course of my research to interview 'Scobie' Breasley, the great Australian rider. Special thanks also to Jane Olivier, Managing Director, and Zarina McCulloch, of Jane Olivier Publicity, London.

I would also like to record grateful thanks for the help and assistance I received from Tony Sweeney, an acknowledged expert on racing facts and statistics and on the essential background data required by any writer in the field of racing and bloodstock matters for so quickly and authoritatively answering the many queries I put to him, extending back to the days when Vincent O'Brien's father, Dan, was training and embracing also Vincent's career as a trainer from the early 'forties right down to the present day.

The Appendices setting out 'The Fabulous Vincent O'Brien Record' at the end of this book represent the painstaking work of Tony Sweeney and his wife, Annie. I feel it will prove an invaluable record for all those who want to see for the first time in tabulated and easy readable form all the big-race successes and title wins of The Master of Ballydoyle.

I deeply appreciate the depth of knowledge and experience that my colleague, Tom MacGinty, Racing Correspondent of the Irish Independent, brought to the task of reading and checking the manuscript.

I could not have gathered as much essential material during the exhaustive research I pursued in the Churchtown and Buttevant areas into Vincent O'Brien's family background and early days and the start of his career as a trainer without the help that I received from D. A. (Tony) O'Neill of Buttevant and Noel and Margaret O'Brien of Churchtown House. I shall always cherish the memory of the days I spent in this area of County Cork which became the base for Vincent O'Brien's initial successful onslaughts on the Cheltenham Festival meeting.

Grateful thanks to John Magnier for the facilities he so kindly laid on for me during my research in the Bluegrass country of Kentucky and also for the co-operation I received from him and from Bob Lanigan and Richard Henry when researching the background to the establishment of the Coolmore Stud complex.

I deeply appreciate the time that Vincent's brothers, Dermot and Phonsie, and his sister, Pauline, so willingly gave me in the course of my research. This book could not have been completed to the planned structure I envisaged without their co-operation and the hours I spent talking to them in their homes. Likewise I thank most sincerely Vincent's own children, including David, who made such a lasting mark in a short period as a trainer. And, of course, Vincent and Jacqueline merit my deepest thanks and appreciation for giving so much of their time, even at the height of the Flat season, to facilitate me in every way.

There are many others who were excited by the idea of a full-length biography of The Master of Ballydoyle and who responded magnificently to helping me in a venture that extended over two years. I proffer my deepest thanks to Lester Piggott and Robert Sangster and also to all the others who have been closely associated with Vincent O'Brien and who readily talked to me for this book.

I acknowledge special thanks to Aengus Fanning, Editor of the *Sunday Independent*, and Paddy McMahon, Personnel Manager of Independent Newspapers, who were both very forthcoming in meeting my request for the leave of absence needed to complete the writing of this work. I thank the staffs of the Independent Library, also Eugene Webber, News Librarian and the other members of the staff of the Press Association Library in Fleet Street and the Express Newspapers Library, London. I thank also the various photographers who provided valuable prints, including Ed Byrne, London, Bernard Parkin, Cheltenham, Caroline Norris, Newbridge and Charlie Collins, Dublin, and the people who lent me photographs from their collections and albums. In the field of assisting with the photographic sections, Jacqueline O'Brien, an outstanding professional photographer in her own right, was most co-operative.

I know how much my friend Joe Walsh, a pioneer in his own field, admires the pioneering achievements of Vincent O'Brien in the Sport of Kings over half a century and I thank JWT Travel for providing facilities in helping me to meet the deadline set by the publishers. I also extend a word of special gratitude to my friends Terence and Annette Sweeney, and to Hugh Flaherty, now a judge of the Supreme Court.

My thanks also to the editors of newspapers and racing papers and magazines and other publications for permission to quote from various interviews, reports and features and also for photos made available to me.

I should also like particularly to thank my editor, Gill Gibbins of Virgin Books, for the professionalism she brought to editing the text.

I could not have devoted the time demanded by this biography without the understanding of my wife, Sheila, and I am grateful too for the patience of Stephen and Bairbre.

Finally, I dedicate the book to the memory of my father, Henry L. Smith, who put me on the road to a career in writing and was himself a keen follower of racing always.

RAYMOND SMITH

PART ONE

THE HINGE OF DESTINY

1

'It Has Got To Be Vincent'

The great Australian jockey turned trainer, Arthur 'Scobie' Breasley was sitting at the Clubroom reception at the Garrison Savannah racecourse in Bridgetown, Barbados, on Friday evening, 10 March 1989. It was the eve of the Caribbean island's biggest event of the racing year, the Cockspur Gold Cup.

Scobie, in a smart blue tropical silk shirt and looking very fit and sprightly for one preparing to celebrate his 75th birthday in May, was asked by one of the English racing writers in my company: 'Who was the greatest trainer you rode for?'

The Man from Wagga Wagga, who had 3000 winners behind him when he quit as a jockey at the age of 54 in 1968, and who was a grandad of 50 when he rode Santa Claus to a superbly-judged victory in the Epsom Derby of 1964 (his first success in the classic in thirteen years of trying) paused and then replied with total conviction in his voice: 'It has got to be Vincent.'

That was a far greater tribute to the Master of Ballydoyle than might appear at first glance.

For when Sir Gordon Richards set up as a trainer at Beckhampton in 1955 (moving to Ogbourne Maisey after one season), the man he signed as his first jockey – for the highest retainer ever paid up to that time to a rider in Britain – was Scobie Breasley. Their association saw Scobie end the 1956 season with 143 winners and in 1957 he increased his total to 173, becoming champion jockey in Britain for the first time (he was also the first Australian to land the honour since the peerless Frank Wootton 45 years earlier).

Scobie was so much in demand in his prime that he had a first retainer with Sir Gordon, a second with Jack Clayton, who managed Norman Bertie's stable and a third with the Duke and Duchess of Norfolk. In addition, he would have ridden from time to time for all the 'name' trainers of his era during a career that stretched over 40 years and embraced Australia, England, France, Ireland and the United States, Sir Cecil Boyd-Rochfort, Paddy Prendergast, Mick Rogers, Etienne Pollet, Alec Head, Noel Cannon, Bill Smyth and later his son Gordon, Arthur Budgett, Atty Persse, Staff Ingham, Stanley Wootton, Captain Peter Hastings-Bass.

Yet, when it came down to naming just one trainer above all the rest, it is significant that Scobie set diplomatic niceties aside and was totally honest and frank in plumping for Vincent O'Brien – the man who trained Ballymoss, the colt he named as 'the best I ever rode', after storming home a two-lengths winner of the Prix de l'Arc de Triomphe in the Longchamp mud in 1958.

After his 1964 Epsom Derby win, Breasley (incidentally, he acquired the nickname 'Scobie' after the late James Scobie, the greatest Australian trainer of his time), who was reputed to have been able to ride a horse at the age of four, would couple the Mick Rogers-trained Santa Claus with Ballymoss in the course of interviews he gave to the media when asked to pinpoint the greatest horses he had ridden. But when I pinned him down on that point, he said that Santa Claus was the best three-year-old he had ever ridden while Ballymoss had no equal among the four-year-olds and older horses he rode.

Three decades on from the Ballymoss season of glory, I watched Scobie Breasley out on the Garrison Savannah track being acclaimed in the Caribbean sunshine by a crowd of over 25,000 – the stands rising to him – after his charge, the David Seale-owned import from Britain,

4

Sandford Prince (Tap on Wood – Sandford Lady) had landed the Cockspur Gold Cup.

As Barbadian racing enthusiasts danced with joy at a 'local' owner-trainer-jockey triumph (Trinidad had been eclipsed!) and cried 'Good Old Scobie', I could not but reflect back to what it must have been like at Longchamp 30 years earlier when, with the rains pouring down, the carefully-laid plans of Vincent O'Brien to win his first Prix de l'Arc de Triomphe with Ballymoss seemed set to evaporate. And he could have been forgiven if he entertained the thought that the ante-post voucher he held with a 'substantial' sum coming off it might well have been torn up on the spot.

'I remember early on Vincent telling me he was thinking of withdrawing the colt,' Scobie Breasley recalled. 'He went away to ask the stewards and then came back and said that they wouldn't allow him to do so.'

Vincent then tried to get Peter O'Sullevan to do a hedging commission on the bet for him. But, of course, there were no bookmakers then as there are none today on the French tracks and Peter had to admit that he could do nothing about it. If only he could have caught the eye of a friendly bookmaker and whispered the necessary words in his ear.

Scobie rode a filly for Alec Head in a race before the Arc and she finished down the field. As he came in Vincent O'Brien could see that he was depressed and obviously Scobie had concluded that the ground had cost his mount any chance she had of winning.

'However, it transpired that the filly had burst a blood vessel,' said Vincent O'Brien. 'I was able to raise his spirits by telling him this before he got on Ballymoss.'

In the last quick tactical exchange between them, Scobie reminded Vincent that he thought that Ballymoss in the hands of T. P. Burns had handled the soft going well enough when quickening well to beat Court Harwell (with Scobie himself in the saddle) and the favourite Brioche in the St Leger at Doncaster the previous season – Ballymoss having drifted out from 6–1 to start at 8–1 (odds that

5

punters would never again get about the Mossborough colt).

And Scobie told Vincent: 'If I find that Ballymoss is not handling the ground, I will not knock him about.'

It was later that Vincent O'Brien would discover that Longchamp, because of the special quality of its surface, can take far more rain than he imagined on that day in 1958.

After Breasley had mastered the French challengers Fric and Cherasco for the £37,925 first prize – bringing Ballymoss's total winnings in Ireland, England and France to £98,650 (thus surpassing the record set by Tulyar in 1951–52 by £22,233), Vincent O'Brien had reason to feel glad that Peter O'Sullevan had failed to hedge that antepost bet for him and gladder still that there were no rails bookmakers at the Longchamp track.

Sitting on the patio of his bungalow-style home along what they know locally in Barbados as 'The Golden Coast', or 'The Platinum Coast', Scobie elaborated on the qualities that made Vincent O'Brien unique as a trainer.

'Vincent could train anything. Look, you will get trainers who are very good with jumpers but who would never make the transition in a million years to turning out top-class two-year-old winners that, in turn, developed into Classic horses, as Vincent made the transition. He was a law unto himself in this respect. The only one I would compare with him as a trainer happened to be an Australian, Lou Robertson.

'I think Vincent thought of the horse first. He turned out his horses looking a picture always. He studied the individual traits of each animal and knew the special requirements each demanded. Lack of condition could never be advanced as the reason for failure when he went after a big prize. He would never rush a horse of his or force it in order to win quick or easy pickings, preferring to aim at big targets, even though they might be twelve months and even longer away.

'He was a great man also to discuss things with you, being happy to listen to your viewpoint and that, again, is the mark of the true professional. For example, when I won the Eclipse on Ballymoss, I said to Vincent, "Let that be his work for the King George", which was only one week away. He nodded and I knew he had taken in every word of what I had said.

'He had this wonderful attention to detail, leaving absolutely nothing to chance.

'I remember on the eve of the 1958 Washington International, at Laurel Park, Vincent studying tapes of previous runnings of the race with me. I remarked to him that I wouldn't have any worries on the score of interference and that was the only way Ballymoss could get beat. Naturally, I was confident after that smashing win in the Arc but I wouldn't agree, as was inferred by some commentators subsequently, that over-confidence or a too-relaxed approach on my part resulted in the defeat of Ballymoss.

'We were interfered with going into the first turn and I had to snatch him up. I will not say it was deliberate. But, remember, in those days there was resentment among the American riders against jockeys coming in to compete in their big races and it certainly wasn't liked if one of their own was "jocked off" for an outside rider. It's completely different now, of course, with racing having become so international and the Breeders' Cup bringing the top horses and top jockeys from both sides of the Atlantic into contention every November.

'Anyway, I recovered from that incident and decided to track Lester coming into the straight for the first time. I thought to myself, "He's one who won't get into trouble".

'There was no running rail then on the inside of the turf track, only a hedge. As we rounded the bend past the stands the sun, which was low in the sky at that stage, caught Lester straight in the eyes and he was so blinded by it that his horse ran into the hedge and almost stopped completely. I ran up his backside.

'Ballymoss was catapulted out into the middle of the track, becoming completely unbalanced. My horse not only lost a lot of valuable ground but also got a real fright. By the time I got him going again, the field was half-way down the back stretch on this sharp 7-furlong circuit. I have no doubt that Ballymoss would have won but for the sun getting into Lester's eyes. What bugged me most of all was that if I had ridden a bad race and taken Ballymoss the longest way round, I would have missed all the trouble.

'Racing's a funny old game.'

Scobie had been married on the day in 1935 that Lester Piggott was born and for years there had been talk of a feud between the two of them, springing no doubt from their fierce tussles for the jockeys' championship in Britain – no greater battle than the 1963 showdown which went right to the final day of the season.

At the now-defunct Manchester racecourse, Lester Piggott walked across the weigh-room and held out his hand in congratulation to Scobie after conceding the title by just one winning ride – 176 to 175. And Scobie was a 'venerable' 49 that same afternoon.

Of course, talk of a feud was all so much poppycock. It was simply two superb professionals throwing down the gauntlet to each other, with no quarter asked or given, and if Lester was reputed to have said one day as he went for the rails, 'Move over grandad', it may have been apocryphal but it was sufficient to highlight colourfully the intensity of that rivalry.

However, the mutual respect and friendship built between them lasted through thick and thin. While Lester was in prison, Scobie wrote to him more than once and Lester replied. And later when Lester was released, Scobie – while on a visit to England – rang him at his Newmarket home and enquired: 'I hope they didn't treat you badly inside. How was it anyway?'

'A waste of time,' came Lester's laconic reply.

Vincent O'Brien's presence at the wedding of Lester's daughter, Maureen, had a deep significance also, proving that the bonds built up between them could never be shattered.

Vincent has admitted that he was closer to Lester through the years of their highly successful association than to anyone else – outside of his wife Jacqueline. He recognised in Lester a total commitment to winning, a professionalism matching his own, for Lester was driven by a burning, indeed awesome, will to win. In a word, they were kindred spirits.

Lester was the embodiment of the stoic countenance, smiling at best in victory but never displaying intense jubilation even after powering to a brilliant Derby victory on a Sir Ivor or Nijinsky but, equally, never breaking his whip, so to speak, in a display of petulant emotion in defeat.

It was the same with Vincent and never was the control of his emotions shown better than on the day at Epsom in 1984 when his 'wonder colt', El Gran Senor, was beaten in a photo finish by Secreto, trained by his son, David.

Both Lester and Vincent had to live with crowds in the hurly-burly of big race days. However, they were both very private men and there was a point beyond which few, if any, could penetrate.

Vincent, in one of his most revealing moments, has confessed to being an introvert – 'but not by choice'.

'I'd love to be an extrovert. I'd love to be the sort of person who's the life and soul of the party. They have a much better time, don't they?'

His brother, Phonsie, is the perfect foil, for Phonsie is the complete extrovert and admitted to me that when he is in company with Vincent and Robert Sangster and John Magnier and others, he can do the balancing act for Vincent's shyness.

There were perfect examples of that in Lexington during the Keeneland July Sales in 1988.

2

Lester On The Master

Now the scene switches to Lester Piggott's home in New-market on a day in February, 1989.

Lester, it is evident, is a man who has acquired a new inner calmness, a wider outlook on life, a deep sense of conviction from the traumatic events he has been through, from being stripped of the treasured OBE, awarded to him in the 1975 New Year's Honours List for services to sport – 'A high point in my life,' he had said – to the terrible distress he experienced when Susan lay seriously ill in Addenbrook's Hospital in Cambridge after a fall from a horse during early-morning exercise on the Newmarket gallops.

And, of course, there was all he had to suffer at the hands of the 'popular' media, who disseminated the most mind-boggling fiction about his alleged doings in prison when they could not garner any hard facts (a man could be forgiven if he craved for the type of legislation that would protect the individual in a democratic society from such machinations by the Fourth Estate).

The sun streams in the window of the spacious but in no way ostentatious drawing-room of the bungalow-style house, so easily recognisable as a racing man's home by the flanking stone models of two jockeys in their coloured silks at the entrance.

More than by the trophies, one's eye is caught by the remarkable life-size study of Lester in a corner of the room

10

– a painting evoking the stance in racing silks of The Maestro with riding whip in hand when he was 'King' of the Classics (he would garner a total of 29 in Britain alone, including nine Epsom Derby successes, and ride 5000 winners before his retirement).

In a strange way it dominates the room, bringing your eye back again and again to those lean, almost gaunt features. And you conclude that ultimately, as with all great artists, it is the memory of the talent that will endure, overshadowing all else in assessments of this man.

For, as in the case of Vincent O'Brien, he stood out beyond the march of time itself on a pedestal apart.

Conversation ranges over the high peaks of what the dynamic partnership between Vincent and Lester achieved, especially in those Epsom Derby triumphs through Sir Ivor (1968), Nijinsky (1970), Roberto (1972) and The Minstrel (1977) and through Alleged in the Prix de l'Arc de Triomphe (1977 and 1978), but principally it is concerned with how Lester saw Vincent and the qualities that impressed him over and above everything else.

'He had to have ambition to achieve all he did achieve,' said Lester. 'Every top-class trainer displays that quality anyway. In Vincent's case, the aspects that set him apart went far deeper. What struck me most forcibly about him was his approach to the profession of training. He was *totally* dedicated. For every minute of the day, he put his mind into the responsibilities of training.

'Of course, he had to make time to socialise in the sense that he had to meet current owners and set out to acquire new ones. But he didn't socialise simply in the manner of spending time in bars drinking just for the sake of it.

'Because of many successful coups he landed when he was establishing himself initially as a trainer, I know there are those who would say he was "a gambler" in those days. I would prefer to describe him as "an investor". He liked to bet when he knew he had a stone in hand; and that was not just in strict weight terms – he knew the horse he had laid out to win a particular race had a stone in hand in terms of ability or class over the rest of the field.

'They didn't all win, of course. That is the law of averages in this game – a great leveller of persons and reputations. In Vincent's case, however, if he got beat, you could rest assured that the average of winners over losers was far, far higher and so at the end of each year the ledger invariably showed a profit and a substantial one at that.

'Perhaps the greatest tribute I can pay him is this: if the horses that he put through his hands were good, he got the very best out of them. If certain horses were no good, you might never even see them on a racecourse. It wasn't Vincent's way to waste time trying to unearth ability where he knew there was none, having given them every chance.'

The scene switches again – to Lexington and the Keeneland July Sales in 1988.

D. Wayne Lukas, current kingpin of the American racing scene (he turned out three winners on Breeders' Cup Day 1988 at Churchill Downs when a crowd of 71,237 bet $10,995,103 in one afternoon), considered the question, 'What in your estimation made Vincent O'Brien such a great trainer?'

'Longevity,' came the cryptic response. 'Many in this game can have a good year, maybe even a few good years. But what makes Vincent O'Brien one of the greatest trainers in the history of racing globally is that he has stood the test of time. The records show that he was turning out champions over the jumps as far back as 1948 and 40 years later he still commanded the deepest respect among racing folk, though now training exclusively on the Flat.

'A good horse can make anybody look good. In Vincent O'Brien's case, however, he did not just depend on one great animal to catapult him on to a level where his name became known in every corner of the world. There was this constant search for excellence. He displayed qualities that can only be recognised as true genius.

'When I first came into this game Vincent was setting the standards for most of us to follow. I know there are American trainers who would say they had been out-standingly successful if they achieved even half of the goals that Vincent O'Brien has achieved.

'The cruel reality that emerges from a close study of the history of racing is that nobody can buy success. In a word, money alone doesn't guarantee Classic or big-race victories. Vincent O'Brien picked them out when he had nothing like the money at his back that would come later in his career. Let me repeat – it takes genius to accomplish all that he has accomplished in a lifetime at the game.'

Woody Stevens and Charlie Whittingham, who both answer to the Wayne Lukas dictum of 'longevity' in the scope and range of their training successes over a span of years, were unanimous in expressing their recognition of the fabulous Vincent O'Brien record, while Colin S. Hayes, the ace Australian trainer, said that Vincent was as well known down under as in the States and it took some record to make one become a household name right around the globe.

The admiration for Vincent O'Brien extends to France and the great French jockey, Yves Saint-Martin, who rode for Vincent more than once and was never as brilliant in a finish than when winning the Prix Daphnis at Evry in 1983 on Glenstal by a short neck from Luderic, said of the Master of Ballydoyle: 'Vincent O'Brien is a great trainer and a wonderful professional and, equally important, a true gentleman.'

And Alec Head, who retired from training in 1984, leaving his daughter, Criquette, firmly at the head, said of Vincent O'Brien to Desmond Stoneham in the course of an interview for the *Irish Racing Annual*: 'One of the greatest trainers I have ever met is Vincent O'Brien. He is an exceptional judge of horses and what a man to have trained three Grand National, six Derby and three Arc de Triomphe winners. He could handle anything and what a beautiful preparation he gave to Alleged to win the Arc in 1977 and 1978.'

Pat Eddery, who succeeded Lester Piggott as first jockey

13

to the Ballydoyle stable, said: 'Those five years riding for a marvellous trainer are five years I will always remember. We got on really well together. I am grateful to him for all the experience I gained. It was invaluable. To sum up, let me put it this way: you get outstanding jockeys and outstanding trainers. Now and then one comes along with a unique gift. Lester Piggott was specially gifted as a jockey and Vincent O'Brien in the same way as a trainer. You cannot express their kind of flair in so many words. They just had the knack of doing the impossible.'

The American, Cash Asmussen, who followed Pat Eddery at Ballydoyle, said that he fulfilled one of his great ambitions when he signed up to ride for 'one of the "genius" trainers of modern times'.

'I have always been a student of this game, I know also that you can constantly advance your knowledge in your chosen profession. For that very reason, I regard the year I spent at Ballydoyle as incalculable in the experience I gained from working under Dr O'Brien. A lot, I know, has been said about his attention to detail. The big difference in his case is that he knows the details to which to give attention and there is a great difference between that and getting caught up in unnecessary details.'

T. P. Burns was associated with some of Vincent O'Brien's finest triumphs in the Gloucestershire Hurdle at Cheltenham, rode Ballymoss to victory in the Irish Derby and English St Leger and then for seven years was Assistant Trainer at Ballydoyle before joining the Dermot Weld stable in the same capacity.

'What impressed me always was Vincent's wonderful grasp of the whole business of training. His insight was phenomenal, his patience quite extraordinary. It meant nothing to him to earmark a horse in his charge for a target a year ahead, maybe even longer. It was no trouble to him to put away a horse when he was going for bigger things.

'He was ahead of his time all the time, yes, a step ahead of the others. I rode for him a lot over a period of nearly twenty years, though not on a retainer for the stable. The stable had to gamble. The money in jumping in those days was peanuts compared with the prize money today for the major events. I rode five to victory in the Gloucestershire Hurdle. They were all gambled on without exception. You knew the money was down. When there is gambling, there is always pressure. You felt the pressure. And, believe me, the pressure was far greater then, far more intense than when Vincent was turning out Derby winners for wealthy patrons.

'Vincent knew to a tee what was required to win that race. He had brought it to a fine art. It was a tremendous feat to win not just one Division but two – like winning the Epsom Derby over a succession of seasons, and probably harder in a way, because you had to pick out a particular type of horse and then you never knew what you would run up against in a hurdle race of this kind.

'Vincent wasn't going to allow the big gambles at Cheltenham to go astray because his challengers could not jump. He took infinite patience in teaching them. One of the greatest attributes of all of a Vincent O'Brien-trained horse in National Hunt races, especially hurdle races was that they could jump. They would invariably gain that vital length in jumping. The only horse of Vincent's I ever fell on was Stroller and that was not his own fault.

'Vincent didn't give vent to any displays of emotion in victory and likewise he wasn't one of those to apportion blame when a gamble became unstuck. His attitude was: "It's lost, we'll get it back." In a word, that day was finished and it was on to a new day.

'I was always amazed at the way he seemed to know everything about the opposition in each particular race. He could read how a race would go in advance in uncanny fashion.

'Having ensured that you were acquainted with the horses you rode for him, he didn't burden you with a book of instructions once he had come to trust your judgement and professional skill. It was a pleasure to ride for him, as he was a true professional himself, always.

'As Assistant Trainer, I found that if he trusted you, he left things to you. He expected you to know your business and that there would be no slip-ups. You were on your honour and there could be no messing. His demands were pretty high. He expected you to keep up with them, for the standards he set for others, he maintained himself. There was no place in his set-up if you could not meet these standards.'

At noon on a morning towards the end of February 1989 John Magnier, son-in-law of Vincent O'Brien, sits in his office in the headquarters of the Coolmore Stud complex near Fethard in County Tipperary.

He has come a long way since he got involved with Robert Sangster and his father-in-law as the key trio in the famous partnership (Tim Vigors was central to it in the founding stage) to oversee the operations of Coolmore; and that same year – 1975 – saw the birth of 'The Syndicate' that would make such a dramatic impact on the face of things at the Keeneland Sales and on breeding operations internationally.

In fact, John Magnier is today, with Vincent O'Brien and Robert Sangster, involved not just in a major Irish stud complex but in what could more aptly be described as an empire, the tentacles of which stretch to Kentucky, where the Coolmore arm is the Ashford Stud, standing El Gran Senor (at $100,000 a service) and Storm Bird. They reach also down under, where an arrangement has been reached with Colin Hayes's Lindsay Park Stud outside Adelaide that sees stallions operating in two hemispheres in the same year – to the marked benefit of shareholders and breeders alike. Ahonoora was operating in New South Wales when he shattered a leg during exercise in a freak paddock accident in September 1989, and had to be put down.

Everybody who is anybody seems to beat a path to Coolmore, which stands today some of the world's most valuable stallions. They include Northern Dancer's son, Sadler's Wells, whose first crop of two-year-olds made such an impact during 1988 (for example, his sons, Prince of Dance and Scenic, dead-heated for the Three Chimneys Dewhurst Stakes) and Northern Dancer's grandson, Caerleon (by Nijinsky), who was responsible for Corwyn Bay, winner of the first running of the Cartier Million at the Phoenix Park and champion Flat sire for 1988, despite being represented on-course by only his first two crops.

The framed letters and coloured prints remind one of the very special days at Coolmore and the Ashford Stud. There is the letter to Bob Lanigan on behalf of The Queen after her visit to the Ashford Stud in May 1986: 'The Queen has commanded me to send her warm thanks for giving her the opportunity to visit Ashford . . .' Then the personal letter from the Australian Prime Minister, Bob Hawke, to John Magnier after his visit to Coolmore in November 1987 when on an official trip to Ireland: 'Thank you for your welcome. . . . I was delighted to have the opportunity to visit your stud and see some of the world's leading stallions.' And a picture of the Aga Khan on the day he came to see Kadissya, the dam of dual Derby winner, Kahyasi.

John Magnier sees Vincent O'Brien as 'the elder statesman' in the Coolmore set-up. 'He is a major asset here, an international thinker, who has so much to contribute and who I can truthfully say has no equal on breeding matters.

'Vincent can take a beating better than any man I know in this business. If it is a sign of greatness to be able to lose, then I can only say that he is a terrific loser. If something goes wrong and he ascertains that it wasn't any fault of his, or anyone else closely associated with a particular situation, then he will put defeat out of his mind and go out the next day as if it never happened. Give him the worst possible news and you find that he is fully capable of taking it on the chin. You end up feeling sorry for yourself as he tells you "not to worry".

'Amazingly enough, I have never seen him in worse humour than the year – 1975 – when he won six races with seven runners at Royal Ascot. You see, he was already worrying about what he was going to aim at next with each of those winners.

'You have to have guts to take it as a trainer and breeder at his level. His brother, Dermot, said of him once that whatever is inside the man can only be likened to four

Rolls-Royce engines rolled into one. 'Dermot, after being part and parcel of Vincent's stable set-up for 23 years, took the easy route and set up as a breeder himself. That is understandable, as Dermot was there through thick and thin – a man who stayed out of the central limelight but, as many are not aware, had a tremendous input into Vincent's success story.

'Vincent has shown that he can stand the racket – the ups and downs. You have got to be able to take it mentally and physically. I suppose in this respect he was unique in many ways as a trainer, when you consider all the water that has flowed under the bridge since he came into the game initially and all he has been through from the late 'thirties to the end of the 'eighties – a span of fifty years.

'Not only would I describe him as a great trainer – he is on a plane apart when it comes to breeding matters. Vincent can compete with anybody in buying on looks alone. He could, I am certain, pick a potential winner, even a future champion, without even looking at the pedigree.

'But he has always taken the view that the yearlings you really go after *must* have a pedigree to match their looks and conformation. If they don't have a pedigree, it's unlikely they will prove attractive as sires to breeders, who place tremendous importance on the genetic bank. In fact, it's rare in the world of breeding that those put to stud that do fail to answer the cruel demands of the genetic bank will emerge as top sires.'

Choosing every word deliberately, John Magnier said, 'Nobody before Vincent, or likely to come after him, could ever match his knowledge of pedigrees and bloodlines. It's uncanny really. People can today, with the benefit of the computer, call up statistics and other vital data that will prove very beneficial to those making vital decisions at yearling sales.

'In Vincent's case, however, it's almost as if all this knowledge was inbuilt. He will take it, as it were, subconsciously into account as he reaches his decisions. He will

18

look at a colt and say, "That is a Buckpasser head" and although he never trained Buckpasser he will know everything that you need to know about the Buckpasser line. He leaves you gasping in wonder at his knowledge.'

John Magnier then went on to relate how Vincent in an inspired moment – which in itself showed the intuitive brilliance that stemmed from a masterful eye for selecting potential champions – came to pick out Nijinsky when there was absolutely no prior thought of going for the bloodline this champion of champions represented.

'Vincent, at the behest of Charlie Englehard, went to look at a Ribot colt at Edward P. Taylor's Windfields Farm in Canada but ended up advising Englehard that he buy a colt by Northern Dancer out of Flaming Page. The colt was purchased by Englehard's representative for 84,000 guineas, a Canadian record at the time.

'Vincent has often told me that from the moment he first saw Nijinsky the colt "filled his eye" and struck him as a real champion in the making. This was the perfect example of Vincent bringing all his accumulated knowledge into play, his penchant for spotting that vital "something" that would later emerge maybe in Classic success.

'At the time Northern Dancer had not, as yet, arrived as a name sire. Nijinsky was one of his second crop. The era when he would become the single most dominant force in the world of breeding was still some years away. And Vincent, by picking colts like Nijinsky and The Minstrel, helped establish the reputation of Northern Dancer on this side of the Atlantic.

'Vincent, as I have already indicated, had no doubts in the case of Nijinsky. But before purchasing The Minstrel he was riven with doubt. I remember as vividly as if it were only yesterday the team arriving in Kentucky for the 1975 Keeneland Sales. Naturally, The Minstrel was a prime target, being by Northern Dancer, Nijinsky's sire and out of Fleur, daughter of Nijinsky's dam, Flaming Page. But there were immediate and obvious worries about how small he was and, even worse, that this flashy chestnut had four white legs and feet.'

John Magnier did not have to spell out the significance

of those four white feet, or quote the old breeding maxim: 'One white foot, buy a horse; two white feet, try a horse; three white feet, look well about him; four white feet, do without him'.

It would have been so easy for Vincent O'Brien to 'do without him' but it is the person who, having accepted all the advice against the purchase, and having had all the negative points impressed upon him – whether it is the size or those white feet – can still decide to go ahead and buy, who deserves a very special accolade.

'Vincent did just that when he went to $200,000 for The Minstrel,' John Magnier went on. 'He allowed Lyphard to be led out of the ring unsold at Newmarket because of his size and didn't lose sleep over that decision, though subsequently Lyphard, after a successful racing career in France, went on to become a very big success as a sire in America. He picked The Minstrel despite his size and had the satisfaction of seeing him valued at $9 million. Yes, the $200,000 buy had turned out to be some investment.'

John Magnier said that if you were to look at racing results around the globe, you just could not get away from the influence of the great horses Vincent had trained that had gone on to make their mark at stud, their progeny in turn creating their own impact (as in the case of Nijinsky and Caerleon). It was the same when you examined the catalogues at the yearling sales. In a word, it was a monument in itself to the profound influence Vincent had had on breeding world-wide that his great horses had such an effect on bloodlines globally.

John concluded by recalling a trip back from the Keeneland Sales. 'We were taking a plane to Dulles when we found that we were actually on a flight to Dallas, Texas. The plane was ready to taxi down the runway. Vincent got us all off that plane, baggage and all, and we made our connection to Dulles.

'I never did get around to asking him how he managed it. An amazing man really.'

3

A 'Crazy' Moment At Keeneland

At the Keeneland Select Sales in July 1988 all eyes were on Lot 269, a Nijinsky colt out of Crimson Saint. When Californian trainer D. Wayne Lukas, who had $15 million to spend, signalled a bid of $3.4 million with his right hand, it seemed that he had beaten the man the American media had dubbed 'The County Tipperary Wizard'. But Vincent O'Brien, in yellow shirt and white boater, having gone 'into the trenches' for this battle, quietly responded with a $3.5 million bid on behalf of Classic Thoroughbreds. He confessed afterwards that he would not have gone any higher.

Spotter Pete McCormick from Ontario gave an enquiring glance at D. Wayne Lukas, but Lukas signalled this time that he was finished. American racing's Mr Goldfinger had lost out to the Master of Ballydoyle.

However, that moment of drama had been far outstripped in 1985 by ten of the most hectic minutes ever experienced at Keeneland. A bid of $13.1 million – a new world record – made on behalf of the Robert Sangster-Vincent O'Brien Syndicate secured a colt by Nijinsky, later named Seattle Dancer and put into training at Ballydoyle. In the space of 24 bids the British Bloodstock Agency, acting for 'The Syndicate', purchased the bay Nijinsky colt (out of My Charmer), a half-brother to American Triple Crown winner Seattle Slew, and to Sangster's own English 2000 Guineas winner Lomond.

Even before Lot 215 was led into the ring, the buzz was already rising right around the packed auditorium. But although the high rollers knew that this was *it* the spotters down on the floor – those like Pete McCormick, who know at first hand everyone who is likely to make a bid and who make you wonder as they snap their fingers so professionally whether you will be called for a bid of $25,000 if you merely raise your finger to your nose – showed not the least sign that this would be different for them from any other sale in the catalogue. Constantly they would swing between concentrated glances at the tiered rows in their particular section of the auditorium to looking quickly towards the man behind the mike on the rostrum – the man who would ultimately bring down the hammer – and these spotters would reveal, by their shouting of the bids, how the action would develop.

An audible stir, a hum of anticipation as Seattle Dancer is led into the small roped-off ring. There is not an empty seat in the Press Box. Vincent O'Brien sits quietly beside Robert Sangster.

Even the most knowledgeable ones in Lexington on that never-to-be-forgotten July day were hardly prepared – and could never have predicted – the scale and adrenalin-pumping climax to the bidding. When it reached $9.8 million the sense of drama was intense. Excitement mounted in anticipation that the previous world record was about to be shattered. 'The Lord loves a cheerful giver,' quipped auctioneer Tom Caldwell when the bids went to $10 million. 'Hot dog,' someone exclaimed, 'we're going to get a new world record.' Applause broke out when the previous record was passed. Then D. Wayne Lukas bid $13 million and it seemed that nothing could thwart him.

However, the Sangster team put in a final bid of $13.1 million and Tom Caldwell brought down his hammer to a spontaneous roar.

'I suppose looking back on it now, it might appear crazy to have paid that much money for a yearling when you had no certainty how it would turn out,' said Robert Sangster, three years on from that record-breaking night.

'We will probably never see that figure reached again in our lifetimes.

'We had Seattle Dancer valued between $8 and $15 million. We would have been willing to go as high as $15 million.'

The colt had been consigned by Warner L. Jones, Jun., of Hermitage Farm at Goshen in Oldham County, then Chairman of the Board of Churchill Downs. He sold eight yearlings for a total of $19.4 million.

In a way Seattle Dancer was a disappointment on the racecourse considering his looks and his breeding. He was retired to stud at the Ashford Farm in Kentucky. His first crop of yearlings were due to reach the sales in 1990.

Vincent O'Brien never flinched when the going got hottest at the Keeneland Sales. You might say it was all in the day's work for him.

It was a far, far cry from the time when in order to get some ready cash, he used to breed a few greyhounds in his native Clashganniff, Churchtown, County Cork and made a pound or two selling them to England. He sold three greyhounds to one Englishman. 'But when the Second World War broke out, the three greyhounds were returned to me. The bottom fell out of the export trade and it actually ceased altogether, so that I was stuck with three greyhounds,' Vincent recalled. 'I finally managed to sell one for £8 but after waiting two years to get paid, I accepted an offer of £4 on the advice of my solicitor, who was David Nagle's father. It was all I had in the world.

'I put every penny of it on a grey mare called White Squirrel by Grey Squirrel. Actually, she was not a thoroughbred but a three-quarter bred, so she did not figure in the Stud Book.'

Vincent had been schooling this mare for point-to-points and in a way it was the first horse he ever actually trained himself – and prepared for a gamble. Initially, his hope was that she would win a point-to-point but when foot-and-mouth disease broke out in the spring of 1941 all fixtures were cancelled. It was when the mare showed up particularly well at work with flat horses in his father's

23

stable that Vincent decided that White Squirrel might have a future in racing and decided to go for 'a touch'.

The race he chose for his first gamble was the Sportsman's Plate, an amateur flat race – or 'bumper' as styled in Ireland – at Clonmel on 8 May, 1941 and, with a field of 27 runners, a good betting event was assured. Vincent decided that he would ride her himself. He was first granted a Gentleman Rider's permit or Amateur licence under both Rules in 1934. However, he had to wait until 7 November, 1940 to ride his first winner – on Hallowment, owned and trained by his father, in a 2-mile bumper at Limerick. Before he quit as a rider after 1941, Vincent had ridden three winners in all. He did not renew his Amateur licence after 1941.

A close friend of his had accompanied Vincent to the Powerstown Park meeting. Vincent's father, if he thought one of the horses he trained himself had a chance of winning, loved nothing better than to tell all his friends about it. For that very reason, Vincent made up his mind that his best hope of getting a good price to his money was to wait until he got to the race meeting itself before advising his father to have a flutter. Before the bookmakers had formed a market on the Sportsman's Plate, he told his friend to go to his father and tell him that he should have a bet on the mare. 'My father, who wasn't a gambler, gave my friend a tenner and he got on at 20–1. Of course, that started a rush and I had to be content with the 10–1 my friend took to my £4.'

White Squirrel duly beat her 27 rivals to win by a comfortable 1½ lengths. 'I was thrilled that we had been successful with my first gamble and it was the one that got me started,' he said.

Incidentally, Vincent had his last ride in public on this same mare in the Moyode Plate at Galway – Plate Day – on 30 July 1941. White Squirrel, starting at 20–1, was unplaced to the 2–7 favourite, Ardenode.

What was of deep significance about the gamble Vincent brought off at Clonmel was that from that moment on he trusted his own judgement far more than previously, and was prepared to back it to the hilt. His brother, Dermot, recalled that one of the biggest coups of all was landed on Gladness in the Broughton Plate at Manchester on 16 November 1956. 'There was this Irish punter standing under William Hill's perch and when he saw me coming, he put two and two together and moved in quickly to get his bet on before I got in. I said to William Hill's representative, "The best odds to £1000," and he replied, "You have evens to £200." '

A bet of £1000 in 1956 represented some wager just for openers. As the money poured on Gladness as if there was no day of reckoning, her price was slashed to 8–11. Considering that in subsequent seasons she would win the Irish Champion Stakes, the Sunninghill Park Stakes, the Ascot Gold Cup, the Goodwood Cup, the Ebor Handicap by 7 lengths with top weight (9 stone 7 pounds) and finished second in the King George VI and Queen Elizabeth Stakes, you can imagine what a cold-stone certainty she was in that big field of maidens over 12 furlongs at Manchester. Her only previous run had seen her finishing unplaced exactly twelve months earlier in the Swilly Maiden at the Curragh.

After a trial with T. P. Burns up against first-class material at Gowran Park, Vincent knew there was no way she could get beat – bar a fall. And he bet accordingly in an era when betting was the only route he knew to meet outgoings and put some money in the bank.

The world of stocks and shares meant nothing to Vincent O'Brien then. He could never have imagined that 49 years on from the day he won £40 at Clonmel, he would be at the Keeneland Sales buying for a company called Classic Thoroughbreds plc, which was quoted on the Stock Exchange. More important still, it would have been beyond his wildest dreams to contemplate that he would have reached the point where thousands of ordinary punters would have such faith in his judgement that they would literally fall over themselves to get a stake in the company when it was launched in Dublin in 1987.

Classic Thoroughbreds had been set up as a £10 million bloodstock investment company. The break-down of that initial float saw £3 million earmarked for the promoter-directors, £5 million taken up by the financial institutions and the remaining £2 million offered to the public, all of whom had the option of increasing holdings by 50 per cent by June 1988.

There were familiar names among the promoter-directors. Vincent O'Brien was Chairman and staked nearly £1 million in the company; Coolmore's John Magnier, his son-in-law, put in £600,000, as did Robert Sangster and Dr Michael Smurfit, head of the multi-million Smurfit Group, while meat baron John Horgan accounted for £250,000. With a one-for-two rights issues, the company was enlarged by a further £5.7 million in mid–1988, with the express purpose of providing the finance for yearling purchases in the 1988 season.

Before the close of 1987, IR£7.6 million had been spent on Classic Thoroughbreds' yearling portfolio. The company started the 1988 season with interests in 38 juveniles (29 colts and 9 fillies) in training at Ballydoyle with Vincent O'Brien. These had been acquired at yearling sales in the United States and Europe. At the close of the first season's racing, 23 of them had been out, providing 9 winners of 12 races. In 1988 Classic acquired interest in a further 16 yearlings – 4 fillies and 12 colts.

When Classic's shares came to the Smaller Companies Market of the Stock Exchange on 22 October 1987 they traded initially at 30p a share, but 'Black Monday' had its effect on them as on many other shares before temporary recovery set in.

In advance of the 1989 English 2000 Guineas investors pushed the price up to 41p on the Thursday before the race in anticipation that Saratogan (who had been beaten just half a length by the dead-heaters Prince of Dance and Scenic in the Dewhurst Stakes) would justify stable confidence. His failure in this race and in the Irish 2000 Guineas, coupled with the subsequent failure of Classic Secret and an injury to the highly-regarded sprinting prospect, Puissance, in the count-down to Royal Ascot, resulted in the shares dropping dramatically to 16p, to level out around mid-June at 17½p.

26

The company had been valued before Saratogan's English 2000 Guineas failure at £23.67 million at the peak 41p-a-share price and it was estimated that the asset value would have increased by an equivalent of approximately £4 million if the El Gran Senor colt had triumphed at Newmarket (Classic Thoroughbreds owned 50 per cent of the colt). In fact, the market estimates were that El Gran Senor's value would have jumped to $12 million if he had been successful.

For that reason observers of the money markets saw Saratogan's failure as a serious setback, but from the very outset, Vincent O'Brien had emphasised that investors were going into a high-risk business in buying shares in Classic Thoroughbreds and if many went in in the hope of a quick 'killing', then the Master of Ballydoyle was warning them against seeing gold at the end of the rainbow. If anyone got his fingers caught in the wringer, at least he had to admit that he had been warned.

There's an Irish irony in the success of the launching as a public company of Classic Thoroughbreds. It takes your natural Irish wit to conjure up the vision of a man with £300 in shares in the company coming up to Vincent O'Brien and, as he touches his cap, politely enquiring, 'How are *my* horses coming along, Boss?'

Millionaire owners are still central to Vincent O'Brien's training and breeding empire, none closer to him than Robert Sangster, whose base may be the Isle of Man but whose bloodstock 'empire' stretches right around the globe from Ireland and Britain to Australia and who has an interest in anything up to 1500 horses, counting what he owns himself and jointly with syndicates. 'I cannot put an exact figure on the overall total,' admits the man who sold the family football pools firm, Vernons, for over £92 million and who makes the world his oyster as he commutes constantly from his home, The Nunnery, to British, Irish or French racecourses; who can be found at yearling sales in Kentucky or Saratoga or Deauville or Goffs or in Australia, and who in January will find relaxation playing golf on the Sandy Lane course in Barbados, where the Sangsters have a house just beside the course.

The partnership between Vincent O'Brien and Robert Sangster was cemented in the 'seventies and flowered in invincible days through a triumvirate, that also comprised the incomparable Lester Piggott in the saddle, and later, in the early 'eighties, Pat Eddery.

The Sangster-O'Brien partnership has survived every setback. And there certainly have been a few since the heady days when colts like The Minstrel and Alleged were carrying all before them in Sangster's famous green and blue silks.

Vincent's brother, Dermot, recalled that their father, Dan O'Brien, had a very good eye for picking out a nice horse. 'Vincent owes an awful lot to his father; he went around a great deal with him and I am sure that it was then that he developed his own unerring eye for spotting potential champions. He picked them, you must realise, when he had nothing like the money behind him that he would have in later years at Ballydoyle.

'My father had no patience with horses. That was his main weakness. He would buy a very nice horse and would improve its condition so much that you would hardly think it was the same animal that had arrived in the yard some months earlier. He would be in a hurry to find out what he might expect from the horse and that can be fatal in this business. Vincent always showed infinite patience. Time didn't matter to him once he knew that the latent ability was there.'

But for an amazing twist of fate, Vincent O'Brien might never have pursued a career as a trainer, might never have got to the point where he could outbid Sheikh Mohammed and D. Wayne Lukas at Keeneland if he so desired. If he owed a lot to his father, he owed much also to a man with a passion for horses, one Jackie O'Brien from Fermoy, who rarely figures today in the many profiles that appear of the Master of Ballydoyle.

Jackie O'Brien stepped into Vincent's life at the most crucial juncture of all – after his father died in May 1943 – when he was undecided where his future lay, though deep down he desperately wanted to pursue the one life he had known with his father: training horses.

In September of that same year, Jackie O'Brien approached Vincent at Limerick Junction. What evolved from that meeting was to have a dramatic and lasting impact on racing and bloodstock history and on the shaping of future records in the National Hunt and Flat racing spheres, and also on breeding world-wide.

4

'What Is To Be, Will Be'

'I had no doubt about training as the career I should pursue once I was approached by Jackie O'Brien at Limerick Junction races in September of 1943 and asked if I would like to train a few horses for Frank Vickerman.'

Thus did Vincent O'Brien recall the fateful moment that he came into contact with Jackie O'Brien and through him Frank Vickerman. These two men would exercise an immense influence in guiding him along the road to initial fame primarily as a National Hunt trainer, though from the very beginning he mixed flat and jumping with commendable success.

Vincent had reached a critical point with the death of his father on 6 May 1943. He was then 26. The family farm had passed to his step-brother, Donal, and all the horses that had been trained by Dan O'Brien were sold off. Vincent was at his wit's end contemplating what to do, though naturally he wanted more than anything else to be a full-time trainer.

Tom Tierney, one of Vincent's teachers and Principal of Churchtown National School, had said of him, 'This lad is something different.' Not, mark you, an academic brilliance but a presence, a spark that the teacher identified with the unerring instinct of the wise old owl sitting in the oak.

When Jackie O'Brien asked Vincent at Limerick Junction races if he would like to train a few horses, it was as if the pieces of a jig-saw were falling into place as fate decreed them. As my friend, 'Chawkie', put it, serving me a Pina Colada one evening in the bar of the Discovery Bay Hotel in Barbados: 'What is to be, will be.'

If you are a believer in the destiny that shapes our ends, then you will understand that events can happen at one point in time that may well affect developments in a person's life some years later. In a word, time in the accepted sense has no bearing on the movement of one's star in the hands of one's Maker. Some would see it as pure chance, others would find deeper, even spiritual elements.

First fate decreed that wealthy Frank Vickerman, a native of Stroud in Gloucestershire, should decide to switch his wool business from Yorkshire to Dublin. Jackie O'Brien, who combined farming with his wool business in the Fermoy area of County Cork, became his principal agent in the South of Ireland. Now Jackie O'Brien was a born character, moving at ease in racing circles, and Phonsie O'Brien remembers that the first time O'Brien horses were transported by plane from Shannon Airport to Bristol in 1949 to run at the Cheltenham Festival – comprising the trio Cottage Rake, Hatton's Grace and Castledermot – Jackie had become so much part of the O'Brien set-up that he came along for the fun and 'the crack'.

'He had a face like Barry Fitzgerald,' recalled Phonsie. 'The last memory I have of him is of walking into the bar of the Grand Hotel in Fermoy and there was the bould Jackie sitting up on a high stool and a terrier on another stool beside him – with a cigar stuck in its mouth.'

Jackie, for whom hunting and point-to-pointing represented part of the very essence of life, was an excellent judge of horseflesh and kept some point-to-pointers himself. One he had picked out – China Cottage – won the Champion Hunters' Chase at Mullacurry with P. P. Hogan in the saddle. In his home in Rathcannon, Kilmallock, County Limerick P.P. pulled out an old scrapbook and there was Jackie O'Brien, proud as punch, leading in China Cottage. 'You would think he had won the Cheltenham Gold Cup, he was so full of himself after that success

31

as an owner,' said P.P. 'I was happ   ɔ ride for him any time he asked, for there was no finer or more generous character.'

He came of a family steeped in the tradition of the horse, one of six brothers. One of them, Willie, was killed riding at a point-to-point meeting. Jackie's brother, Tommy, was Master of the Avondhu Hunt, Jackie himself the Whip. He rode to hounds with an enthusiasm that was infectious and he knew, from the knowledge bred in his bones, what you had to look for in a horse that would make a first-class point-to-pointer or potential star chaser.

His nephew, Willie O'Brien of Buttevant, who had an outstanding record as an amateur rider, winning no less than 200 races, and who also rode work for Vincent O'Brien when he was based in Churchtown, recalled: 'Jackie picked up The Harrier for my father, James, and they still talk to this day about the record of this horse. He ran in 22 point-to-points and won 20 of them. Yes, he had a great eye for a horse. I remember my father telling me that before Frank Vickerman really came to know Jackie and put full trust in his judgement, he bought three horses in Tramore. When Jackie saw them he said to Frank, "You might as well return them." It was Jackie who was instrumental in alerting Frank to the potential of Cottage Rake when the horse was owned by Dr Otto Vaughan of Fermoy.'

Jackie O'Brien had a store in Fermoy and one in Tallow, County Waterford. The farmers would bring in their wool and he would pay them for it, then store it before it was transferred to Frank Vickerman, who duly settled with him. Jackie was more than a mere agent for Frank Vickerman. In fact, a deep mutual respect and friendship developed between them and when Jackie married rather late in life the Vickermans were special guests at the wedding.

Invariably on his rounds Jackie O'Brien kept his eyes open for a bargain – a store that might catch his fancy on some farm. He was even reputed to carry on his person a bundle of open cheques signed by Frank Vickerman so that there would be no hiccups, no delays from the moment he clinched a deal. That story may be apocryphal, as Jackie was not short of money himself. However, it is indicative in itself of the relationship between the two men. It was Jackie's approach that once he made up his mind to buy a horse, he would take out his cheque book, fill in the name of the vendor on the spot and thus avoid any possibility of a change of mind, which could so easily happen if he announced that he would come back some days later with the money.

Once, in a moment of inspired intuition as darkness descended on the fair in Fermoy, a dealer pressed Jackie to buy a horse from him. 'I'll take it anyway,' he told the dealer – though in the fading light he could not be certain. When he saw the animal the next day, he knew he had scored. For £25 he had picked up one that became a champion point-to-pointer.

The Second World War hit racing very badly in Britain. The Cheltenham Festival meeting was suspended in 1942. The bottom fell out of the export market for Irish horses and it was not until 1946 that it got back to normal. You could pick up a very promising horse for the proverbial song. Jackie O'Brien would invariably go to the sales with Frank Vickerman.

Vickerman's son, Brian, was serving with the British Army in the desert campaign against Rommel in North Africa and Frank, who at that stage was not into racing himself, thought it would be nice to give him a few horses as a welcoming-home present. Sadly, the boy never did return. He died of malaria in Africa.

Jackie O'Brien had purchased six yearlings at give-away prices by today's standards. He suggested to Frank Vickerman that he give at least a couple of them to Vincent O'Brien to train. Vincent's budding talent was known to the wool agent from Fermoy, for he was a judge not only of horseflesh but also of trainers and jockeys.

And thus evolved that fateful approach at Limerick Junction. Vincent did not hesitate to answer in the affirmative.

He was on his way.

Vincent O'Brien sent out only one runner in 1943 – but it was a winner. Oversway, running in his own name and with Noel Sleator in the saddle, took the Elton Plate, a 1 mile 1 furlong flat race at Limerick Junction worth £74 by 1½ lengths from Galway Girl. The winner was returned at 6–1 but paid 27s for a 2s stake on the Tote or odds of 100–8. Oversway was sold by Vincent to Archie Willis, who sent him to the Curragh to be trained by Aubrey Brabazon's father, Cecil.

The following year, at the age of 27, Vincent made the big-name Curragh trainers rub their eyes in astonishment and at the same time landed his first important betting coup as a public trainer in his own right when he sent out from Churchtown the winners of the Irish Autumn Double. On 7 October 1944 Drybob (Morny Wing) dead-heated with Dawross (Jimmy Eddery) in a field of 26 in the Irish Cambridgeshire, 3 lengths ahead of The Abbot of Hainsault (Phil Canty), owned by Willie Robinson's mother and trained by his father, George Robinson. Drybob was returned at 20–1.

Then in the Irish Cesarewitch on 4 November at the Phoenix Park (it had been transferred there that year from the Curragh), 30 horses went to the post. Free Trade started at 6–1 favourite but was beaten a neck by Good Days (Morny Wing) at 20–1, with Distel, destined to win the Champion Hurdle two years later, third. Other famous jumpers that were unplaced that day included Prince Regent and The Gripper.

Vincent did not have the resources to have a good old-fashioned tilt at the ring himself on Drybob and Good Days, but he advised Frank Vickerman that both horses were ready to run for their lives. Frank had £10 each-way at odds of 800–1.

Looking back 46 years later, Vincent said, 'There was a part of me that found it difficult to believe that such a double could come off. So I modestly said to myself, "I'll have £2 each way." '

If Drybob had won outright instead of dead-heating, Frank's winnings would have come to £10,000 and Vincent's to £2000. In the end they had to settle for £5000

34

and £1000 respectively. Yes, that dead-heat in the Cambridgeshire made a lot of difference, as the odds were halved.

Still, Vincent had got the nest-egg that would make a world of difference to him: it was out of the £5000 he netted that Frank Vickerman acquired Cottage Rake in due course and started the cycle that would see Vincent O'Brien become the 'king' of Cheltenham for well over a decade – nothing, according to Dermot, matching his record in the Gloucestershire Hurdle, today known as the Waterford Crystal Supreme Novices' Hurdle.

What most racing folk forgot, after the 'unknown' young trainer from County Cork had made his spectacular double-pronged assault on two big handicaps at the back-end of the 1944 season, was that Vincent had done it already with Solford in the 1938 Irish Cambridgeshire and in 1941 with Astrometer in the Irish Cesarewitch. 'Trained D. P. O'Brien' is entered after each horse in the record books. Vincent, however, as assistant to his father, was really the inspiration, the guiding genius behind those notable successes. He was only 21 at the time of Solford's success and 24 when Astrometer triumphed in 1941.

In the case of Solford, you can see Vincent already employing the training methods that would stand him in such good stead later with horses like Cottage Rake, Knock Hard and Hatton's Grace – in effect, showing that they could win over the obstacles and at the same time be sharpened up to take big handicap races on the Flat. And he was already, too, displaying the infinite patience, when he realised that he had something special under his care, that enabled him to wait a full year, if necessary, before the build-up was made to a special target.

In all this he was prepared to stay in the background and let his father enjoy the limelight – and there was no prouder man in County Cork after Solford's success than Dan O'Brien, for the *Cork Examiner* gave special headline treatment to this success by a 'local' trainer.

They even composed a ballad about it, one verse of which went:

I'll raise my glass to Moylan
May his glory ever shine
To Solford and his owner
The genial Dan O'Brien
And I won't forget the trainer
Whenever I relate
How Solford won the 'Cambershire' of '38

Solford was an unbroken three-year-old bay (by Sol-dennis out of the Swynford mare, Margaret Beaufort) when purchased by Dan O'Brien and his breeder, Jack Hartigan of County Limerick. From the outset he showed distinct promise, winning three races on the Flat at four and five, but then he broke down when, with Vincent in the saddle, he started 2–7 favourite in a field of three for the Fermoy Plate at Mallow on 17 June 1936 and was beaten 4 lengths by the 8–1 outsider, Owen Mor.

Solford was not rushed back, being off the course for the entire following season. After his return he won over hurdles at Naas in March 1938 and was then trained specifically for the Flat – the long-term target being the Cambridgeshire at the back-end. He ran up a sequence of six wins and, not surprisingly, was allotted 9 stone 9 pounds in the Cambridgeshire. Ridden by Jack Moylan, he carried this burden to a length victory over Ajar in a field of fifteen with Seedling (Willie Howard), the 3–1 favourite unplaced. Behind the scenes this triumph gave immense pleasure to young Vincent, who saw that a good horse can shoulder weight and still win; in 1950 Hatton's Grace would win the Irish Cesarewitch with 10 stone and the same season Knock Hard put up an excellent weight-carrying performance when taking the Irish Lincolnshire.

The Cambridgeshire success by Solford immediately resulted in the cheque books being brought out. He was bought as a seven-year-old gelding by Curragh trainer Charlie Rogers on behalf of Miss Dorothy Paget, who put him into training, with most of her other jumpers, at the stables of Owen Anthony at Letcombe Bassett, near Wantage. Solford fell in the lead at the last flight in the 1939 Champion Hurdle but atoned by winning it in 1940.

At home in Churchtown, Vincent had reason to be proud of his role in the making of Solford as a champion-to-be.

In the case of Astrometer's Irish Cesarewitch triumph in 1941, Vincent O'Brien proved to himself that a three-year-old could win against the older horses in a big field. Astrometer was handicapped on the 7 stone 6 pounds mark in a field of 25. Ridden by Robin Hardwidge, he won by a short head from Bold Maid. Willie Howard rode the unplaced 4–1 favourite, Tom Mix. Incidentally, Bold Maid subsequently produced Red Winter, who carried the colours of Sir Winston Churchill to victory in the 1954 Ulster Derby. In 1943 Astrometer dead-heated with Point D'Atout in the Irish Cesarewitch, when owned by Dorothy Paget and trained by Charlie Rogers.

So, when his father died in 1943 and he started on his own, Vincent O'Brien was far more experienced and indirectly had already achieved much more than could have been known to the general body of racegoers in Ireland. In a word, he was not simply arriving out of the blue. The Autumn Double coup with Drybob and Good Days in 1944 was certainly not going to prove to be just one golden hour.

After his father's death, his step-brother, Donal, had taken over the family farm at Clashganniff and Vincent rented gallops, stables and grazing from him, the arrangement continuing from 1943 until Vincent moved to Ballydoyle in 1951. Vincent, as time went on, rented extra gallops from Michael Lynch of Cregane, Churchtown, a good friend of the family.

In between Drybob dead-heating for the Irish Cambridgeshire and Good Days winning the Irish Cesarewitch, Vincent sent out Wren Boy from Churchtown on 12 October 1944 to gain his first success under National Hunt Rules by taking a hurdle race at Limerick Junction worth £74. The owner of the winner was W. J. Gleeson.

Aubrey Brabazon was in the saddle when Vincent won his first steeplechase on 14 June 1945 with Panay in the Templemore Plate at Thurles. The owner of Panay was given as 'Mr. D. G. B. O'Brien' but in reality it was Frank

Vickerman (it was possible then to register an assumed name with the Turf Club). By the time Cottage Rake became his property, he was proud to be listed as the owner of this champion chaser.

The year 1945 was to be in many ways the most fateful in Vincent O'Brien's life. It was the year that Dr Timothy J. 'Otto' Vaughan of Mallow approached him and asked him to train Cottage Rake for him. If great horses help to make trainers by putting a new spotlight on them internationally, then Cottage Rake was to place Vincent O'Brien firmly on the rung of the ladder that saw his name becoming known to a vast new racing public in Britain.

But before we detail the new heights Vincent began to scale once Cottage Rake arrived at Churchtown, let us turn back the clock to discover that from the time he sat as a young child on his father's knee, he was learning about horses and their breeding. Indeed, it could almost be said that he could be put to sleep more easily by being told the pedigrees of the horses in his father's stable than nursery rhymes and bed-time stories.

5

The Fifth Of Seven Sons

Helena O'Brien died as she was giving birth to her fifth child in an upstairs room in Clashganniff House in Churchtown, County Cork, on 28 October 1914. She was 36. In that era in Ireland babies were as likely to be born at home as in a nursing home. There was nothing unusual about it. Big families were the norm – six, seven, eight and even ten children. It was not unknown to find families of fourteen and fifteen. 'What God ordains, God will provide for,' was the dictum of the Catholic Church. People of simple faith accepted it without demur. Any form of contraception, even the most basic and natural, was seen as meriting an eternity in Hell's fire. The Church did not choose to enlighten its flock, even in cases where the mother's health was endangered by continuous pregnancies. And ordinary folk were loath to go against the ruling of the Church in such matters. 'We suffer and we bear,' was the fatalistic outlook. 'It will all be right in the next life.'

The Duhallows were hunting in the Churchtown area on the day Helena O'Brien died. The baying hounds entered the front field and Dan O'Brien came out and quietly told the Whip that there had been a death in the family. The hunt was immediately called off.

Daniel P. O'Brien – just Dan to his friends – was married again on 4 March 1916 at the age of 47 to his late wife's first cousin, Kathleen Toomey. Kathleen was no stranger to Clashganniff. She and Helena were close. Helena seems to have put her on her honour that if anything ever happened to her, then Kathleen would play her part in helping to see the family through difficult days.

Vincent was the eldest of the four children of the second marriage – three boys and a girl, Pauline (who was to become Pauline Fogarty, married to John, a businessman and a member of a well-known County Wicklow family). Vincent's brother, Dermot, was for 23 years his right-hand man, both in Churchtown and Ballydoyle, and now runs his own Derrygrath Stud near Cahir, County Tipperary. His other brother, Phonsie, was actually christened Alphonsus Septimus, the Septimus being for the seventh son.

There had been four boys by Dan's first marriage, Donal, John, Ignatius and James. At the time of writing this book in 1989 Ignatius was the only surviving one of the four and was in poor health in the Nazareth Home in Mallow. Donal died on 23 July 1988 aged 79. His son, Noel O'Brien, lives today with his wife, Margaret, and their four children in the original family homestead, Clashganniff House. He farms the land where once Vincent and his father before him had their gallops. I stood with him on a beautiful morning in April 1989 in 'The Galloping Field' and he pointed out to me how the horses would finish up on sharply-rising ground for all the world like the hill at Cheltenham. I could almost hear the sound of horses' hooves in the early morning as, in my mind's eye, I saw Cottage Rake and Hatton's Grace in their final gallops as Vincent prepared to go into battle for the first time at the Cheltenham Festival.

Noel O'Brien is into dairying in a substantial way. And he breeds horses. He is extremely proud of the traditions surrounding this place and the aura that hangs over Clashganniff and, indeed, over the whole Churchtown district because of what Vincent O'Brien achieved here first when assistant to Dan and later on his own. He would consider it unthinkable that there are not horses about the place.

When Dan O'Brien died in 1943 the farm, under a marriage settlement, passed to Vincent's eldest step-brothers, Donal and John. John later sold his interest to Donal. Normally, where a girl married into a farm, a legal document was drawn up committing the farm to go to the eldest son. It could not be sold or transferred to anybody else while the eldest son was alive. Even though Dan O'Brien must have known before his death that Vincent would have dearly loved to take over the farm, with which he had become so closely identified with his father, the marriage settlement document was sacrosanct. Thus, in the Irish way of doing things, the farm could not be willed to Vincent.

After Donal married in 1950 Vincent settled on the area in County Tipperary in the shadow of Slievenamon that was to accommodate the famous Ballydoyle stables. He had been looking out for a place of his own for some years before buying Ballydoyle. The move was made in 1951.

Vincent O'Brien was born in Clashganniff House on 9 April 1917. The weather is reputed to have been very unseasonal when he was christened in Churchtown. 'I often heard them say at home that the snow was hedge-high the day Vincent was brought to St Nicholas's Church,' recalled Dermot. He was given the names 'Michael Vincent' – thus the 'M.V.' – and in the baptismal records produced for me by the Parish Priest, Father Patrick Twohig, the parents are listed as 'Daniel O'Brien' and 'Kathleen M. Toomey'.

Clashganniff House is within walking distance – not more than half a mile – of the village of Churchtown, which today has a population of 450, though there are 1300 people in the combined parish of Churchtown-Liscarroll. Churchtown – Brugh Thuinne in the Gaelic form – is proud to claim that it was the birthplace of Robert O'Meara, who was the doctor to Napoleon on St Helena. A noted Irish poet of the first half of the eighteenth century, one Sean Clarach Mac Domhnaill also hailed from the village, while the family of Maeve Binchy, today an international best-selling novelist and *Irish Times* columnist came from the area. In the last century, an excellent type of hard red marble was mined near the village and it found its way into pillars in some of the great churches. Sadly, it was never developed to the point where modern machinery was utilised and Churchtown, instead of continuing to be famous for red marble, became famous instead as the place that gave Vincent O'Brien to the world of racing.

The village has a butcher's shop, Gaffney's (Vincent O'Brien was their biggest customer when training in Churchtown) and two pubs, O'Brien's (no relation of Vincent) and O'Sullivan's (formerly Flannery's). O'Brien's pub, in typical Irish country style, also combines a super-mart and Tom can be seen selling rashers, sausages and black pudding in one half of it, while his brother Pat, is pulling a creamy pint within hailing distance in the bar section. They had a successful racehorse which Tom trained and it was very aptly named Ask Pat, because when someone in the supermart didn't know the price of something, the reaction automatically was to shout across and 'ask Pat'.

Once the village had three pubs but O'Keeffe's, which shared the glory days when Cottage Rake came back to a victory parade, first in Buttevant and then in Churchtown, after that first Gold Cup win in 1948, no longer serves spirits, beer or stout. The old-timers still remember the bonfires blazing and, as Jimmy O'Sullivan put it to me, 'Churchtown being drunk dry' and Vincent O'Brien 'being carried shoulder-high round the village' as they acclaimed him for his first big Cheltenham Festival triumph. They remember how Frank Vickerman, the owner of Cottage Rake – 'a very generous man' – went around all the pubs in advance and told them to stock up and that he would meet the bill. They remember 'nine barrells of stout out on the street' being tapped to cater for the hundreds who gathered in the village to join in the celebrations, which went on into the early hours of the morning. And they remember, too, how Frank Vickerman and his wife, Constance, went to the old National School with the original owner of Cottage Rake, Dr 'Otto' Vaughan of Mallow and

Vincent O'Brien and, after dispensing 'gallons of sweets', they signed the school register, as did Vincent and Dr Vaughan. The Vickermans' entry can still be read today: 'Our visit has given us great pleasure. . . . the essays written on Cottage Rake were really excellent.'

'It was a pity Vincent ever left Churchtown,' said Jimmy O'Sullivan with a definite hint of nostalgia in his voice for times past. 'The whole area was a horse-conditioned region while he was training at Churchtown. He was the biggest employer by far. Everything revolved around his stable and it was never the same once he moved to Ballydoyle.'

They could never have envisaged the impact this lad would make on the life of a community when he started his schooling in the old National School in Churchtown (now a Community Hall) on Monday, 13 September 1920.

Clashganniff, the townland from which he hailed, means 'The Sandy Furrow' – great land for rearing horses and training them because of its special limestone qualities.

Dan O'Brien gave his profession in the school register as 'farmer'. Fortunately, the school records are extant to this day. They could so easily have been pulped. During the Second World War, because of the shortage of paper, an order went out from Dublin for the return of all the school record books to the Department of Education. The order, for some reason, does not seem to have penetrated as far as Churchtown and across the bottom of the page carrying the entries on Vincent O'Brien, from the time he started in 'Infants' to the day he left on 6 September 1930 when finishing in 'Sixth Class', someone wrote years later – 'Horse Trainer, Ballydoyle, County Tipperary'. There is a world of significance behind that five-word entry.

The fathers of most of the children were listed as either 'labourers' or 'farmers'. Labourers dominated – a sign of the depressed times when Ireland was in the middle of the War for Independence and the affluent sixties were a long way away as yet.

School photographs were taken by a photographer

doing the rounds on his bicycle and he would stand his box camera on the familiar tripod and vanish momentarily behind 'the bag' as he snapped a group picture. The group picture would probably cost 6d but if a boy could promise to bring in an extra 6d the next day, the photographer would oblige by taking him and his brother, where there were two members of the one family in a school. Vincent and Dermot knew that their father could afford that extra 6d, so I was able to unearth a print of the two of them together during their school days.

Pat Fennessy, current Principal over the new National School (built in 1947), preserves the old school register with loving care, realising full well the historical significance of the entries in it.

The area into which Vincent O'Brien was born and which was to establish him in time as a trainer was steeped in racing lore and renowned not alone for the horses it produced, but the natural horsemen who hailed from the area.

It embraces the Dashing Duhallows country (Vincent hunted with them from an early age in the traditional black jacket). The Duhallow is actually the oldest Hunt existing in Ireland. At the time when Charles Edward Louis Philip Casimer, commonly called 'The Young Pretender', was raising the standard in Scotland, Mr Henry Wrixon of Ballygibbin kept a pack of hounds. It is on record that the Wrixon family hunted in 1745 and a button was found later with the inscription 'Duhallow Hunt Revived, 1880'.

The Churchtown area is equally renowned for shooting and fishing, pastimes which had always been accepted as an integral part of life itself in the O'Brien family, though Vincent's eldest son, David, after acquiring the bug from his father and going shooting from time-to-time with him, decided to give it up – 'as I reached a point where I did not like killing things'.

Cahirmee Fair (Caheramee is the local pronunciation) held in Buttevant about the third week of July each year was

44

Vincent O'Brien's parents,
Dan and Kathleen,
pictured at Clashganniff,
Churchtown, Co. Cork.

REGISTER OF *Churchtown B.* NATIONAL SCHOOL.

Date of Entrance. 1920.	Register Number.	Pupils' Names in Full.	Age of Pupil last Birth Day.	Religious Denomination.	Residence.	Occupation or Means of Living of Parents.	State the Name and County of the last National School at which the Pupil attended; and the Class in which he last passed.		
							School.	County.	Class.
June 8th	931	1 Callaghan Matt.	21.12.13	R.C	Rath	Labourer	Never at school before		
June 15th	932	2 Murphy Thomas	9.4.14	"	Ballychristy	"	"		
Sep 6th	933	3 Tierney John C.	19.15	"	Churchtown	Nat. Teacher	"		
Sep 7th	934	4 OLeary Denis	3.9.14	"	Egmont	Labourer	"		
Sep 13th	935	5 OBrien Mc Vincent	9.4.07	"	Clashganniff	Farmer	"		

Name of Pupil.	Year ending	No. of Attendances made in the Year.	Class in which Enrolled.	Precise Date of Admission to that Class.	Class in which Examined.	Results of Examination.								Extra Branches, insert Name.	State whether Pupil passed or failed.	If Pupil be struck off, give date.	If Pupil be re-admitted, give date.
						Reading, &c.	Spelling, &c.	Writing, &c.	Arithmetic.	Grammar.	Geography.	Needlework.					

The Old National School (*below, with author*) in Churchtown where Vincent O'Brien started his schooldays on Monday, 13 September 1920, and (*above*) the school register showing Vincent's name. The school is now a Community Hall.

The class of 1923. Vincent O'Brien (*ringed*) is in the second row from the back, and his teacher, Tom Tierney, the principal, is at the extreme left. It was he who said of Vincent, 'This lad is something different.' *Left*: Dinny Fisher, one of Vincent's schoolmates, in 1988.

Vincent's only sister, Pauline Fogarty and (*below*) their childhood home, Clashganniff House, as it is today.

Vincent (on left), aged 17, with his brother Dermot, cutting a dash of sartorial elegance. *Below*: On an Alpine holiday, close friends (left to right) Martin Molony, the late Jim Blake and Vincent.

Dan O'Brien chatting with Jimmy Canty, father of Curragh trainer Phil Canty, and (*below*) leading in Hallowment after the horse, which he trained, had won the November Plate (bumper) at Limerick on 7 November 1940. It was Vincent's first winning ride as an amateur. *Right*: Aubrey Brabazon leading over the last hurdle on Hatton's Grace to win the Champion Hurdle for the first time in 1949.

Martin Molony (*above*) shows his style as a jump jockey, and (*right*) powering Hatton's Grace home to beat Knock Hard in the 1949 Irish Cesarewitch. *Below*: Molony wins the race again the following year for Vincent O'Brien, coming with a tremendous late run on the inside, despite a welter burden of 10 stone.

once the greatest in Europe, lasting for a week or so where now it only lasts a day. It reputedly dates back to the days of King Brian Boru, who drove the Danes out of Ireland in the Battle of Clontarf in 1014.

It was said that each cavalry battle on the Continent meant money for the farmer-breeders of the area but once the dragoon and hussar regiments switched to tanks, that outlet dried up like a spent oil-well.

According to local legend, the 600 gallant horses of the Light Brigade had left their farms to clatter into Buttevant to be sold at the Cahirmee Fair. And earlier still, they will tell you, the pride of the Fair was a horse which eventually became famous as Marengo, Napoleon's favourite white charger.

Con O'Brien, 'The Bard of Ballyhea', who they will tell you locally was 'a bit of a genius in his own way' and who was related to Vincent O'Brien from another side of the family, was inspired to write a ballad about it – and the sadness of its fall. He described 'the sunshine blazing down on all, on dealers great and blockers small' and 'jarveys steering through the throng, with passengers the whole day long' and the hotels packed day and night 'with money flying left and right'.

A magazine correspondent who visited the Fair 35 years ago wrote how Buttevant 'which has the quiet abandoned look of many a Munster town – small shops down a long street' comes to life each July with the horse-fair and is 'shaken with a tremendous hustle'.

'Knots of horses trot along the road in a cloud of lime-stone dust, with drovers whooping behind. Spring carts and sulkies rattle by. At the cross-roads on the edge of the town, groups of men sprawl on the little green or prop up the signpost to Mallow. Their attitude is lazy but their eyes are sharp watching the hunters, the cobs, the Connemara ponies streaming past . . .

'The town fills with newcomers, whiskey-faced men with breeches and crops, ladies who have the sound as well as the look of horses, shabby copers with a reputation for being worth "gallons of gold", escapologists, wheel-of-fortune operators, sellers of web halters, and the vagrant horse-dealers whose caravans are parked in a line along the verge of the Limerick road.'

Cahirmee Fair lives on in a very modified fashion, only a pale shadow now of the great event it was – 'echoing with foreign haggling' – in other times. It will live as the Fair of Ballinasloe and Puck Fair in Killorglin will live – as long as Ireland breeds horses.

Buttevant publican, Tony O'Neill, for long a friend of the O'Brien family and a storehouse of knowledge on the history of the area, recalled that this area gave the word 'steeplechase' to National Hunt racing.

The O'Brien homestead in Clashganniff, looking east to the Ballyhoura mountains, lies three miles from the steeple of St John's Church in Castlelands, Buttevant.

In 1752 two local gentlemen, Cornelius O'Callaghan and Edmund Blake, were to take part in what is accepted as the first steeplechase on record. The race was 'to settle a bet of a hog's head of wine'.

The approach was to pick a line of country and then set an objective towards which the contestants would race – and what was more suitable and more easy to see in the distance than the steeple of a church?

Messrs O'Callaghan and Blake were to race over four-and-a-half miles of country from Buttevant Church to the St Leger Church in Doneraile and because it was from steeple to steeple, it gave rise to the word 'steeplechase' in the racing vernacular to this day.

The challenge was won by O'Callaghan, who was a direct descendant, on the mother's side, of Willie McLernon, a leading amateur rider.

Two hundred years on from the first recorded steeplechase, it was decided to stage a repeat. The original race had been from Buttevant to Doneraile but the historical renewal (arranged primarily by the Buttevant Tostal Council and the Duhallow Hunt with the blessing of the I.N.H.S.) on 23 April 1954 was run from Doneraile to Buttevant. John Huston, a great advocate of the Hunt in the West of Ireland, was one of those who competed.

The race was won on a horse called Baypark II by P. P.

Hogan who was later to play such a significant role in the fortunes of Robert Sangster. Willie O'Brien, a nephew of Jackie O'Brien was second and W. A. (Billy) McLernon third, Brian McLernon fourth and John Twomey fifth. The field comprised 30 participants.

In P. P. Hogan's home in Rathcannon, I was shown the Tostal trophy which he received for his victory.

They are proud in Buttevant and Churchtown of the outstanding jockeys who have direct links with this area of County Cork. Jack Moylan rode for Dan O'Brien and later for Vincent and his daughter married Jimmy Eddery, Pat's father.

Jimmy 'Corky' Mullane, who had the most perfect 'sit' of any jockey of his era on a two-year-old, was born near Buttevant and in time was to ride as first jockey to the powerful Paddy ('Darkie') Prendergast stable.

The Duhallow Pony Club was the nursery for outstanding jump jockeys like Jonjo O'Neill and Brendan Powell. Jonjo's birthplace, Castletownroche, is just 15 miles from Buttevant.

Michael Collins, father of highly successful and very shrewd Curragh trainer, Con Collins, trained with a commendable strike rate at Springfort House (now a well-known restaurant, outside Buttevant). Con was actually born there. Incidentally, Michael Collins helped lay out Mallow racetrack. He subsequently moved to the Curragh, trained for Joe McGrath and won the Irish Triple Crown with Windsor Slipper.

The Churchtown area became renowned for the classic horses it produced. Loch Lomond, which was trained by the legendary J. J. Parkinson at Maddenstown Lodge to win the 1919 Irish Derby, was bred here. And exactly 60 years later that tradition was maintained when Dickens Hill, which was bred at the Flannery's Egmont Stud, finished second to Troy in the Epsom Derby (1979) and was runner-up to the same colt in the Irish Derby.

The Flannerys once had a stud in the village itself, Churchtown Stud, founded in 1850 and reputed to be the oldest stud in Ireland. They also had the Egmont Stud at the edge of the village, dating from 1870.

The late Frank Flannery and his wife, Nell, always maintained very close ties with Clashganniff House. In fact, Frank's friendship with Dan O'Brien led to Dan acquiring a mare that was to bring him great good fortune. Once when Frank Flannery was going to the Newmarket Sales, Dan asked him to keep an eye out for a good mare and told him to purchase it if he thought fit.

Frank duly bought the mare, Golden Emblem, for 35 guineas in foal to Tetrameter. Her first foal, Golden Meter showed a lot of speed but did not stay. Dan bred her to Vesington Star, which was standing at the Flannery's Churchtown Stud and the result was first Astrometer and then Astrologer – two colts that turned out to be prolific winners, as we shall see.

The Egmont Stud, so steeped in proud tradition, is run today by Edward Flannery who, with his wife Mary, maintains the close links with Clashganniff House that have stood the test of time. Christy Stack, who was born in the area and worked for the O'Briens, is now his Head Man. There are roughly 15 to 16 mares at the Egmont Stud but they do not stand any stallions.

The Stud had the distinction, when Dickens Hill won the 1979 Irish Two Thousand Guineas on the way to being second in the Epsom Derby and Irish Derby, of also breeding the runner-up in the first Irish classic that season, Brother Philips, trained by Con Collins.

You cannot escape the conclusion, then, that Vincent O'Brien was reared in an atmosphere permeated with a love of horses and racing, also with following the hounds and with shooting and fishing in their respective seasons.

Vincent knew 'almost from the cradle', as they say in Munster, how to sit astride a pony and later a hunter. He remembers before he actually began following the hunt in the formal manner, going out with young friends of his and experiencing the sheer exhilaration of jumping ditches – 'and it was such fine expansive country that we never had to jump the same ditch twice'.

Years later – towards the end of the eighties – his brother Dermot recalled going out on winter days with Vincent. With them would be Ned Fitzgerald, Danny O'Sullivan and Maurice O'Callaghan – 'three excellent lads' – as they schooled point-to-pointers. 'It was marvellous. I can never forget the wonderful memories left by those days as we went, maybe, four miles over natural jumping country and it meant that horses just had to jump. It was better and more exciting than any hunt. Vincent loved it like the rest of us.'

Locals who remember Vincent from those days recall him as 'a good rider' – 'a natural in the saddle'.

Vincent grew up in a happy household like any normal lad in a country area. It did not matter whether the lads who went to school with you were the sons of labourers or farmers, you played with them in the school yard and you played with them after school. Ireland in its rural heartlands, in its towns, is unique in the sense that its national schools and its secondary schools, too, provide the platform for all classes to mingle and 'townies' learn how to mix with their 'country cousins'. And that is why its born politicians, who are products of this same school system, have the common touch and invariably amaze visitors with the way they can so readily win a response from their 'constituents', whether it is in the street, the pub or at some race meeting.

Dinny Fisher, who was in school with Vincent, said, 'After school we would play hurling in a field in front of Vincent's house. He was a great hurler. I think he could have gone on to win All-Ireland honours with Cork if he had kept at it.'

Dan Flynn, retired postman and living in a comfortable Churchtown cottage next to Dinny Fisher's said that as he was 74, he would have been a few years ahead of Vincent in school. 'He was a strong young chap and very adept with the hurley.'

Jimmy O'Sullivan, who would later work for Vincent O'Brien, and whose brother, Danny, was an outstanding work rider initially and later head lad, talked in his cottage at the turn of the bend beyond Clashganniff House with

Jack Murphy, whose brother, Bill, was in the same class as Vincent. 'I am 69 now,' said Jimmy. 'I was in the same class as Dermot but Vincent was a couple of classes ahead of us. I remember Vincent as a very good hurler especially when there were matches between Clashganniff and Churchtown.'

The goalposts can be seen from Clashganniff House in the field where these friendly matches took place. Once Clashganniff were short of a player and it was agreed by mutual consent between both sides that Katherine Cowhey, who had been an outstanding camogie player, would be allowed to play in goal. She was an inspiration as Clashganniff, with Vincent O'Brien playing a very prominent role up front – 'He had a great eye and a great shot,' said Jack Murphy – beat the lads from Churchtown.

Confirmation day is always a day to remember for Catholic boys and girls in Ireland. In the old days it was when most boys first got long trousers and then they did the rounds and received 'presents' from relatives and from neighbours and friends. The traditions persist to this day – though they do not wait until Confirmation day to get into long trousers. Vincent O'Brien was confirmed with his school pals of around the same age on 9 May 1928. He was rather young, however, at eleven for Confirmation. He had the honour of being Confirmed by Bishop Robert Browne, who had won distinction as President of Maynooth College.

Vincent had started going to school when Ireland was in the throes of the War for Independence. County Cork was one of the greatest hot-beds of guerilla warfare against the regular British units and the Black and Tans, who did not always observe the letter, or even the spirit, of the Geneva Convention.

'I remember on my way home from school, we would hear the sound of one of the Crossley tenders carrying a unit of the Black and Tans and we would hide behind some ditch until they had passed by; we would lie there in fear, our hearts stopping at the thought that if they spotted us they might begin firing indiscriminately,' Vincent recalled.

As a youth Vincent went everywhere with his father –
'To races, to sales and round the country to various farms
looking for young stock to make hunters, point-to-
pointers and chasers.' Vincent smiles now when he recalls
that once he had the audacity in the hearing of grown-
ups to advise his father quite seriously against buying a
particular animal in a field because of something he had
spotted about its forelegs. He was already on the road,
without realising it, to Lexington and the Keeneland Sales
– half a century before he actually made the initial
onslaught with 'The Syndicate' in 1975.

He would never forget the debt he owed his father for
introducing him so young to the world of the judgement
of horseflesh – for helping him acquire 'an eye' that can
be acquired in no university or any seat of learning but
only in the hard school of experience.

'Whatever knowledge I may have of horses, I owe a
great deal of it to my father. I learnt so much in those
years going around with him and I have no doubt my
father realised my great interest in and love for horses
and that he fostered it.'

6

'A Thorough Gentleman'

'A thorough gentleman, a pure old toff,' is the memory that Tony O'Neill of Buttevant has of Dan O'Brien, Vincent's father. There is a photo extant of him in cap and overcoat (reaching down well below the knees, as was the fashion of the times) and the inevitable tweeds, leading in Hallowment at Limerick on a November day in 1940, with Vincent in the saddle. Dan owned the horse and trained it to win that day.

Dan O'Brien was born in Clashganniff House, where the family had farmed before him. In the 1893 *Munster Directory*, he is listed with eight other people under the heading 'Churchtown – Gentlemen and Clergy'. The Directory had a separate section for those listed as 'Farmers' solely.

Vincent's great grandfather, Daniel O'Brien, when a widower spent the last six to eight years of his life in the Cistercian Monastery, Mount Melleray, near Cappoquin, not as a full monk but as an 'Associate' or 'Familiar'. A document compiled by one of the monks in 1971 and presented to the O'Brien family, reveals that Daniel O'Brien was a benefactor of the Monastery and before he finally entered made a week's retreat every year. 'When he came to reside here,' the document goes on, 'he had his temporal affairs settled and his family reared; one of his sons being a priest in the American Mission and four of his daughters being professed nuns in Ireland. His

52

death was a most holy and tranquil one. He had attained a great age.' On his death in January 1877, he was buried not apart from the monks but in the same plot – behind the altar of St Brigid in the Abbey Church. And the cross over his grave was the same as that over the graves of the monks.

Dan O'Brien was tall and well-built and carried himself in the local community with that quiet dignity that made him extremely popular. In some pictures, he bears a striking resemblance to Dermot. He was a down-to-earth personality, with no airs or graces, a man of the people. A man, too, with a keen sense of humour, a wonderful mimic and with a remarkable fund of stories, which his daughter, Pauline, regrets were never written down and preserved for posterity.

'He loved to dress well,' she recalls. 'Tweeds were his special fancy. He had quite a selection, too, of the type of shirts that were so popular in his day, the ones with the studs and a few collars. There could be great difficulty, I remember, getting those collars on.'

The theatre and music – light opera especially – meant a great deal to him, and he would never miss a presentation by one of Ireland's best-ever and most popular comedians, Jimmy O'Dea, at the old Cork Opera House, a building long since gone that helped create the operatic tradition for which the City by the Lee became famous (local tenors in the gods would show in the interval of an operatic production how 'La donna e mobile' really should be sung).

Dan O'Brien never drove himself. His son, Donal, would be seen at the wheel of the maroon-coloured, fluid-drive, bull-nosed Dodge. Whenever there was a good show in the southern capital that attracted him, the big Dodge would be on its way and friends in Buttevant would be heard to remark; 'There's Dan off again to the theatre.'

'Yes, Father had a great ear for music,' said Pauline. 'If you hummed a tune he didn't know, he would be able to get it within a few minutes on the piano or on the melodeon which was his pride and joy. Mother, too, was very good at the piano, so there was always the sound of music in our house. And when the piano wasn't being played or the melodeon, Father would put on a John McCormack record or a Gracie Fields record, like "The Biggest Aspidistra in the World" and hum it to himself or sing it aloud with real gusto. How he loved those old records.

'Nothing gave him more pleasure than the magnificent voice of John McCormack. Whenever there was an opportunity of listening to him in concert in Cork, he would be there. He deeply admired Count McCormack's singular rendering of appealing Irish numbers like "The Bard of Armagh", "I Hear You Calling Me", "Mother Machree", "Kathleen Mavourneen" and "Macushla". He cherished his 78s and they were played over and over again.'

Dan and John McCormack became friends, probably through the famous tenor's interest in racing (he actually owned a number of indifferent racehorses at one stage and dissipated quite a deal of his money on the Sport of Kings) and would, when his schedule permitted him to do so, go racing on the Metropolitan circuit, particularly at the Curragh. Dan was generous in giving tips when he fancied one of his own and, no doubt, put his friend on to a winner or two.

Pauline, Vincent's only sister, displays the same effervescence, vivaciousness and bonhomie in her character as Phonsie (she was at one stage a 6-handicap golfer and Junior All-Ireland champion). She unfolded in relaxed and easy manner the world of Dan O'Brien – the great family man – and his wife, who chose to stay as much as possible in the background and yet was a wonderful mother to her children, despite delicate health all through her life.

'Mother was frail, gentle and retiring, but of a very sweet and endearing disposition. She was always there to help us when we needed her; so wise, so far-seeing and so full of love for us all, especially my step-brothers. Each night after the evening meal she would see to it that we all knelt down and said the Family Rosary (and the trimmings). This was never overlooked, never once forgotten, never set aside.

'When Vincent married, Mother moved from Ballydoyle to a house – "Windswept" – which the family procured for her in Clonmel. She used to come to visit us a lot here and I would go down to Clonmel and stay with her. Even though her health was never good, she out-lived Father by thirty years.

'When I was seven, I went as a boarder to the Ursuline Convent in Cork, where one of Father's relations was Reverend Mother. I stayed there until I was seventeen and then finished in Drishane Convent in Millstreet. I was only home for holidays at Christmas, Easter and for the summer. Father was very Victorian in his ways, believing that girls should be seen and not heard. While I was always interested in horses, I wasn't allowed to ride to the hunt. That, of course, would never be the case today.

'Father, I remember, was superstitious also. He hated to see a ginger-haired woman if he was on his way to the races and had a fancied runner. If one of the horses got beaten and he had seen a ginger-haired woman that morning, he would put it down to the ill-luck she brought.

'The fruit-sellers at the races had great affection for him. They would greet him going in with the cry, "Ah, Mr O'Brien it's yourself – what is going to win today? We will keep the best fruit for you." Of course, he would blurt out a tip if he expected one of his own to win. Whether he won or lost, it didn't greatly affect his outlook or the warmth of his personality. "There's always a next time" summed up his philosophy in defeat. There was no better loser, ever. I feel he passed on that philosophy to Vincent and the rest of us.

'He would bring us home large quantities of fruit that he had bought from the fruit-sellers on his way out from the races. Baskets of strawberries in season. Sweets and chocolate – he never came home empty-handed. Father was a big man in his outlook. Money, for him, was never an end in itself but a means of enjoying the good things of life, of making others happy.

'Father liked nothing better in life than a game of cards

with his friends. The games they played generally were nap, poker or "45". They would adjourn to the drawing-room and at midnight Mother would make tea for them. Father could drink tea till the cows came home. He never drank alcohol. His favourite drink was grapefruit juice. He would take a large glass of this when playing cards. He poured the whiskey as lavishly as if it was grapefruit juice. I remember the laughter and the repartee emanating from the drawing-room as the drinks had their effect.

'Yes, I remember those times as very good times, very happy times. Our parents gave us a lot of love.'

Dan O'Brien raised dry stock on his farm but really horses were his life. He raced and trained them for the pleasure of it. His main interest was picking out good horses and breaking them. He put all types through his hands, from good-class flat to jumpers and hunters. One of the best was the useful flat handicapper, Holy Fooks, named after a famous local character who lived back in the last century around Kanturk. When fighting a duel on horseback one day, he rattled a seasoned pig's bladder which had lead in it in the face of his adversary and it made such a horrible sound that it frightened the opponent's horse. He turned tail and as he ran for his life, Holy Fooks could be heard exclaiming: 'Come back you coward!' Holy Fooks – the horse that is – was sold to Florrie Burke to go jumping and was afterwards ridden to victory by Joe Canty in the 1924 Galway Hurdle.

In the late 'thirties Dan O'Brien mated his mare Golden Meter with Vestington Star. Out of these matings came three excellent handicappers, Astrometer, Astrologer and Astromonic who, between them, won fourteen races on the flat from 5 furlongs up to 2 miles, not all of them in his ownership. Already we have seen how Astrometer won the Irish Cesarewitch while Astrologer, when owned by Jimmy McVey, gave John Oxx his first big handicap in the 1943 Irish Cambridgeshire.

Jimmy O'Sullivan described Dan O'Brien as, 'The best man I ever saw to clip a horse. He would go off some-where and come back with a horse that he had bought and that you wouldn't give tuppence for, but when he had finished trimming it and pulling the mane and tail, you could hardly believe it was the same animal.'

Dermot revealed that his father could be difficult to buy from, putting a high value on his own stock, particularly ones he had bred. 'Tom O'Donnell, a famous horse dealer in Buttevant, once picked up the tail of a horse for which my father had asked a price that Tom thought was excessively high and, peering under the tail, enquired, "Dan, where are the diamonds concealed?" '

'My Father belonged to an era of sportsmen,' summed up Phonsie O'Brien, who was thirteen when Dan O'Brien died. 'The thing he loved most of all was to go to the races, see his horses running and meet his friends. He loved the day out and his group of friends looked on a race meeting as a chance to entertain each other. They were not in the horses for money – you had sportsmen and their horses. My father particularly loved going to Killarney because, in addition to the races, he could stay down there and play cards. He had been known to play all night buying drinks most generously for his friends, though he did not drink himself.'

In *Horse Racing*, edited by Finbarr Slattery, Phonsie says: 'How different it is now when the racecourses are thinking what they must put on to entertain people. We seem to have lost something along the way.'

Pauline recalls her father's last visit to the Curragh in 1943, and its aftermath: 'I remember it as well as if it was only yesterday as that day's racing preceded his death. And because it was such a beautiful day, it probably hastened his end, as I shall explain.

'The arrangement was that my parents would come back to Arklow with us after the races and stay some time with us. Phonsie, who was a boarder in Wicklow Dominican Convent school, was due to be Confirmed. Father wouldn't have missed that occasion for anything as Phonsie, being the youngest, was his pet.

'Father had Astrologer running in the Irish Lincoln, with Jack Moylan up. There was a big field of about 26 runners. Astrologer was beaten half a length by Foam-crest, trained by Cecil Brabazon and ridden by Tommy Burns, T.P.'s father. Foamcrest, as far as I can recall, was getting 7 pounds and it was a tremendously exciting finish. I recall Father saying, "If Astrologer had stuck out his tongue he'd have won."

'After the race, Father gathered all his friends around him and invited them upstairs to the Owners and Train-ers. I remember that Henry O'Brien from Fedamore, his bosom pal, was there, also the Hartys of Patrickswell and the Flannerys. It was such a lovely day, so warm that all the men had taken off their coats very early on during racing. Father did so, even though he was always extremely careful in such matters after contracting pneu-monia twice from wettings he got at fairs. Mother pon-dered aloud the wisdom of taking off his coat but he laughed and said, "Now, now, I'm as young as the rest of you."

'A man came up to him while we were having tea and said that he had very good oats for sale – that he would be putting the oats up for public auction during the following week. He promised to give Father first option. That decided Father in favour of going back home on the train, and leaving Mother to come on with us to Arklow. It was agreed there and then that my husband, John, would be at Kingsbridge (now Heuston Station) to meet him off the train and drive him to Arklow on the following Monday.

'I remember Father gave me an extra kiss before we parted that day at the Curragh. I never thought it would be the last time I would see him. I recall John taking the phone call from Churchtown that fateful Monday morn-ing, and when he put down the phone he was strangely silent for a moment. Then he came to me and said quietly, "Pauline, I'm afraid I have bad news for you. Your father is dead."

'Later I heard the full story. Going back from the Cur-ragh he told his friends that he was not in the mood to play cards with them. That was very strange, as he never turned down the chance of a hand of cards. He went to bed that night complaining of feeling cold. Dr Corbett came next day – Sunday – and said he would have to stay in bed. He got the medication that people got in those days for threatened pneumonia but his condition deteriorated rapidly. He died very suddenly late that evening. Penicillin became available the following September.

'Instead of there being a great reunion in Arklow, we found ourselves heading for Churchtown and the funeral. We were all so sad, especially after he had seemed so full of life at the Curragh on that glorious Saturday afternoon.'

There is a story that became something of a legend in Irish racing circles that it was because his father was broken by the bookmakers that Vincent O'Brien set out to exact his revenge on them by landing some of the most spectacular and carefully-planned coups in the annals of the Turf. I put the question straight to Vincent himself in Ballydoyle House and he flatly refuted it. 'If my Father had £5 on a horse, he would consider that a big amount.'

Dan O'Brien had money when fellow farmers in the area were forced to sell off their cattle in order to meet their rates bills. They went to the fair knowing in their hearts that they could not bring the animals home again. They had to take what was offered. Vincent had seen it happen when accompanying his father to fairs and it left an indelible imprint on his mind. 'The tariff walls that the British Government put up against us during the Economic War meant for a very bad situation,' he would recall years later. 'I remember seeing big bullocks weighing, maybe, 10 or 12 hundredweights being sold for 10s. And calves for five bob. The skins and hides were worth more than the animals themselves. They skinned them on the spot and threw the carcasses over the hedge.'

Tony O'Neill recalled a farmer in the area failing to dispose of a two-year-old bullock at Buttevant Fair and then selling it for the price of a good round of drinks by today's standards to a few men who played a hand of poker for it. 'They sportingly let him sit in and dealt him a hand but he didn't succeed in winning back the bullock. He was content, however, to have got something for the animal and a game of cards into the bargain before he went home to his wife and family.'

Dan O'Brien came into money, not by gambling, but again through the hinge of fate that was indirectly influencing every step in Vincent's climb up the ladder to fulfilling what his teacher had predicted when he said, 'This lad is something special.'

7

A Legacy From America

Dan O'Brien received a legacy from America in 1929 of £30,000, equivalent to £888,869 today. When men and women in the States were jumping off high buildings in despair after learning that their fortunes had evaporated overnight in the Wall Street crash, Dan O'Brien found himself coming into a bequest from a relative which could have placed him in the position – if he desired it – that he could have bought up all the land that was for sale in the Churchtown-Buttevant area and much further afield. And through the 'thirties, when farming was so depressed in Ireland, there was many a farmer who would have been only too willing to part with his holding for ready cash. Dan O'Brien, however, was not a grasping man and treasured very much the popularity he enjoyed in the community.

Vincent held to the philosophy of the sacredness of land in Ireland inculcated in him by his father. When the Coolmore Stud found it necessary to expand, great care was taken by both Vincent and his son-in-law, John Magnier, to ensure that no land bordering the existing acreage was purchased without the total willingness and consent of those who had it to sell and, furthermore, that they were entirely happy with the price. The same approach was adopted when Vincent was expanding his Ballydoyle stables.

The employment given today by Coolmore in the

various studs in the complex and also at Ballydoyle, and the revenues accruing directly and indirectly from their operations on such a wide scale, mean more to the area than any sizable industry. Industries, even those set up by multi-nationals, have a way of closing, whereas there is continuing remunerative employment at Coolmore and Ballydoyle for many hundreds.

Perhaps if Dan O'Brien had bought an extra farm specially for Vincent, it would have saved the first son of his second marriage a deal of mental torment as he pondered where his future lay once the lands of Clashganniff House passed to Donal and John (who subsequently sold his interest to Donal).

Denis Gaffney, the local butcher in Churchtown, said that he often heard his father speak of the day when Dan O'Brien arrived from Clashganniff House and in a room off the shop showed him a cheque for £17,000. That would seem to indicate that Dan did not get the whole £30,000 in the one lump sum but that the rest of it came later. And there were even suggestions that he would have got more from the will if he had gone to the States to collect it personally, and that a portion of what he was bequeathed was in stocks and shares and could have got caught up in the Wall Street crash.

Eamon de Valera as Taoiseach (Premier) over the Fianna Fail Government, that had been elected in 1932, had decided to try and force certain concessions from Britain – like the eventual winning back of the ports – through fighting an Economic War. However, while he had the support of a majority of the people for his policies, it meant immense hardship on the farming community. Heavy tariffs were imposed by Britain, all but wiping out for a time the export trade in live cattle. Animals not disposed of for give-away prices on the domestic market were slaughtered. Dan O'Brien facilitated friends of his in the area by giving them joints from the animals he killed, rather than allowing the meat to go completely to waste.

Anyway, the money from America arrived at a most timely juncture in Dan O'Brien's life and helped him to get through the Economic War in the 'thirties without having to endure the hardship that others in the neighbourhood and in Ireland generally had to suffer.

He could live quite comfortably and there is ample evidence to show that he liked the life of a gentleman farmer-cum-trainer. He kept a good staff and paid them well and also fed them well. However, he was not a born manager where money matters were concerned and certainly, but for the legacy, he would have been in serious difficulties financially. The five-figure sum he received provided him with the funds to send his children to boarding school.

Vincent was enabled to go to Mungret College in County Limerick. He stalled at leaving home unless Dermot went with him.

'I was three years younger than Vincent,' Dermot recalled. 'Vincent was twelve when we departed from Churchtown in 1929. There were a lot of tears that day, as Vincent was very close to his father. Tim Molony, Martin's brother, sat in the same desk beside me in Mungret.' Tim, who died in September 1989, would later ride Hatton's Grace to victory for Vincent in the 1951 Champion Hurdle and power Knock Hard to a memorable triumph in the 1953 Gold Cup.

Vincent stayed just two years in Mungret College, where he acquired an interest in rugby that was to remain with him throughout his life (he goes to Dublin for international matches and normally has an after-match reception for friends in the Berkeley Court Hotel).

'I hated the confines of the schoolroom.' Vincent confessed. 'I almost felt as if I was in prison. I wanted to feel, again, the air in my lungs on the farm in Churchtown. I wanted very much also to be with my father and the horses, going to point-to-points and, of course, following the hunt.' His father released him from the 'prison' of formal schooling when he was fourteen. But he had to serve his apprenticeship and was sent to Fred Clarke's establishment at Leopardstown, Foxrock, County Dublin, pursuing at night school the studies he missed out by leaving college. He became a proficient amateur rider, riding at point-to-points and also under both Rules and entering the winner's enclosure three times.

Martin Molony recalls riding on the same afternoon when Vincent O'Brien had the mount on Knight's Crest in a bumper race at Rathkeale, County Limerick. Rathkeale had a track in those days in the early part of the Second World War and Martin Molony actually rode his first hurdle winner there in 1942. It was Thursday, 19 March, the Rathkeale Plate, a 1½-mile Maiden Hurdle. The horse was named Prince John and was owned by Mrs E. J. King. Prince John had been brought back from England and Martin Molony won by a short head from Mrs Peg Watt's Border Knight, ridden by Willie T. O'Grady, father of Edward O'Grady.

Martin Molony and Vincent O'Brien became very good friends. It was a friendship that was to last and which blossomed to the benefit of both when Martin won the Irish Cesarewitch on Hatton's Grace in successive years (1949–50). Vincent and Martin went on an Alpine holiday together with Jim Blake, a close friend of Vincent's (Jim was later the victim of a tragic drowning accident). The picture taken in the Alps showing a very youthful Martin Molony and an equally youthful Vincent O'Brien is one which Martin cherishes very much.

During the seven years that he was Assistant Trainer to his father, Vincent O'Brien became very familiar with the point-to-point circuit and also with the meetings that are styled today the 'Festival round'. When the Irish Cambridgeshire was won with Solford (1938) and the Irish Cesarewitch with Astrometer (1941), the means of transporting horses to the Curragh was a far cry from the manner in which challengers from Ballydoyle are given the red carpet treatment today, down to Ballydoyle having its own landing-strip to fly horses to Britain and Continental destinations. Solford and Astrometer would both have been walked from Churchtown to the local railway station in Buttevant; Vincent, with the bike in the other hand, led the horses earmarked to win the principal autumn handicaps in the Irish racing calendar. 'I would throw the bicycle in the Guard's van and then the horses would be loaded on to the train and I would stay with them for the journey until we reached our destination.'

When the train got into, say, the Curragh, Vincent would retrieve his bicycle and supervise the unloading of the horses and then walk them to the course where they would be stabled. Normally this would be on the eve of racing and, having booked in at some guest-house in Kildare, he would cycle up to the racecourse later in the evening to feed the horses and ensure that they were bedded down comfortably for the night.

Fortunately, there were rail tracks in Dublin and in the suburbs at that time which were submerged without any real thought for the future in an expanding city (how much better the Dart service could be today if proper foresight had been shown).

Phonsie O'Brien said that in the early period, when Vincent was training on his own, horses bound for Leopardstown would be taken right out to Foxrock by rail, and in the case of the now-defunct Baldoyle track, as far as Sutton on the Great Northern line. There was even a rail connection to Naas.

It is amazing that racing was maintained in Ireland during the period of the Second World War, considering the difficulties that had to be overcome with petrol rationing. Turf-burning trains were excruciatingly slow but at least they provided a means of transport in days when any vehicles on the roads were only operating under special permit and coupons for petrol, as in the case of tea, were like gold dust. On the other side of the coin, the days of Emergency – as the period of the Second World War was known in Ireland – had a relaxed ease and pleasantness that left Martin Molony with some of his happiest memories, especially when riding in picturesque Killarney.

'We used to travel in a horse-drawn caravan as it was the only available means of transport. My brother, Tim, also travelled in the caravan along with neighbours, the late Ned Hartigan and the late Henry O'Brien (no relation of Dan O'Brien but a great friend and loved by all the children; he was Dermot's godfather). There were few autos on the road and little traffic of any kind, so the horse could be given his head to go about his business.

'We used to occupy the many hours of the journey by playing solo, both going from and coming back to home at Rathmore, near Croom, County Limerick. Usually we would stop at Castleisland overnight and continue on to Killarney the following morning for the races.

'One of my great memories of the Killarney races was in 1949. On the day prior to the start of the Festival meeting, Michael O'Hehir placed in his newspaper column a tip for punters, admonishing them all who were to have a flutter to do so on each and every one of my rides at the meeting. During this three-day meeting I was fortunate to have five winners and four seconds and ten rides, making Michael a pretty fair prognosticator.

'After racing, many very enjoyable evenings were spent at the Great Southern Hotel listening and dancing to the band of the late Major Watt.'

Jimmy O'Sullivan recalled going with Vincent with three horses to the now-defunct Miltown-Malbay track in County Clare. At Ennis they switched to the West Clare line made famous in the Percy French song ('Are you right there, Michael, are you right?') and because of the narrow gauge they had to put the horses into cattle wagons. The journey was not wasted, as two of the horses won. Timmy Hyde's father, the late Tim Hyde, was the successful rider. Vincent O'Brien got accustomed to being away from home for four or five days for these Festival meetings. Nowadays Curragh-based trainers will drive to Galway and back each day and even do the same in the case of Killarney, Tralee and Listowel.

When Cottage Rake was being transported across to England for his bid to win the King George VI Chase at Kempton in December 1948, having already won his first Gold Cup and the Emblem Chase at Manchester, he was accompanied on the train by Dermot and Danny O'Sullivan. Everything went smoothly from Buttevant to Mallow, where 'The Rake' was switched on to the train for Rosslare.

'We ran into a herd of cattle on the line,' recalled

Dermot. 'Some of the cattle were killed and others were injured. There was a delay while the carcasses were being removed and the train, which had been slightly derailed, was got back on to the tracks by a maintenance unit.

'At Rosslare, where the departure of the ferry had been delayed awaiting his arrival, he was swung in a box container from the quayside up on to the boat and the container was then lashed down. Again they held the passenger train in Fishguard for us and, believe me, some of the passengers, who had no interest in racing, weren't at all pleased when they were informed that the train to London had been delayed specifically to facilitate a horse. The journey to London at the back of that fast passenger train – not made for carrying horses – was equally hairy, I can tell you.'

Incidentally, Cottage Rake duly won the Kempton race. Strange, that Vincent O'Brien never once offered the excuse in those days, when one of his charges was beaten, 'My one didn't travel well.'

March 1949 marked the first time that Vincent O'Brien-trained challengers for the Cheltenham Festival meeting went by air. The Curragh Bloodstock Agency arranged the flight in a reconstructed bomber from Shannon to Bristol. Dermot O'Brien and Danny O'Sullivan accompanied Cottage Rake, Hatton's Grace and Castledermot. Dermot knew that Cottage Rake was a nervous traveller even when taken by road and sea. Now he wondered what would be 'The Rake's' reaction to his first experience of coasting down a runway before take-off.

He warned the pilot to be extra careful, especially when turning round to straighten out actually to face the plane down the runway. But, unfortunately, the plane gave a lurch and Cottage Rake, taking fright, began to go down. 'I knew if he went off his feet we were sunk,' said Dermot. 'There I was holding on to Cottage Rake for dear life, hoping and praying that I could prevent disaster. Danny and I took turns during take-off and during the flight itself swinging, you might say, off his tail and there were some terrible moments when we felt we had an impossible task on our hands. Thank God, we reached Bristol without mishap. But it was a near thing, a very near thing.'

In those day's planes were non-pressurised and, therefore, could not get over the weather. The result was a very rough trip when a plane ran into bad weather. The most hair-raising plane journey of all involved Lucky Dome when being transported with other horses from Ballydoyle to run at Merano, near Milan. Jacqueline O'Brien had made friends with Pierro Richard, head of the Steeplechase Society in Italy. It was agreed that Vincent would send over a number of horses to run at the autumn meeting in Merano, a racecourse set in a basin surrounded by hills.

It was known that Lucky Dome was a bad traveller, so Maxie Cosgrove, the vet, suggested that he be given a sedative that would get him through the worst part of the journey. It had been arranged that the plane would pick up Lord Leigh's horses that were also due to run at Merano but, unfortunately, that took longer than anticipated – 1½ hours in fact – and as the plane flew over France, the effect of the sedative began to wear off.

The plane was due to touch down at Lyon to refuel before making the final leg of the journey to Milan. It ran into a thunderstorm and with Lucky Dome already beginning to get fractious, the pilot had no option but to turn back for Paris. On the tarmac in Paris Christy Stack was with Lucky Dome in the back of the plane when suddenly the horse jumped over the barrier in the stall and out on to the tarmac. He landed on all fours – with one eye closed and the other half-closed. Christy Stack was knocked flying as Lucky Dome made his sudden exit from the plane.

The vet was called and pronounced that the horse was sound. 'We spent that night at Alec Head's place. The rest of the party had gone on in the plane to Milan with the other horses and I was left with instructions on how to get Lucky Dome by rail to Milan,' recalled Christy Stack.

On the Saturday Lucky Dome was put on a goods train

at 1.30 p.m. Christy remembers the time exactly, as he does every detail of that long and dramatic journey.

'Someone gave me a long loaf of French bread and a bottle of wine. I had no idea how long the journey to Italy would take. I suppose I thought the loaf of bread and bottle of wine would suffice to see me through. The stalls were old-fashioned. I remember falling asleep and Lucky Dome had his head under me. We came on to the border of France and Italy. I remember that journey by the place names we passed or the stations we stopped at. On Sunday night we pulled into a siding. It was now six o'clock in the evening. Some fellow came along and took me for an Espresso coffee.

'We journeyed on and I remember we went through a long tunnel. It seemed like eternity. The bread and the wine were gone. We stopped again and I went out and picked a bucket of apples and shared them with Lucky Dome. Now we were in the mountains. I think it was Monday night when we reached Turin. Now the place names were in Italian. Later I heard that the people who had gone on to Milan were frantic, wondering what had happened to me. They were putting out messages, right down along the line to Paris.

'The track narrowed and I learned from someone who had English that we were not all that far away from Milan. But with mountains all around, I couldn't imagine a racetrack. I didn't realise that the Merano track was set among surrounding hills.

'On the Tuesday we finally pulled into Merano station. Dermot O'Brien, Paddy Norris, John A. Woods, the owner of Lucky Dome, they were all out to greet me. I felt like a VIP. I was feeling a bit hungry, I must admit, and I asked for a feed of spuds. But to tell the truth, the potatoes were the world's worst – little "cuchains" of things.'

Knock Hard did not win at Merano – but Lucky Dome, despite all he went through and the one eye closed and the other half-closed that he had suffered in his leap from the plane in Paris, won a ladies' race with Signora Grisi in the saddle.

Phonsie O'Brien remembers rough journeys to England, too. 'I remember horses being loaded at night at the North Wall, being put on the boat, after the cattle had been loaded first. Danny O'Sullivan and I would travel with the horses, down in the hold where the cattle were. We would rig up a tarpaulin to keep the cattle away from the horses. We slept on the straw beside the horses. It would be 6.30 in the morning when we hit Birkenhead; usually it was customary for the horses to be let off before the cattle. They would then be put in a horsebox for the journey of about six or seven hours to Gerald Balding's place in Bishop's Canning. They were always housed there for Cheltenham. Gerald, of course, was Toby's father.'

These journeys on the cattle boat from the North Wall to Liverpool, sleeping on straw, left Phonsie with the ability to walk with Presidents and yet retain a so-natural touch. He prefers not to talk about it, but he has been on Airforce One with President Bush, a close friend of his for many years now, and they have gone fishing together. Phonsie saw George Bush as a certainty to win the US Presidential Election, as he reckoned that Michael Dukakis peaked too soon at the Democratic Convention, and he went for 'a touch' that would have done credit to some of Vincent's old-style gambles on the Gloucestershire Hurdle.

He smiles the smile of a man who loves life and lives it with zest and gusto, whether it be playing golf with Robert Sangster and John Magnier over the Sandy Lane course in Barbados or standing in relaxed mood at the bar in the Hyatt Regency Hotel in Lexington, swapping yarns and being simply the life and soul of the party. When he survived a bout of cancer some years back, he came to view life in a new light – seeing every new dawn as a bonus and reckoning that one of the most important things was a sense of the *joie de vivre*.

The Emergency saw Vincent O'Brien and his step-brother, Donal, joining the Local Defence Force (LDF), Ireland's equivalent of the Home Guard in Britain. Dermot was in the Army, a Lieutenant serving in County Kerry – 'You could say I went to university in Kerry,' he said with a smile.

'For the Emergency I was in the Waterville area, guarding the cable station on Valentia Island. The late Bill Shanks was a comrade-in-arms and close friend of mine. They were great days.'

Vincent encouraged those working in the stables – Danny O'Sullivan and his brother, Jimmy, and Maurice O'Callaghan – to do their bit for Ireland, as the saying went then. Eamon de Valera had decided on a policy of neutrality and got the full backing of the people in the General Elections during the period of the Second World War. The Opposition Parties in Dail Eireann also supported the Republic's neutral stance.

The LDF were willing to 'die for flag and country', if needs be, though the means at their disposal and the regular Army also were pathetic when viewed beside the might of the German Army. It would have been like an elephant stamping on a mouse. Jack Murphy of Churchtown, who was in the LDF with his brother, Bill, said that they had only six rifles between the whole unit. He laughed when he recalled 'Lord Haw Haw' saying one night that when Hitler was finished with Churchill, he would 'deal with de Valera's cabbage garden'.

Vincent O'Brien, in his brown LDF uniform, would have learned from Sergeant Flaherty of the regular Army how to throw a hand grenade – 'A big moment when we were shown how to pull out the pin,' said Jack Murphy. Jimmy O'Sullivan recalled the big manoeuvres that were held at one stage involving both the Army and LDF. 'I remember the "enemy" advancing and we were told that if they crossed Mallow bridge, we were beaten.'

On another occasion, a plane crash-landed in a field that was used as gallops by Vincent O'Brien. 'John Sheehy and myself, dressed in our LDF outfits, guarded the plane through the night until regular Irish Army personnel arrived at around 6.30 a.m. We didn't ride work at all that day,' said Jimmy.

Jimmy recalled the days of compulsory tillage, the shortage of tea and sugar, the rationing coupons. 'It was all brown bread, mostly coffee, very little tea, though most people preferred tea to coffee. There were even clothes coupons but you had plenty of those as there was no rush to buy new clothes then. You could hardly get a cigarette for love nor money and people improvised making their own.'

Jimmy rode a bit himself in his younger days. It was £2 or £3 for a ride. He remembers carrying the bag when Vincent O'Brien was out shooting. 'Vincent was a great shot,' he said simply.

'Yes, a wonderful natural shot,' brother Dermot concurred – and he was speaking from experience, as he often went out with Vincent. And they also went fishing together.

It was a great area for duck, snipe, pheasant, woodcock. The pheasant season opened on 1 November, the duck season on 1 September. It was said of Vincent that he was adept at bagging a pair – that is of snipe, the true test of a great shot.

Early on he fished the Awbeg – trout and pike – but later on he had his favourite stretches along the Blackwater, wonderful for salmon fishing. 'He loved fishing. I would say it has always been his favourite pastime,' said Dermot. 'He trained himself to cut himself off from the pressures of training and he discovered early on that there was no better way of doing it than by indulging in a day's fishing.'

The day Chamour defeated Alcaeus to win the 1960 Irish Derby before a crowd of 10,000 in sweltering heat at the Curragh, Vincent O'Brien was under suspension for allegedly doping the colt when he won the £202 Ballysax Plate at the Curragh on 19 April. In the record book Chamour appears as 'Trained A. S. O'Brien', that is by Vincent's brother, Phonsie. Vincent was declared a disqualified person and could not attend the Derby – or any other race meeting – even if he had wished to do so. He went fishing along his favourite stretch of the Blackwater, a portable radio at his side.

Daughter Susan, seven years old then, was with him that day and she remembers vividly that after Chamour had passed the post in front, she could hear on the radio people exclaiming: 'We want Vincent, we want Vincent.' Vincent went on fishing, oblivious to the amazing wave of sympathy spilling over at the Curragh. Fishing was always his way of getting relief from intense pressure. And it stood him well in the darkest days of his career.

8

A Disease Called 'Cheltenhamitis'

Vincent O'Brien trained at Churchtown from 1943 to 1951 and from there launched his first successful assaults on the big Curragh handicaps like the Lincolnshire, the Cambridgeshire and the Cesarewitch.

The 1951 Cheltenham challengers – including Hatton's Grace, who won the Champion Hurdle for the third successive year – left Clashganniff to run at the Festival meeting but when they returned to Ireland it was to Vincent's new establishment at Ballydoyle, County Tipperary.

At the turn of each New Year from the moment Vincent began to make his mark at Cheltenham, the stable would be hit by the disease which both Dermot and Phonsie O'Brien describe succinctly in one word: 'Cheltenhamitis'.

'A terrible disease,' said Phonsie, with an amused gleam in his eye. 'Not alone was Vincent affected by it himself but everybody working for him was hit with it also. No stone was left unturned in the count-down to Cheltenham to ensure that failure could not be laid at the door of human error. Vincent was totally analytical in his approach to every facet of getting the horses ready for their particular races and he knew, of course, that the money would be going on them – big money – and in his mind there was no place for excuses once he knew he had the material for the job. The pressure was intense, terribly so.'

'No one talked of getting ulcers,' said Dermot, 'but we

74

all suffered from the disease I coined as Cheltenhamitis. It would hit us immediately after Christmas and there would be no respite until the horses were on their way to Cheltenham. Vincent would be pretty uptight as his mind became totally fixed on the Festival meeting. Everything was geared to it. And, remember, to lift a race valued £8000 meant winning a prize worth many times that amount today.

'There were no prizes in Ireland to compare with the Cheltenham events. Cheltenham also presented the opportunity for good old-fashioned tilts at the ring, before the English bookmakers came to really fear Vincent and began to quote very short prices – ridiculous at times – about some of the Festival challengers, especially in the Gloucestershire Hurdle.

'We really made money the first year Cottage Rake won the Gold Cup and started at 10–1. And also when Hatton's Grace took the first of his three successive Champion Hurdles. He went off at 100–7. They had been backed at much longer odds ante-post.'

Dermot recalled bookmaker William Hill saying to Vincent and himself once: 'Never back odds-on, boys. Always try and get a price to your money.'

William Hill was not aware when he said that of the fact that Vincent had got a price to his money when he landed his first gamble at Clonmel on White Squirrel and when he brought off the Irish autumn double on Drybob and Good Days.

There came a moment at York in 1958 – the season that Vincent, through the successes of Gladness and Ballymoss, could do no wrong – when William Hill walked over to the Master of Ballydoyle, who was chatting with Sir Noel Murless and Sir Cecil Boyd-Rochfort.

Hill remarked to him in the hearing of the other two: 'I would have saved myself literally thousands of pounds if I had had you done away with ten years ago.'

'We had to gamble to survive,' said Vincent quite frankly.

He had owners who had the 'readies' and who loved to have a bet when Vincent told them one was 'expected'.

They could afford to put on £500 or £1000 and more and not find themselves in deep water if a gamble became unstuck.

'I had to come up with the goods to stay in business. It was me against the bookies and though the pressure was enormous, we did all right,' he said.

'We did all right.' Never was there such an under-statement.

Dermot assisted Vincent in keeping a complete ledger of all bets made at the time. Even though they invariably came out right at the end of each season, it certainly was not wine and roses all the way.

'I remember one season when the going was very hard and we backed a string of losers. When the big gambles came off, people tended to forget the setbacks.'

Vincent had a couple of people he had complete faith in to put the money down whether for himself and a couple of close friends or any owner who wanted 'a monkey' (£500) on. Nat McNabb of Dublin and the late Bob Mulrooney (died 1989) of Limerick were the trusted lieutenants who entered the firing line against the book-ies. Nat McNabb said that when he crossed over to England he had accounts with all the leading rails bookies and had no trouble in executing his bets 'on the nod'. Dermot would sometimes step in, too, to fire a salvo or two on days of fearless gambles in England.

There was a priest in Churchtown who used to bless the horses before they departed for the Festival meeting or other big races. He was never told when one was regarded as a near-certainty. He either got a cheque in the post – or a note telling him how much he owed when the odd one went down. Of course, most often it was a cheque.

'If a person gave us a few gallons of petrol during the Emergency,' said Dermot, 'instead of giving them a tip, we would put them on for a little; and they were quite happy when they received a cheque. All these types of bets – the bets for the priest and the garage owner with the petrol pumps – were recorded in the ledger.'

If something went badly wrong in cases where the

bookmakers were expected to be taken to the cleaners, then Vincent would want to know why.

'Having satisfied himself that it wasn't the fault of the horse or the jockey, he would never mention the matter again. Where Vincent was concerned there was no crying over spilt milk. He just went forward.'

Of the Cheltenham bets recorded in Vincent's ledger, the biggest one of all was that on Ahaburn to win the County Handicap Hurdle in 1952. The amount invested was £1452, equivalent to £20,114 by 1989 values. Aubrey Brabazon was riding. In the parade ring beforehand, Vincent said quietly to 'The Brab': 'I think this one should win.' When Vincent ventured something like that Aubrey knew that the horse was fancied no end.

'We were only cantering at the second last and I said to myself – 'This is going to be easier than Vincent himself imagined.' Then Ahaburn suddenly stopped as if he had been shot and finished in the ruck in ninth place,' recalled Aubrey.

'I could see that Vincent was mystified and very dejected at what had happened. He would never say a word to me in a situation like that. He kept his feelings bottled up and I have never known him in all the years we were associated with each other to vent anger or disappointment. That day he was just strangely quiet and I realised it was bothering him deeply that Ahaburn should have stopped to nothing.

'It wasn't until two days later that we discovered what had happened – when Ahaburn was on his way back to Ireland. The man travelling with him noticed the stone-black droppings. The horse had burst a blood vessel internally. In such situations instead of bleeding from the nose, the blood will be retained in the system and it's the droppings that reveal to you what has happened.'

Aubrey added that Ahaburn was injected for the problem and made amends by winning the Irish Cesarewitch later that year.

Ahaburn, incidentally, was the medium of a very successful gamble in 1955 when with T. P. Burns in the saddle he won the Birdlip Hurdle – the selling hurdle later withdrawn from the Festival programme. Ahaburn was subsequently bought in at the auction for 950 guineas.

The County Handicap Hurdle was the kind of Cheltenham event that Vincent O'Brien liked to have a 'cut' at, yet something always seemed to go wrong and the nearest he came to winning it was when Pat Taaffe finished third on Stroller in 1954. This one, having won a Division of the Gloucestershire Hurdle at the same Festival meeting, was beaten a head by Clair Soleil in the Champion Hurdle the following season. He went back in 1956 and, though falling three out in the Champion Hurdle, came out the following day and won the Spa Hurdle with Harry Sprague in the saddle.

T. P. Burns who rode Stroller in the Champion Hurdle in 1956 – the year he won the two Divisions of the Gloucestershire Hurdle on Boys Hurrah and Pelargos – told me that a swinging hurdle caught his mount and brought him down in the 'Champion' that year. It was the only fall he ever had on an O'Brien-trained horse and he rode hundreds for Vincent.

Dermot O'Brien revealed to me something that has never emerged in all that has been written about Vincent and especially about the manner in which he rocked the ring at Cheltenham over a decade. Alberoni, backed as if defeat was out of the question in the County Handicap Hurdle in 1950 was 'got at'.

'When we searched for a reason why he finished out of the money, we discovered that someone had placed acid under his shoes. There was a hole showing in each foot where the acid had burned into the foot. That cost us a good bit of money,' he said.

Vincent had wisely instructed his staff that when anyone enquired the name of a horse running at Cheltenham, they were to mix a cocktail, so to speak, in responding to the inquisitive. Thus, Alberoni became Hatton's Grace and Hatton's Grace became Alberoni. The 'Tipperary cocktail' worked in the sense that it saved Hatton's Grace, 5–2 favourite to win his second successive Champion Hurdle, from being 'done'. My research into this episode has convinced me that the nobblers believed they were ending the victory hopes of Hatton's Grace when they put the acid under Alberoni's shoes.

'Ginger' Dyson was brought over from England to ride Ahaburn in the 1951 Irish Cesarewitch. He started evens favourite after a whirlwind gamble but could only finish third in a seventeen-runner field, beaten 2 lengths and 5 lengths by Le Roi Soleil and Sontogo. 'He ran into all sorts of trouble,' said Dermot O'Brien. 'I could have bought myself a nice small farm with what I lost on him that day.'

Dermot thinks that the outstanding achievement of Vincent's career was the unparalleled strike-rate he set in the Gloucestershire Hurdle. Now the Supreme Novices' Hurdle, it used to be run in two Divisions as the curtain-raiser to the Festival meeting. The record reads: ten winners out of twelve runners in the period 1952–1959. The other two, Knockabout and Courts Appeal, finished second. In an era when the French were playing a strong role over hurdles as well as on the Flat, Tasmin, ridden by René Amery and trained in France, started the 5–1 second favourite and got up on the line to beat Knockabout (T. P. Burns), the 7–4 favourite by a head. The winner was third next time out to Prince Charlemagne in the Triumph Hurdle at Hurst Park.

Albergo (Doug Page) was backed from 100–8 to 9–1 and beat the even-money favourite, Courts Appeal (T. P. Burns), by 6 lengths. The following year he was runner-up to the Paddy Sleator-trained Another Flash in the Champion Hurdle and was one of the outstanding horses trained by the now-retired Clem Magnier.

Phonsie O'Brien, while agreeing with Dermot that the Gloucestershire Hurdle record was 'out of this world', still, amazing as it may seem, pinpoints another achievement as *the* greatest of Vincent's career. It was the winning of nine races with seven horses over the Christmas period in 1950.

Vincent took one race at Leopardstown, the Shankill Hurdle – with Hatton's Grace. And he won eight at Limerick with The Beetle (Greenpark Maiden Hurdle), Little Boy Blue (Holiday Handicap Hurdle), Dashing Lady (Mungret Novice Chase), Lucky Dome (Rineanna Plate), Airlift

(County Maiden Hurdle), Little Boy Blue (City Handicap Hurdle), Dashing Lady (Thomond Handicap Chase) and Silk Cottage (Southern Plate).

'I rode seven of those winners at Limerick,' recalled Phonsie O'Brien. 'I was unable to do the weight on Little Boy Blue in the Holiday Handicap Hurdle and Eddie Kennedy had the ride.'

The consistency Vincent showed at Cheltenham has never been emulated by any other Irish trainer in the history of National Hunt racing. He ended up with 23 winners – only two behind the leading Irish trainer at the Festival meeting, the late Tom Dreaper, but Vincent's total was compressed into roughly a decade (1948–59) as against a span of 25 years (1948–71) in Tom's period of turning out winners.

Vincent's first runner was Cottage Rake in 1948 – a winner. In fact, his first five runners (1948–51) all won and Hatton's Grace was the only challenger in 1951. Nine out of twelve runners sent over in the years 1948–52 were successful. The last Vincent O'Brien-trained challengers at the Festival meeting were York Fair and Courts Appeal in the two Divisions of the Gloucestershire Hurdle in 1959. T. P. Burns rode York Fair to victory in the first Division while, as we have seen, Court's Appeal was second in the other Division.

The bookmakers first reeled under a Vincent O'Brien onslaught on the Gloucestershire Hurdle when Cockatoo, with Phonsie up, won Division One of this event in 1952, starting at 4–1.

Dermot recalled: 'Cockatoo had only one side to his mouth which meant he was a very difficult ride, so we decided to drop him out at the start and give Phonsie every chance to steer him. He gave away 100 yards at the start but still landed the gamble. Unfortunately, we never got the same odds in the race again.'

Vincent names Saffron Tartan as the best of his Gloucestershire Hurdle winners and T. P. Burns said of him: 'He was the best of them all, the finest novice that ever left the stable; he had the rest of the field stone cold from the top of the hill and beat Predominate as if he was a selling plater.'

It is hardly surprising that both Vincent and T. P. Burns should rate Saffron Tartan so highly when one reflects on this horse's subsequent achievements and also those of the horse he pulverised, Predominate. When Vincent switched from training jumpers to concentrate completely on the Flat, Saffron Tartan was sent to Don Butchers, who trained him to win the 1961 Gold Cup in the hands of Fred Winter from the 1960 victor, Pas Seul, and Mandarin. And Mandarin was the winner in 1962 from Fortria and Duke of York.

As T. P. Burns pointed out, Predominate also turned out to be a very good horse. Bought in Dublin as a yearling for 1150 guineas by Ken Cundell for Mrs G. Trimmer-Thompson (for whom he won seven races, including two hurdle races), his most memorable performances came when he was bought by Jim Joel, who had him racing solely on the Flat. Then trained by Ted Leader, he was second in the Cesarewitch, won the Queen Alexandra Stakes, the Goodwood Stakes three years running and climaxed his career by taking the Goodwood Cup at nine. In all, the gelding won fourteen races worth over £17,000 in prize money and he had the distinction of winning at Goodwood four years running.

Vincent's tremendous strike rate in the Gloucestershire Hurdle, according to Phonsie, could be attributed to the schooling over obstacles the horses were given. 'You might say that they were taught to jump before they could gallop. The ones aimed at this particular event had the jumping ability of handicap hurdlers before they were entered for this very competitive race. Once the going became good to soft in September, Vincent would have four hurdles and four fences put out. Every horse that was going to have a dual purpose in life jumped eight hurdles or eight fences every Tuesday and Friday. It was a case of jumping the four and then coming back and jumping them again. No other trainer schooled his horses to jump as Vincent did.

'He maintained that it was very difficult to teach horses

81

to jump after they began to run races on the Flat. You might then find yourself trying to eradicate faults which might not have developed if you had made your horses proficient jumpers from the outset.

'Once a horse of Vincent's reached handicap class as a chaser, he was never schooled over fences again. A chaser might be popped over the four fences before his first run of the season simply to sharpen him and then just given a 'pop' occasionally to keep the eye in.

'In the case of the Aintree Grand National challengers, he didn't school them over jumps similar to Becher's, Valentine's or The Chair. They would never have seen anything like these jumps before they got to Aintree; yet they were so well schooled early on in their jumping careers that they had the ability ingrained in them to jump any jump, no matter how formidable.

'The National fences were much tougher in those days than they are now. Vincent knew exactly the type of horse required for the race. He knew they had to be able to jump. If they did not meet this requirement, then other attributes would not suffice at Aintree.'

Phonsie summed up by saying that 'everything' would have to be right before Vincent would allow one to take its chance in a bid for an important prize, like those rich Cheltenham races or the Grand National. There were no 'ifs' and 'buts' in his vocabulary. He was a perfectionist through and through.

Dermot said that from the very beginning Vincent was ahead of his time in his attention to detail. 'He would leave absolutely nothing to chance. Martin Molony was riding a lot in England and became very friendly with Bob Turnell. On one occasion Bob and Martin's brother, Tim, came over for a spell of shooting. I was with them in the hotel in Mallow one evening at dinner and we were detailing for Bob Turnell the exactitude that Vincent brought to his training methods. Bob threw his hands in the air and remarked, 'If I had to do all that, I wouldn't consider it worth the price in the pressure it would mean, no matter how much success it brought.'

'For Vincent all the bits and pieces had to fit in. You might end up concluding that the finished job was perfect but you would have failed to notice how the small details – so patiently observed – all added up to the achievement of that perfection.

'Later that attention to detail would reveal itself again in the way he put cotton wool plugs in The Minstrel's ears when he feared the colt might be upset by all the pre-race hustle and bustle of Derby Day at Epsom.'

Dermot added that Vincent never spared expense where his horses were concerned. 'The cheap ones got the same treatment as those that were bought big at Keeneland. He was always terribly caring where the horses under his care were concerned. There was always the additional consideration, of course, in the case of the top Flat horses that you could be talking about potential sires, whose eventual value would run into millions of pounds. That too created an additional burden.'

Dermot stressed that Vincent had the knack from the very outset of growing with the challenges that he came to face. 'He always kept his sights high. He kept aiming higher and higher.'

Aubrey Brabazon, who had such a highly successful relationship riding for Vincent, leading to some of the most memorable triumphs at Cheltenham, said: 'For me the number-one attribute that put Vincent ahead of all others as a trainer was thoroughness. I remember in the era when horses were brought to race meetings in primitive looking trailers, Vincent would see to it that he always had a spare one standing by in case of a breakdown. He was never caught out.

'Also, where he had runners in important chasing and hurdle events, he saw to it that he had alerted a jockey to be on hand and ready, in case his number-one choice had a fall in an earlier event and could not take the mount. The more I reflect back to those days, the more I am convinced that from the very outset he was way ahead of the field in the sheer professionalism he displayed.'

Paddy Norris, who was Vincent's Travelling Head Man for years and whose son is now attached to the Ballydoyle stables in a veterinary capacity, said that when Vincent put his trust in someone he expected that trust to be observed right down the line. 'He was very exacting on himself and he expected total professionalism from those working for him. If you fell down on the job, if his trust in you was misplaced, then you knew there was no place for you in a stable where the standards set were so high. You knew in your heart it was time for you to go, without Vincent having to tell you to go.'

In a majority of cases the men who passed through Churchtown and Ballydoyle did not end simply being run-of-the-mill journeymen. It was akin to attending one of the great universities of the horse and his 'college' left an indelible mark on all who passed its portals. Men found something in working with The Master.

The names spring easily to mind: Christy Kinane, Danny Kinane, Tony Redmond, Jimmy Gordon, David Murray Smith, Paddy Norris, Michael Kauntze, John Gosden and, of course, Michael Dickinson. They gained the confidence to go out and set up on their own and each and every one of them remembers his spell with Vincent in a special way – and with gratitude for what he acquired.

Michael Dickinson, talking during the 1988 Keeneland Select July Sales, said: 'It was very flattering for me when I had the first five home in the Gold Cup in 1983, Bregawn's year, that comparisons were drawn with some of Vincent's outstanding achievements in the National Hunt arena. I know I would never have pulled off that record without all the knowledge I acquired at Ballydoyle and so indirectly Vincent left his special mark on that particular achievement of mine.

'From the time I first began to learn about racehorses, I looked up to him like a God. I read all about the big races he had won. Then later, when I was riding over the jumps, I wrote to him asking him if he could give me a job for the summer, as I wanted to further my education. Initially, my approach didn't succeed as he wrote back to say he had no vacancy at that time. I persevered and it was one of my proudest moments when eventually I passed through the gates of Ballydoyle. I spent two summers, 1973 and 1974 working there – two of the happiest years I have ever enjoyed. And also the most informative. I was made to feel that I was one of the family, and I will always be grateful to Vincent and Jacqueline for that.'

Michael Dickinson, now training at Fairhill, Florida (the breach with Robert Sangster and the bitter departure from Manton are things he prefers not to talk about), summed up what he saw as placing Vincent O'Brien on a pedestal apart: 'He does not make mistakes. Everything is so well organised at Ballydoyle, from the boxes to the gallops themselves, that you are talking about sheer perfection, a perfection that is stunning. His knowledge of horses, of breeding, is immense – overwhelming, in fact – and when it comes to an eye for picking potential champions, few if any can match him. From my own experience there, I would say that the "Ballydoyle way" will get the very best out of a horse – if it has the ability.'

Vincent said frankly one day, 'I always went for top jockeys.' His approach was that if he felt he had the material to win big prizes – over the jumps or on the Flat – he was not going to miss out by not having the right jockey up.

He picked horsemen like Bryan Marshall and Pat Taaffe for his three Grand National winners. He had Aubrey Brabazon, a jockey with a wonderful pair of hands, versatile enough to ride with the best on the Flat as well as over the jumps, to win the Gold Cup three times on Cottage Rake and the Champion Hurdle twice on Hatton's Grace. Tim Molony was on Hatton's Grace when the gelding won the Champion Hurdle for the third time and this fine horseman rode Vincent's fourth Gold Cup winner, Knock Hard.

Of course, he utilised the immense talents of Martin Molony and struck up a tremendous partnership with T. P. Burns, son of 'The Scotsman', Tommy Burns. T. P. rode five of the ten Gloucestershire Hurdle winners and won the Irish Derby and English St Leger on Ballymoss.

On the domestic front he employed the talents and vast experience of Liam Ward. Liam rode Nijinsky to victory in the 1970 Irish Derby, won the Irish Oaks on Aurabella (1965) and Gaia (1969) and the Irish St Leger on White Gloves (1966) and Reindeer (1969). Christy Roche, who had a number of Classic triumphs during his time as stable jockey to 'Darkie' Prendergast, later became associated with the Ballydoyle stable, though not on a retained basis. When Vincent's son David set up as a trainer on his own Roche became stable jockey and on Secreto ended the unbeaten run of 'wonder colt' El Gran Senor in the photo finish to the 1984 Epsom Derby.

Vincent engaged 'Scobie' Breasley for Ballymoss when T. P. could not take the ride because of injury and two other Australians for whom he had an immense respect were Jack Purtell and Garnie Bougoure (Phonsie thinks that Bougoure was one of the most artistic jockeys ever associated with Ballydoyle and it was simply amazing how often the verdict went his way in a photo finish).

'The best Australian jockey could win a race by a neck or half a length for you with 7 pounds or more in hand. And, of course, they were very good judges of pace,' said Vincent.

Vincent and Robert Sangster utilised the immense talent of Pat Eddery over a five-year period (the only real setback being the defeat of El Gran Senor) before Arab money saw him start another chapter of a career that has him rated today one of the best big-race jockeys of all.

Undoubtedly the most successful partnership of all was that with Lester Piggott and Vincent has never hidden his admiration for Lester's power and skill in a finish – as on Roberto and The Minstrel in the Epsom Derby.

9

The Rake's Progress To Triple Triumph

It was Gold Cup Day at Cheltenham 1948 and Vincent O'Brien was, understandably, tense and very uptight. Cottage Rake was his first-ever challenger at the Festival meeting and represented his bid to break into the big-time in Britain.

Aubrey Brabazon had no ride in the race before the Gold Cup, the third event on the card. 'As people were crowding up on to the stands for the second race, I could see Vincent standing all alone, very pent-up looking,' recalled Aubrey. 'I said to him casually, "Well, how are we going?" He replied, "I know where I am going now. This is the only time that you are likely to get the bars fairly empty. I'm going for a brandy. I think I could do with one. And we can have a chat together while we're waiting for the big race."

'Normally Vincent would never have a drink like that before a race. So you can imagine how he must have felt when he decided to try and ease the tension with a stiff brandy.'

Forty-one years on from that day, I had come in from the gallops at Ballydoyle with Vincent on a morning in March 1987 after watching Seattle Dancer, then the pre-season pride of the stable, being put through his paces. It was just four days before the Master of Ballydoyle celebrated his 70th birthday and suddenly, with a definite feeling of nostalgia in the air, he pointed to the spot where the box used to stand that once accommodated Cottage Rake. Now it has merged into a modern office, as has the one that housed Hatton's Grace.

There was no mistaking that morning the affection Vincent retained for the chaser who started the golden era for him at Cheltenham that made him 'king' of the Festival meeting for a decade. The prints of Cottage Rake have a special place in the O'Brien home. And no wonder.

Having won the Naas November Handicap in 1946 and the Irish Cesarewitch in 1947, Cottage Rake, by taking the Gold Cup in 1948, put Vincent O'Brien very firmly on the map in the eyes of racing followers in Britain. Suddenly they began to recognise a unique talent. It was no longer a case of Vincent remarking, as he did after his father's death five years earlier, 'Nobody knows me'.

Cottage Rake was buried in McCarthy's field in Fermoy, the field to which he retired after suffering the terrible ignominy of ending up, after leaving Vincent's stable, as something of a rehabilitated crock running in the Shrewsbury Chase (3 miles) at Wolverhampton worth a paltry £204. Ridden by Dick Francis on that December day in 1953, he could finish only third to Holly Bank under 11 stone 10 pounds, beaten a total of 25 lengths. And that brought the curtain down finally on a career which Aubrey Brabazon had no hesitation in saying should have ended 'in honourable retirement' much earlier.

There was no doubt a desire to win a few more races with him when he had transferred to England – to call back the glory he had known. But he had reached the stage in his career when he could no longer do himself justice. After finishing fourth under 12 stone 7 pounds in the 1950 Irish Grand National, he developed tendon trouble from a freak accident while out on grass at Churchtown at the end of the season. He had a bosom pal, a donkey. One morning when he looked up and did not immediately spot it, as it had got in among some cattle grazing in the same Lawn Field (the lad who normally took the cattle out of the field had not shown up that morning), he thought for a moment he had lost his best pal and nearly went berserk. In wildly circling the field looking for the donkey, he got too close to a fence and, kicking out, damaged a tendon.

'I don't think he was ever the same horse again,' said Vincent.

Vincent regrets that some kind of commemorative stone was not erected where Cottage Rake was buried. The idea of erecting a bronze of the great chaser seems to have been mooted after the third of Cottage Rake's Gold Cup triumphs but it never reached fruition. Aubrey Brabazon was sent a poem by Ellen Sheehan of Mallow titled simply 'Cottage Rake' and it captures the reason why in witty fashion:

> In memory of this gallant steed
> A figure of bronze was planned
> To stand outside Mallow Station
> But the project was duly banned
> 'A horse would be out of place'
> Said a Councillor at the time
> 'Might even be disrespectful
> To the nearby Marian Shrine'
> The Rake's sponsor most indignant
> Full of impatience and remorse
> Shouted 'Since when did the Virgin Mary
> Take umbrage to a horse'
> Yet the bronze was never placed
> To the matchless Cottage Rake
> Who took the Gold at Cheltenham
> Three times without a break

However, Aubrey Brabazon was immortalised in a ballad of the period just as the balladeers would sing of Dawn Run's never-to-be-forgotten Gold Cup triumph 38 years later and Peter O'Sullevan-style commentaries became the order at gatherings of racing folk (one friend of mine in the Irish Diplomatic Service brings it off from the last with rare gusto).

> Aubrey's up, the money's down,
> The frightened bookies quake,
> 'Come on, me lads, and give a cheer,
> Begod 'tis Cottage Rake!'

Aubrey looks back to 1948: 'That first year Cottage Rake was practically an outsider, starting at 10–1, and Martin Molony and I had a great duel for the last mile. He was on Happy Home for Miss Dorothy Paget and he knew as well as I did that the only way he could win was to make the then inexperienced Cottage Rake stand off too far at one of the last three fences and either fall or make a bad mistake and that I would not have time to let him get balanced again before the winning post arrived. But "The Rake" had such speed that I could afford to ease him up at these last few fences and still pass Miss Paget's good horse halfway up the final hill.'

Vincent O'Brien was standing down at the last fence as Happy Home and Cottage Rake rose to it together. Men who were there that day and who know what horsemanship is all about, still talk in awe of the way Martin Molony drove Happy Home into the last, knowing that his only hope of beating Cottage Rake and Aubrey Brabazon was to come out of it in front. He did – gaining a length to a length and a half with one of the most fearless jumps he had every essayed. 'But Cottage Rake beat my one for speed in the run to the finish,' said Martin factually. The verdict was one and a half lengths.

Asked what he considers the best race he had ever ridden over the jumps, Martin Molony replied unhesitatingly that it was in defeat in that 1948 Gold Cup. 'God gave me great courage,' he said simply, no doubt thinking inwardly of the manner in which he powered Happy Home into the last.

Aubrey Brabazon, in a generous tribute to Martin Molony's fearlessness at the last, said: 'I remember remarking at the time on the wonderful plucky ride that Martin gave Happy Home into that last fence. I doubt if any one of us would have ridden at it with such sheer guts and gusto.'

With no racecourse commentary in those days, Vincent O'Brien had no idea what had won. He guessed from the tumult and the shouting that it was a terrific battle to the line and he could only hope that Cottage Rake's finishing speed had enabled him to get up. His heart was in his mouth as he made his way back to the stands. 'It was when I saw Aubrey touching his cap to acknowledge the cheers of the crowd that I knew we had pulled it off.'

Just as he would later have very mixed feelings when Secreto, trained by his son, David, beat El Gran Senor a short head in the 1984 Epsom Derby, Vincent would have been left to ponder the might-have-beens if Happy Home had held on.

'Happy Home was out of a mare called Golden Emblem, whom my father bought and sold on to Michael Magnier, John's grandfather. He stood the top jumping sire, Cottage, at the time, so mated the pair, and Happy Home was the resultant produce. He so nearly made us regret ever selling the mare,' recalled Vincent.

Aubrey Brabazon still cherishes the menu from the famous Jammet's Restaurant in Dublin where the celebratory dinner was held on Easter Monday night, 29 March 1948 to mark 'The Rake's' first victory in the Cheltenham Gold Cup. The opening course was appropriately styled 'Le Saumon Fumé Churchtown' and there was also 'Le Potage Vincent' on the menu and the main dish was a choice between 'Les Paupiettes de Sole Cheltenham' or 'Les Poussins à la Rake garnis'.

They drank Möet et Chandon 1938 and the toasts were to 'Ireland', 'The Horse', 'The Trainer' and 'The Jockey'. On the back of the menu they listed 'The Rake's Progress' to that first Cheltenham Gold Cup win on 4 March, 1948. Among the autographs on 'The Brab's' menu, still legible over 40 years on, is that of Vincent O'Brien.

The 1948 race marked the first pulsating Cheltenham duel in Aubrey Brabazon's *mano a mano* with Martin Molony – two outstandingly gifted horsemen and two jockeys who did not have to use the whip to get that winning drive from their mounts, either over the jumps or on the Flat.

'I never once hit Cottage Rake with the whip,' said Aubrey. 'Martin Molony was not what you would term "a whip merchant" either. These days there is a lot of controversy about the use of the whip. All right, you can shake the whip at a tiring horse to keep him going but you don't have to punish him. I can tell you that you won't find a photograph of Martin Molony and myself giving our horses "the treatment" even as we battled it out from the last on Gold Cup Day in 1948.'

Martin Molony always rode long because it came natural to him to ride that way and it is not surprising that no less a judge than Vincent O'Brien should refer to his power in a finish. Vincent had nothing but the highest admiration also for the supreme touch, the superb control he exercised with his hands and the horseman's brain of Aubrey Brabazon. Martin and Aubrey were horsemen through and through.

Cottage Rake had taken the Emblem Handicap Chase (3 miles) under 12 stone 7 pounds at Manchester and the King George VI Chase at Kempton before he bid for his second Gold Cup in 1949.

Looking back on 1949 Aubrey Brabazon said: 'It had both tragic and joyful memories for me. The tragic part was that the jockey who was second to me was my very good friend, the late P.J. (Joe) Murphy, who died as a result of a fall in a chase, and the horse he rode was an old favourite of mine Cool Customer.

'The joyful thing, apart from winning the race, was that it was also just after my wedding and Eithne was at Cheltenham for the first time. I very nearly missed the ride altogether, as my plane from Nice was held up on the previous day. We had to charter a plane from London that morning to get to Cheltenham in time. Had the Air France flight not left Nice, I would not have made it, as it was too late to come by train to Paris and we only had a few francs left. Even if we had had the money, it would have cost half the Gold Cup prize money to charter a private plane from the Riviera to Cheltenham.'

Cottage Rake, although winning in the end by 2 lengths, had a very tough race. He had just recovered in time from a bout of equine flu which would definitely have prevented him taking his place in the field had not Gold Cup day been lost during the Festival meeting itself because of frost. The extra month provided the precious time for Cottage Rake to recover. Cool Customer looked all over a winner as he took a 2 length lead coming to the last. Again, however, 'The Rake' produced a brilliant burst of finishing speed.

Cool Customer was owned by Major 'Cuddie' Stirling-Stuart, an outstanding sportsman from Yorkshire. It is hard to gauge what his feelings must have been as he saw Cottage Rake catch Cool Customer in the searching uphill run from the last. Tony Riddle-Martin had negotiated a deal that could have procured Cottage Rake for Major Stirling-Stuart at £3500. On the advice of the almost legendary Maxie Cosgrove, whose name would always be linked later with the mightly Arkle, Cuddie Stirling-Stuart decided against going through with the purchase. The vet's professional judgement was – and it was shown later that he was right in this – that Cottage Rake had a problem with his wind.

So, ironically, the champion chaser that could have come into the ownership of a great Yorkshire sportsman was later to deny the Major winning the prize he so dearly wanted to win.

The destiny which had worked from the outset to bring Vincent O'Brien to the very top internationally was working to ensure that he would first get Cottage Rake to train – and then not lose him out of his stable until he had won three successive Gold Cups.

Dr 'Otto' Vaughan of Mallow had acquired Cottage Rake from his brother, Dick, who bred him at his Hunting Hall Stud in County Cork. In fact, 'The Rake' might well have been sold before he ever arrived at Vincent O'Brien's stable but luckily for Vincent he was brought back to Mallow, the good Doctor having failed to dispose of him at Goff's Sales (then held in Ballsbridge).

'The Rake' arrived at Vincent O'Brien's stable in Churchtown in 1945 as a six-year-old and 'Otto' Vaughan appeared to be of the state of mind that once he had won an amateur flat race or maiden hurdle race, the horse would be put on the market again. Vincent sent Cottage Rake to Limerick on 27 December 1945 to win the County Maiden Hurdle with consummate ease at 10–1 with Danny

O'Sullivan in the saddle and then to Leopardstown in February 1946, where P. P. Hogan won the bumper – the Corinthian Maiden Plate – at evens. 'The Rake' was so impressive that day that immediately the cheque books were waving.

Dr Vaughan was very anxious to cash in after these two unbeaten runs. Thwarted more than once by veterinary reports on the horse, he was convinced that someone would be prepared to take a chance. It was now Vincent's job to find a prospective buyer, who would be willing to leave Cottage Rake with him. Vincent realised after Leopardstown that he had a potential champion on his hands – a horse that could put him on an entirely new plane.

And he realised, too, that Cottage Rake was bred to go right to the top. For one thing he was by the outstanding sire of jumpers, Cottage. And, secondly, there was Stella blood in his veins on the dam's (Hartingo) side and Vincent, with his expert knowledge of breeding, knew that Stella was a foundation mare who had to transmit class.

Vincent now turned to Frank Vickerman, who still retained happy memories of the Drybob/Good Days Irish autumn double coup, and he agreed to purchase the horse. He made out a cheque for £1000 to Dr Vaughan as a down payment, only to get word from Vincent that another veterinary examination had revealed a minor problem of rheumatism in the shoulder. Frank Vickerman had decided to cancel the cheque when he learned that Dr Vaughan had already cashed it.

'So Frank Vickerman had no option but to take the horse. Could anything have been as fortunate as that?' mused Vincent aloud.

When Cottage Rake completed the three-timer by winning the Gold Cup again in 1950, it was his most convincing victory of all: he won pulling up by 10 lengths.

'Knowing the horse's terrific acceleration, I took a big gamble that day and it came off,' said Aubrey Brabazon. 'Again, Martin Molony, this time on Lord Bicester's Finnure, represented the main danger. Finnure had beaten us in the King George VI Chase at Kempton and I considered that I had not ridden a clever race that day and must use different tactics next time.

'I decided that the best thing to do was to turn on the speed at the most unlikely place – namely, rounding the sharp turn before the last regulation at the top of the hill. Luck was on my side. Martin's horse made a mistake just then and, aided by the downhill slope, my mount flew for about 100 yards to get 10 lengths in front. Perhaps Finnure did not like the rather slow gallop early on or Cheltenham did not suit him quite as well as Kempton. In the final analysis, Cottage Rake had it over all opposition once it came to the last at Cheltenham and over three memorable seasons his finishing speed proved the trump card.'

How good was Cottage Rake? In the book *Vincent O'Brien's Great Horses*, the Master of Ballydoyle rated him the greatest chaser he put through his hands, adding quite significantly: 'I believe Cottage Rake ranks with Prince Regent, Golden Miller and Arkle as the greatest winners of the Gold Cup.'

His reason for expressing that viewpoint was based on the assumption that Cottage Rake had more speed than Golden Miller, Prince Regent or Arkle – the speed that enabled him to win the Naas November Handicap over 12 furlongs when still a novice chaser and also the Irish Cesarewitch. However, Aubrey Brabazon would only rate Cottage Rake third – after Golden Miller and Arkle.

'My reason for that,' said Aubrey, 'is not just because Golden Miller won the Gold Cup five times, but my friend Harry Beasley (Bobby's father) rode him in a gallop at Newmarket before the Queen Alexandra Stakes at Ascot in the era of Brown Jack and told me that he beat some very good horses a distance. He would have been a certainty to win the race that season but the ground came up rock hard and Basil Briscoe, his trainer, decided not to risk him.'

T. P. Burns said that while Cottage Rake had the class and the speed to win a race like the Gold Cup, he could not give weight away in handicaps in the same manner as Arkle. But still T.P. would describe him as a great chaser, posing the question: 'How many horses have won three successive Gold Cups?'

In fact, before Cottage Rake came on the scene, only Golden Miller had bettered his Cheltenham Gold Cup record. Golden Miller's five Gold Cup wins came in the years 1932–36 (between the ages of five and nine). There was no race in 1937 and he was back in 1938, finishing second that year at the age of eleven years to The Pilot, beaten 2 lengths.

There is a colossal difference between a good horse and a great one, according to Martin Molony.

'Great horses can carry weight, good ones can't,' sums up his philosophy in a nutshell. 'A great horse, especially a great chaser, can give lumps of weight away to lesser animals and still win. Cottage Rake, I am afraid, although he won three successive Gold cups, was not able to give weight away like Prince Regent or Arkle.

'Prince Regent was able to win handicaps with 12 stone 7 pounds on his back and was conceding 42 pounds to Knight's Crest when I rode my mother's horse to a length victory in the 1944 Irish Grand National. Likewise, he was giving away 24 pounds to Lovely Cottage when beaten into third place in the 1946 Aintree Grand National.

'Arkle was able to carry welter weights to victory. I remember meeting the trainer of The Brasher, a good chaser, before the 1965 Whitbread Chase. The Brasher was carrying 10 stone and his trainer was confident he would run a very good race and even entertained hopes of beating Arkle at the weights, as Arkle was carrying 12 stone 7 pounds. But though The Brasher looked to be there with a very good chance at the last, Arkle suddenly sprinted away and won handsomely, despite the concession of 35 pounds.'

Martin Molony and Aubrey Brabazon both agreed that the intervention of the Second World War killed Prince Regent's hopes of gaining real immortality like Golden Miller and Arkle. For example, the Tom Dreaper-trained gelding was eleven when he won the Gold Cup in 1946, with Tim Hyde in the saddle, by 5 lengths and 4 lengths from Poor Flame and Red April. Supposing he had arrived in 1942, the year he won the Irish Grand National under 12 stone 7 pounds – what then? Might we not have been talking of five-in-a-row to equal Golden Miller's record five-timer?

Aubrey Brabazon thinks he was one of the unluckiest losers ever in the Aintree Grand National, in which he carried the welter burden of 12 stone 7 pounds into third place, 7 lengths behind Lovely Cottage (10 stone) after Tim Hyde, faced with the terrible dilemma of a loose horse that could have carried him out at the wing of a fence, was forced to go on much earlier than intended and had used up everything by the time he cleared the last.

In any assessment of Cottage Rake, it must not be over-looked that Silver Fame, named by Martin Molony as 'the greatest chaser I rode', could not beat Vincent O'Brien's charge in the Gold Cup at levels. And when Cottage Rake met him in the Emblem Chase at Manchester in November 1948 he carried 12 stone 7 pounds as against the 12 stone 2 pounds Lord Bicester's horse was set to carry – a concession of 5 pounds. Both were then nine-year-olds. 'The Rake' won by a neck in a thrilling battle from the last, despite the fact that Aubrey Brabazon lost his whip.

Silver Fame was a splendidly bold chestnut who won 26 races during his career. He took the Gold Cup as a twelve-year-old in 1951 when he did not have to contend with Cottage Rake, Martin Molony guiding the gelding to a short-head win over Greenogue.

Despite Cottage Rake's achievements on his raids to England, prize money was so poor in Ireland that Vincent O'Brien has a note he had received from Frank Vickerman round about 1949 suggesting that the trainer find someone willing to buy 'The Rake' for a possible £15,000. This would be equivalent to a chaser being sold for a sum in the range of £100,000 to £120,000 today, which gives some idea of the value placed on Cottage Rake after he had won his second Gold Cup and also the King George VI Chase.

The sale of Cottage Rake to someone willing to leave him with Vincent O'Brien was the alternative to sending him to be trained in England. Frank Vickerman was loyal enough to Vincent that he wanted the horse trained by him and no one else. However, after the third Gold Cup triumph leg trouble had set in to plague this outstanding chaser and he was transferred to the stable of Gerald Balding, father of Toby.

It was sadly all downhill from that point onwards. The blame could certainly not be placed on the shoulders of his new trainer, who was a great friend of Vincent O'Brien. No, he should have been retired rather than being sent to England in the first place. The last four races represented a sad and tragic finale before the curtain fell on a brilliant career.

Cottage Rake was eleven when he won the Gold Cup for the third time in 1950 and, after his long lay-off because of tendon trouble, was fourteen when he fell at the last ditch in the Queen Elizabeth Handicap Chase at the Old Hurst Park course on 25 May 1953, with Aubrey Brabazon in the saddle. He started at 100–6 that day.

Aubrey recalled that the going was very hard. 'I broke my collarbone in that fall,' he said.

Cottage Rake was rising fifteen when he suffered that last ignominious defeat at Wolverhampton on 8 December 1953. The very fact that he started at 9–4 showed that the old horse was not regarded as a lay-down certainty by the books in a chase that would have been at his total mercy in his prime. Three years earlier he had started at 4–6 when winning the King George VI Chase.

There came a day when Vincent O'Brien, having switched to training entirely on the Flat, decided to go after new owners and acquired the patronage of American John McShain, which led in turn to the acquisition of Bally-moss, who catapulted him to fame on an entirely new international plane, just as Cottage Rake had done a decade earlier. But early on in his training career it had not been like that. 'I did not seek jumpers. I took what was offered me,' he reflected 27 years after 'The Rake' had won the Gold Cup for the third successive year.

The real importance of Cottage Rake, however, in the developing Vincent O'Brien success story is that his initial Cheltenham triumph in 1948 alerted other owners to the trainer's genius.

Harry Keogh was in the manufacturing business in Dublin and with his attractive wife, Moya, had horses in training with Barney Nugent. They decided to switch three – Hatton's Grace, Royal Tan and Castledermot – to Vincent's Churchtown stable. Knock Hard would follow later.

Hatton's Grace, bred by J. W. A. Harris at the Victor Stud in County Tipperary, was sold as a yearling on 1 October 1941 at Ballsbridge for 18 guineas to John Kirwan, the County Kilkenny trainer. Knock Hard was bred by T. J. Sheahan and sold by him to Mrs M. G. Scott for 75 guineas at the 1945 Ballsbridge September Sales. The chestnut gelding by Domaha out of Knocksouna (by Beresford) was acquired by Harry and Moya Keogh in 1949.

By the time Hatton's Grace retired with eighteen victories under his belt (twelve National Hunt successes and six on the Flat), he had winnings to his credit that came to just £1150 short of £30,000. Far, far more was won on bets on both these outstanding servants of the Keoghs.

It was Colonel Dan Corry of the Irish Army jumping team, a very prominent personality in racing circles at the time, who acquired Hatton's Grace initially from John Kirwan. Dan Corry actually rode Hatton's Grace, a 1–2 favourite, to a three-quarters-of-a-length victory in the Bellewstown Plate, worth £74 5s at Bellewstown on 3 July 1946. Hatton's Grace was trained then by Dick O'Connell, father of Al O'Connell (who turned out Classical Charm to finish second to Celtic Shot in the 1988 Champion Hurdle). Moya Keogh owned him in partnership for a time with Dan Corry before eventually buying out his share.

While in training with Barney Nugent, Hatton's Grace won the Tower Handicap Hurdle at the Christmas meeting at Leopardstown in 1947 and a few other races but he

99

finished unplaced in the Champion Hurdle of 1948 when ridden by Martin Molony and starting a 20–1 outsider. The glorious chapters in his career would not be written until he was switched to Vincent O'Brien's stable.

'Vincent would only take Hatton's Grace, Royal Tan and Castledermot on condition that they would not see a racecourse for quite some time and I recall him saying that he was prepared to wait a year with the trio, if necessary,' said Mrs Moya Keogh, whose husband died in 1964.

'Vincent was determined that he would be given time to build up the horses we sent him. He wanted to do his own thing. He didn't want to be hurried or rushed into anything. It was in the summer of 1948 that the horses were sent to him and he did not let us see them until October. Vincent's patience was tremendous and, of course, it paid off handsomely.' Vincent was true to his word, as Hatton's Grace did not see a racecourse for five months and had just two outings in 1949 before he won the Champion Hurdle for the first time.

Moya Keogh remembers being in a tented bar before Hatton's Grace went out to withstand the English and French challenge when going for the three-timer in 1951 and a well-wisher remarked to her: 'The Irish are behind you to a man.' 'I don't mind as long as the English and the French are behind me at the finish!' came her witty retort.

If the Festival has today grown into one of the greatest events in the racing calendar, the seeds were sown of the Irish invasion of later years by the assault launched by Vincent O'Brien in 1948. He quickly caught the imagination of the public. People wanted to be there as he threw down the gauntlet to the English bookmakers, watching them visibly squirm in face of a succession of spectacular coups, especially in the Gloucestershire Hurdle.

Charter flights were as yet unknown. The invasion of the Cotswolds that the 'eighties would bring was still a long way off. There was no question of putting a limit on the crowd for Gold Cup Day (now set at 50,000) and certainly no question of selling Club badges in advance for all three days. It would have been unthinkable for the then Manager of Cheltenham racecourse to go to Ireland – as Edward Gillespie did before the 1988 Festival meeting – to explain why they were compelled to go all-ticket.

'We didn't fly initially,' Moya Keogh recalled. 'We went over by boat and took the train on to Cheltenham. Later we would take over the car in the ferry to Liverpool and drive the rest of the journey. The Queen's Hotel and The Plough (now no more) were the centres of much of the action for the Irish. We always stayed outside the town, the first year in an old manor house that had a big blazing fire. Dan and Joan Moore stayed there that year also. Someone said it was haunted. I got a funny feeling myself. We didn't stay there again.

'I remember the gatherings, the O'Briens and their friends and we and our friends. Nat McNabb, of course. Aubrey would be there at dinner. It was like a family gathering. No hectic late nights. Nothing but race talk. They would talk racing until the cows came home. Vincent and Aubrey and Nat McNabb talking about the opposition, talking tactics, and you had to be impressed with the knowledge they showed. You got the feeling of people being keyed up, an air of expectancy about the morrow.

'Before we left the hotel in the morning, we would say nothing to the management about the arrangements for a victory dinner. We didn't believe in making plans in advance. Once, when one of the managers said, "How many can we expect for dinner tonight?" we didn't like it, as we felt it gave the impression that we thought victory was in the bag.

'But once we had won – whether it was Hatton's Grace or Knock Hard – we would ring up from the course and tell the hotel how many to expect. We didn't put a limit on the number we invited. If we met friends at the course and we felt like asking them to join in the celebrations, we did so. But there was nothing wild about the parties.'

Of the horses sent by the Keoghs to Vincent O'Brien, Hatton's Grace was the smallest and most unimposing. But Moya Keogh unhesitatingly described him as 'my pet'. And Martin Molony, who rode him to victory over hurdles, though not in the Champion, would say of the three-times champion: 'He was undoubtedly the best hurdler I rode. He proved his versatility by winning the Irish Cesarewitch two years running (1949–50) and also the Irish Lincoln.'

Martin was in the saddle on both occasions when the Cesarewitch was won – the first being remembered as the day at the Curragh when the O'Brien stable set out to land one of the most spectacular gambles of all.

That is a story in itself.

10

No One Told Martin Not To Try

No one told Martin Molony not to try on Hatton's Grace when he foiled a major O'Brien gamble on stable-companion Knock Hard in the 1949 Irish Cesarewitch. Vincent O'Brien would never dream of asking Martin Molony or any other jockey riding for him to stop any horse. Hatton's Grace and Knock Hard were allowed run totally on their merits that particular day at the Curragh. Anyway as Vincent pointed out: 'We had worked Knock Hard at home with Hatton's Grace and he had pulverised him for speed, so we knew we had something to go to war with.'

Phonsie O'Brien said: 'Knock Hard, we concluded, was a stone-cold certainty if held up to make the best use of his acceleration in the final furlong.'

The man who did the betting for the Keoghs, owners of both Hatton's Grace and Knock Hard, was Nat McNabb. 'A great judge of form and a wonderful judge of a racehorse's ability,' was Moya Keogh's tribute to him. In the picture of Tim Molony bringing Knock Hard into the winner's enclosure after winning the 1953 Gold Cup, Nat McNabb, race glasses in that familiar position down over the front of his raincoat, can be seen waving his hat in triumph.

Moya Keogh said, 'Hatton's Grace had this knack of fooling you at home and he didn't really give of his best on the gallops. He was a different horse on a racecourse and the excitement seemed to electrify him in some strange way and stir him into giving some wonderful displays.'

They met at the Jockey Hall restaurant on the Curragh for lunch on the day of the race – Vincent O'Brien and Dermot, Harry Keogh, Nat McNabb and Dermot McDowell, a Dublin solicitor and a great friend of the Keoghs. Also there was Bob Mulrooney from Limerick, who formed with Nat McNabb the duo Vincent O'Brien entrusted to get the money on when the stable was depending on successful gambles to survive. The lunch that day became, in effect, a council of war – the finalising of the tactical plan to ensure that the best possible price was got about Knock Hard.

Nat McNabb would almost invariably meet Harry Keogh on Friday evenings in Dublin to talk horses and discuss the card for the following day. The Dolphin was then the Mecca of the racing set on Friday nights and after racing on the Saturdays, and Jammet's was also at the height of its glory. Nat McNabb remembers the marble-top bar counter and the roast beef for which the Dolphin was famous – 'the best in Ireland'. He remembers asking the proprietor, Jack Nugent, one evening why it was so wonderful always and Jack confided that he only bought the first three ribs in any side of beef for then he knew he was getting the very best quality. And the 'ferocious games of poker' – Nat McNabb remembers them, too, smiling as he recalls the household names in the racing world who participated in them. •

On the eve of the 1949 Irish Cesarewitch Harry Keogh said to Nat McNabb as they tucked into their roast beef, 'I want you to come down early with me to the Curragh tomorrow. We are meeting Vincent and I have booked a table in the Jockey Hall.' Nat McNabb knew then that there was something really big on.

'We got to the Jockey Hall around noon,' he recalled. 'Over lunch Vincent spelt it out to us – they had worked Knock Hard and Hatton's Grace on the Churchtown gallops and Knock Hard had proved vastly superior. Then he said across the table to me, "Nat, Knock Hard meets Hatton's Grace ᴏn 10 pounds better terms today than in the gallop. What do you think?" My reply w: .s, "Well, Vincent, in that case Knock Hard must be a racing certainty."

'I qualified that statement, however, by adding, "But there is one thing we must not forget, Hatton's Grace is the type of horse that never gives in. He will be staying on when most of the field has cried enough over the 2 miles of the Cesarewitch."

'The plan decided over lunch was that we would go in first on Hatton's Grace in order to push out the price of Knock Hard. And we were going to make sure that those who always had tabs on Bob Mulrooney and myself would be left in no doubt that Hatton's Grace was the one the stable was on.'

Nat McNabb arranged with his wife Eileen that she would position herself in a certain spot on the stand wearing a hat. 'When we had finished the job backing Hatton's Grace and I knew that the price was right on Knock Hard, I would give her a pre-arranged signal from down below in the ring and then she would touch her hat. That would be the sign to the others in the front-line trenches to go over the top.'

Nat knew that it would spoil everything if there was not perfect timing. If one of the team went in even a few minutes before the others, the bookies would be warned of what was happening and the bush telegraph would cause the price to disappear in a twinkling from the boards that mattered. 'We had to act in complete concert, hitting the books together, snapping up the best odds to our money before any of them realised what was happening,' he said.

The overall strategy for the day worked like a dream. Hatton's Grace came down to 3–1 as Knock Hard eased to 6–1, to 7–1 and even to 10–1 on some boards.

As Vincent's trusted lieutenants 'went to war', Nat McNabb and Bob Mulrooney in the van, the bookies were overwhelmed with the rush of money and Knock Hard's price came down to evens while Hatton's Grace drifted out to 8–1.

Phonsie O'Brien had £1000 to £100 on Knock Hard and a small each-way saver on Hatton's Grace.

'Vincent's instructions to Bert Holmes were not to hit the front on Knock Hard until inside the final furlong,' recalled Nat McNabb. 'The horse, however, was going so easily as they turned into the straight that Bert Holmes let him go on. Hatton's Grace was a terrific stayer and he caught Knock Hard within sight of the post and beat him.' It was what one might describe as a typical Martin Molony power finish and when Martin got down to work like that, he could really make horses run for him.

'The money lost was minimal,' said Nat McNabb. 'You see, by backing Hatton's Grace at such good odds early on, we very nearly covered ourselves for the gamble we had on Knock Hard. At worst, we lost no more than £100.'

Legendary bloodstock agent Jack Doyle put it well when he said, 'Vincent O'Brien, like "Darkie" Prendergast, seldom if ever left it behind with the bookmakers. And if a gamble became unstuck, you could say the money was only on loan. Invariably Vincent would get it back – and with interest.'

Five months later he planned to recoup the losses on Knock Hard. And he showed real shrewdness in the way he outwitted the bookmakers. Knock Hard was run in a novice chase at Naas – which he won, incidentally – a fortnight before the Irish Lincoln. Frankly, as Vincent himself said, the aim was 'To get a better price about the horse in the Lincoln'. How many would believe that a horse that had run in a novice chase would win the Lincoln carrying 8 stone 12 pounds?

Pre-race opinion was that betting would take a wide range and 6–1 and better was available about Knock Hard early on. Then, as Louis Gunning reported in the *Irish Press*, 'An avalanche of money hit the bookmakers to make Knock Hard a tight 2–1 favourite'.

The immense stable confidence was completely justified by the race itself as Knock Hard, with T. P. Burns in the saddle, beat the opposition to a frazzle. Once the favourite struck the front, it became a one-horse procession, with young Tommy's father, 'Old' Tommie or 'The Scotsman', taking runner-up position on Signal Service, with Mariner's Light third, Olien's Grace fourth and Rockspring fifth.

The genius of Vincent O'Brien in being prepared to lay out a horse for an old-style gamble in different types of races was never better illustrated than in the case of Knock Hard, whose middle name was 'versatility', as he could win on the Flat, over hurdles and over the major obstacles.

Knock Hard was sent over to run in the Coventry Plate (1 mile 2 furlongs) for amateur riders at Worcester with Phonsie O'Brien in the saddle. The race itself was worth £138, yet the connections took something like £14,000 out of the ring, as the fancied Noholme was beaten.

Nat McNabb put the scale of the gambles and the money won in true perspective when he said, 'We are talking about an era when you could get a new suit for £4 and a pint was only 10d.'

Sitting in front of a warm fire in his comfortable home in Dublin's southside, Nat McNabb reflects on other times, other gambles. It is Aintree Grand National week 1989 and his countenance suddenly clouds over with sadness as he says that Bob Mulrooney had passed on in Limerick a few weeks earlier.

The afternoon had been spent looking at the first day of the Liverpool races on television, his knowledge coming through as he voiced his comments on the performances of individual runners, his mind still as sharp as a razor. 'I never bet on the National – too much of a lottery,' he said.

But then, on his own admission, the man who put on thousands of pounds for Vincent O'Brien and his connections 'never gambled'. He could not have been a heavy gambler anyway, even if he had wanted to be. He had a large family to bring up. He worked as a manufacturer's agent 'in the rag trade', as he put it, when he was not putting on the bets for Vincent O'Brien. He first met Vincent during the Second World War through Willie O'Grady, who introduced the two of them on a train journey from Cork to Dublin. 'We hit it off immediately and our friendship developed from there.'

He smiles when he reflects on his father paying £70 to get him apprenticed. 'You got no pay during your three years' apprenticeship.' And he recalled: 'We had to be down in the store in the old Todd Burns shop by eight o'clock in the morning and we would have to have the whole place swept out and clean by nine. We didn't complain.'

He graduated to the point where Vincent O'Brien had total confidence in him. Initially, as Vincent was making his way up the ladder, just getting established after his father's death, some of the gambles were in cash but later the big bets were 'on the nod', the bookies settling by cheque with Nat McNabb the following week if a coup was landed on a Saturday, and likewise Nat paying by cheque.

'I remember during the War Vincent had three horses running in Limerick. It was Easter Monday and I was all set to go to Fairyhouse for the Irish Grand National. He rang me from Churchtown and asked me to get £200 on the three horses in the S.P. offices as, naturally, he knew that if he put that much on the meeting itself, he might not get any odds to his money.

'It was an awful lot of money, ten times the monthly wage of some workers. There were no cars on the road except those that had special permits and it was almost impossible to get a taxi. So I got on my bike and went around the offices, putting on a fiver here and a tenner there, until I got the whole £200 on. The three horses duly won – that was Vincent, fearless when he knew he had the goods.'

Among the big bookies in the Irish ring then were Dick Power, Jim Rice and Patsy McAlinden.

Nat McNabb recalled that the biggest individual bet he had on a horse in Ireland for Vincent O'Brien was the £3000 he placed on Good Days in a race at Naas in the 'forties. Multiply that by twenty and you get a clearer picture of the 'investment' by today's money values.

'I knew that with that kind of bet I had to get the best price that would obtain that day. I knew, too, that if I began to put it on piecemeal, the market could quickly

Left: Vincent at the Ballsbridge Sales in 1950. *Below*: Vincent with his brothers Dermot and Phonsie on the famous day at Limerick in 1950 when over the Christmas holiday race meeting the stable won eight races and Phonsie rode seven of the winners.

Two men, Jackie O'Brien (*left*) and Dr 'Otto' Vaughan (*below*) who exercised a profound influence on Vincent O'Brien's climb up the ladder to international fame. Jackie O'Brien is pictured with his own point-to-point winner, China Cottage, and Dr Vaughan with Cottage Rake after winning at Leopardstown. P. P. Hogan is up on both horses.

Below: Noel O'Brien points out the rolling acres of The Galloping Field at Churchtown over which Vincent O'Brien exercised his charges when he was establishing himself as a trainer. *Above*: Cows now graze in the field, which in other times constituted the Cheltenham-style uphill climb towards the house that tested a stream of winners at the Festival meeting.

Hatton's Grace (No 4) coming at the last to beat National Spirit (inside) in the 1950 Champion Hurdle, with Martin Molony on the extreme left challenging on Harlech. *Below*: Aubrey Brabazon returns to an Irish roar as Mrs Moya Keogh leads in Hatton's Grace, with Vincent O'Brien directly behind followed by Dermot. To Moya's right (wearing a hat) is her husband Harry.

Martin Molony (*above*) in 1989,
and Michael O'Hehir,
the famous commentator.

Vincent and Jacqueline
on their wedding day
in Dublin on
Saturday, 29 December 1951.

The family man: enjoying the bracing Tipperary air with Jane and David and pet cat, Trickie and pet boxer dog, Moss, named after Ballymoss.

ight: Displaying the catch of the ay with Liz, David and Jane, and *below*) in relaxed mood at home ith Jacqueline and four of the five hildren; (left to right) Susan, Liz, avid and Jane.

'Mincemeat Joe' Griffin (at left) threw fabulous parties at the Adelphi Hotel in Liverpool after the Aintree Grand National triumphs of his horses Early Mist and Royal Tan. He won a small fortune in bets on Early Mist.

Below: Miss Dorothy Paget (at right), who bought Solford from Vincent O'Brien's father, used to bet in telephone numbers. It was nothing to her to put £10,000 on one of her horses.

vanish on me and I might even end up having to take odds on to some of the money. So I had a chat with Patsy McAlinden and I said to him, "I am going to back this horse today and I will be backing it big. What price will you lay me?"

'Patsy did not flinch. His immediate response was, "I'll take the bet and lay you the best available odds provided you don't have another bet." I agreed. Patsy recovered the £3000 and more by backing Good Days around the ring, so we were both happy when he came home a very easy winner,' said Nat.

The period immediately after the Second World War was the boom period for betting, he said, and it was one marked by fearless gamblers and by bookmakers prepared to take them on.

'Our big bets in England were credit bets – on the nod. We had accounts with Hills, Ladbrokes and McLeans,' he said.

He remembered going over to the Liverpool Grand National meeting just after the War, 'And I had my eyes opened to the scale of betting and how much you could take out of the ring if you brought off a successful coup.' He explained that there was 'A phenomenal amount of black market money around in England and the only way it could be laundered was to get a cheque from a bookmaker.'

He recalled standing beside William Hill's perch before one particular race. 'This little Jew boy came in and said "£9000 to £3000" as Hill was shouting "3–1 the field". William Hill never batted an eyelid but continued to shout "3–1 the field". Another chap came in and took "£9000 to £3000". And a third. It was only then that Hill dropped the price to 11–4.

'I had seen nothing like it and I knew in my heart that we had a market once Vincent decided to tilt at the big prizes in England. Before the English bookmakers woke up to how good Vincent really was at preparing a horse to win the race he had it earmarked to win, we took them to the cleaners more than once. Yes, we stung them very badly with Hatton's Grace the first year he won the Champion Hurdle in 1949. I know the starting price was 100–7 but we backed him ante-post at 33–1, 25–1 and 20–1 and continued to back him right down the line.'

Reflecting on the day – 19 November 1952 – that Knock Hard, with Tim Molony up, ran in the Nuneaton Hurdle at Birmingham, Nat said, 'He must have been the greatest certainty of all time when you consider that he had won the Irish Lincolnshire with 8 stone 12 pounds.

'I had £10,000 to put on him,' Nat said, relating how he flew to Birmingham knowing that this was the biggest bet he had ever been entrusted to execute for the O'Brien stable. The last person he would want to see would be anyone from Ireland known to like a bet.

'I was hardly in my seat when I spotted ahead of me Dinny McArdle, who had a public house in South King Street but was a great racing man, a great punter and a great character. Everyone in the game then knew him as "Spitty". He had this way of saying, "A great race, a great race" and then his special little mannerism would show itself. I said to myself, "He must know something about Knock Hard."

' "And what's taking you to Birmingham?" I enquired, as nonchalantly as I could.

'Without as much as the flicker of an eyelid, he told me how he had sold a greyhound to a client in the Birmingham area and was travelling over to get paid – in cash. He then produced an expensive box of cigars, which he said he would be giving to his client as a "luck penny" after he had received his money.

'Then he surprised me by breaking open the box. "Try one, Nat." Cool as a breeze, as he lit up, he remarked with a mischievous smile, "The Customs can't take them off me now – personal use and all that, you know what I mean!"

'As we got off the plane I asked him if by chance he would be making his way to the race meeting in Birmingham after he had collected his cash and, again without the flicker of an eyelid, he remarked, "No, Nat, I want to get back to Dublin as quickly as possible."

'When I got to the racecourse, the first man I met inside was the bould "Spitty" and when we didn't get the price we had hoped to get to our money, I wondered, I just wondered. Knock Hard won even more easily than Gay Future did on an unforgettable occasion at Cartmel. He was actually passing the post when the others were only jumping the last. I couldn't but help notice that "Spitty" was smiling on the plane all the way back to Dublin. I never did get on all the £10,000.'

Nat McNabb went on to relate how Vincent O'Brien went for a real touch on Knock Hard in the 1952 Manchester November Handicap. The plan was to make it an ante-post coup.

'After those early years in Cheltenham and the successes of Cottage Rake and Hatton's Grace and those successful Gloucestershire Hurdle gambles, the English bookmakers were no longer taking any chances with runners from Vincent's stable. I remember Harry Keogh and myself flew over to London specially to back Knock Hard. We picked up the *Sporting Chronicle* to get the prices. We saw that Knock Hard was quoted at between 10–1 and 12–1. We went into Ladbrokes office and we were received by Charlie Simmonds, who had a great welcome for us, as we did a lot of betting with his firm. We told him we wanted to back Knock Hard at the price quoted in their advertisement in the *Sporting Chronicle*. Charlie's response was: "I'm sorry, boys, but that was the price this morning. We had to drop it due to a flood of money. The best I can offer you now is 4–1." We garnered a lot of wisdom from that brief exchange. Of course, we were disgusted at failing to get 10–1 or 12–1 to our money but I do recall that Charlie Simmonds did tell us as we were taking our leave, "There has been strong support also for Summer Rain."

'The name didn't register immediately but I certainly remembered it when Knock Hard failed by a head to this horse, who had finished third in the Epsom Derby of that year.'

Nat McNabb smiled when he recalled how his judgement

was vindicated when Hatton's Grace won the Champion Hurdle in 1949.

Hatton's Grace was an eight-year-old when he joined Vincent O'Brien in the summer of 1948. It was a tremendous feat of training on Vincent's part to turn him out to win his first Champion Hurdle at the age of nine and maintain his appetite for the game so well that he completed the three-timer at eleven and meanwhile also had some outstanding wins in big handicaps on the Flat.

Vincent's attention to detail was again clearly demonstrated in the case of Hatton's Grace at Cheltenham. If you look at the pictures hanging in the hallway of Ballydoyle House of Hatton's Grace winning those three successive Champion Hurdles, you cannot but note that in the case of the third, in particular, as Moya Keogh's gelding arrives at the last, he is on the outside of the English horse. Always on the eve of the start of the Cheltenham Festival Vincent would walk the track with Nat McNabb to assess the going. They were standing at the last hurdle this day and admiring the stiff climb up to the finish when Nat got the idea that from the side of the hurdle where he was standing, the distance to the winning post looked shorter than on the inside.

'I drew Vincent's attention to this and he was suddenly very alert and remarked, "Well, Nat, you might be right."

'We then went back into Cheltenham and bought a tape and returned to the course and actually measured the distance from the last hurdle to the winning post – from the two points, the outside of the hurdle and the inside. We discovered that if you came on the outside, the distance was shorter – by a neck.

' "That could be good enough to win a race," was Vincent's conclusion.'

National Spirit had won the Champion Hurdle two years running (1947 and 1948) when Vincent O'Brien sent Hatton's Grace over to take on the Vic Smith-trained gelding. Just as Desert Orchid would become four decades later, National Spirit was a great favourite with racing enthusiasts in Britain and was a very warm order to complete the hat-trick. On the face of it, Hatton's Grace hardly inspired confidence to be the one to dethrone the champion, as he had been unplaced at 20–1 in the previous year's Champion Hurdle when ridden by Martin Molony.

'Hatton's Grace was with Barney Nugent then,' recalled Nat McNabb. 'He had won at the Leopardstown Christmas meeting and then a handicap hurdle at Naas and was showing such great form at home that Barney Nugent decided to let him take his chance at Cheltenham. Because of a strike, it was not possible to send him over by plane. He had to go by boat, from Rosslare to Fishguard, and was housed in a shed for three days before he resumed his journey to Cheltenham. He didn't eat up, which wasn't surprising after what he had been through. He finished fifth or sixth and I said to myself, "if he can put up a performance like that after hardly eating for three days, then he must win the Champion Hurdle next year." My mind was made up there and then.'

Nat McNabb went on to recall that when the horses entered the parade ring before the 1949 Champion Hurdle many people who had not taken much note of Hatton's Grace before that were turned completely off him and he drifted out to 16–1 in the betting before coming back to start at 100–7. 'In fact, he was rather miserable looking compared to National Spirit, a fine big horse, and if the English thought he was a certainty to complete the three-timer, they were entitled to think so on his performances in the two previous runnings of the race.'

Significantly, however, even though Hatton's Grace had been unplaced in his opening run of the season at Naas, he had later won the Rathcoole Handicap Hurdle under 12 stone 7 pounds at the same course. It was a month before the Champion Hurdle and he started at 7–4.

'They told us we'd never beat National Spirit,' recalled Vincent O'Brien, even though some critics were saying that at the age of eight, National Spirit was getting a bit old. Against that Hatton's Grace was a year older and not many were prepared to back him to win a Champion Hurdle at that stage. Hatton's Grace, showing real pace from the last flight, won easily by 6 lengths.

The following year he started at 5–2 and this time

National Spirit, in blinkers, led him to the last flight but made a bad mistake and Hatton's Grace came away to display again a fine burst of finishing speed, winning by 1½ lengths from Harlech, ridden by Martin Molony.

In 1951 National Spirit, on the inside again, led into the last but blundered in an exact replica of the previous year's error and, losing his balance completely, let Aubrey Brabazon through to win by 5 lengths on the very heavy going from the French horse Pyrrhus III.

Less than a month after winning his first Champion Hurdle, Vincent O'Brien had the inspiration to have a go at the Irish Lincoln with Hatton's Grace – something very few trainers would contemplate doing. Vincent, however, knew the capabilities of Mrs Keogh's horse and knew also that even with 9 stone he was a betting proposition. The O'Brien stable got good odds to their money and eventually Hatton's Grace came down to 6–1.

The jockey who had the ride was Morny Wing, one of the best flat riders in an era marked by tremendous competition between a clutch of riders of exceptional qualities: Morny Wing (22 Irish classics), Tommy Burns (21 Irish classics), Joe Canty (17 Irish classics) and Martin Quirke (9 Irish classics).

Wing, who excelled on two-year-olds, hailed from Yorkshire and served his apprenticeship in England. He fell in love with Ireland and never went back, six victories in the Irish Derby on Ballyheron, Waygood, Rock Star, Rosewell, Windsor Slipper and Bright News helping to cement the relationship.

Vincent O'Brien was being true to his own dictum of using the best every time he utilised the unique talents of Martin Molony. Ironically, Martin foiled that major gamble on Knock Hard when he won the 1949 Irish Cesarewitch on Hatton's Grace – against the expectations of the O'Brien stable. Hatton's Grace carried 9 stone 2 pounds to victory that day. He was allotted 10 stone the following year and started at 10–1.

Martin Molony tends to play it down: 'I got a marvellous run on the inside. That horse had courage.' But it was generally reckoned to have been one of his greatest-ever finishes on the Flat as he won by a short head from Penny On The Jack (to which Hatton's Grace was conceding 36 pounds) and a neck from Pelorus (to which the concession of weight was 35 pounds).

Vincent O'Brien paid Martin the tribute that he was 'a wonderful horseman' and totally dedicated to his profession. 'As a National Hunt rider, he had developed the style of a Flat jockey in a finish and, therefore, could ride a powerful finish at the end of a chase or hurdle race. It gave him a distinct advantage over many of his contemporaries. Like his brother, Tim, he was fearless. We were always great friends apart from our professional association. In fact, there was a strong and lasting friendship between our two families.'

Nat McNabb, who saw the greatest of his era, said unhesitatingly, 'Martin Molony was without question the best jockey I ever saw and I would even put him ahead of Lester. He had strength, he had judgement of pace and horses ran for him in an uncanny manner. I believe that if he was riding today and concentrating totally on the Flat, he would be snapped up by one of the Arab Sheikhs and would be earning even more than Pat Eddery.'

Vincent had provided him with two of his greatest moments on the Flat with Hatton's Grace, and Phonsie was riding in the same race as him at Thurles in 1951 when Martin Molony's career was abruptly ended through a cruel fall. He was on the 4–6 favourite Bursary, who had won at Tralee six days earlier. The race was the Munster Chase and the day was Tuesday, 18 September 1951. He suffered a fractured skull and lay at death's door for a week in Thurles Hospital, the racing world holding its collective breath waiting for bulletins on his progress.

Phonsie vividly remembers the fall and its aftermath: 'The fall happened at the top of the hill. I was immediately behind Martin and was brought down when Bursary came a cropper. I got into the ambulance after Martin had been placed in it. I never saw so much blood. It was streaming out his nose and mouth, which was all busted up.

115

'One of the young ambulance chaps put a plaster over Martin's mouth to try and stop the bleeding. I suddenly noticed that Martin was going blue in the face. I caught the plaster and pulled it off and he gave a big gulp as if gasping for air. He was black from the face down.

'I went to see him every day in hospital. The waiting was awful, as we wondered, would he pull through? Our two families were so close, you know. We were so glad when he did.

'He was good, very, very good. No doubt in the world about that. He never gave up. Going into the last, you might have half a length to spare over him and he would gain half a length, if not more, in the air. Horses ran very well for him. It was a pity to see his career cut short in an ordinary race in Thurles when he had come through so much. But that's what National Hunt jockeys live with, that's what makes them.'

Martin spent six weeks convalescing in bed after emerging from the hospital. Recovery was long and slow. He had a lot of time to think, to ponder his future and where he was going. He travelled across to England for plastic surgery and during that visit saw a specialist who advised him not to ride again. He was only 26 when his career was prematurely ended.

Perhaps if he had still been riding in 1953, he would have been on Knock Hard in the Gold Cup instead of his brother, Tim, who had ridden Hatton's Grace to victory in the 1951 Champion Hurdle. Or, against that, he might have been on one for an English retainer. We shall never know how many more glorious hours he would have enjoyed at Cheltenham or whether Vincent would have had him up on one of his National winners. Certainly, there was a lot more he could have achieved.

Moya Keogh's Knock Hard, the horse with the doubtful heart, was never a natural chaser, never really in love with the game but once he jumped the last he had the speed of a Flat horse to carry him to victory, though, of course, he could never rank in the same league with Cottage Rake when it came to analysing the pros and cons of Vincent's Cup horses.

Vincent remembers him, however, with a special fondness for the gambles he landed, such as the Irish Lincolnshire win in 1950 and the Coventry Plate win at Worcester in 1952, at a time when the stable needed to gamble successfully.

Knock Hard, a 5–1 chance that year – with Freebooter, the 1950 Aintree Grand National winner, favourite – was cantering under Phonsie O'Brien when he fell two out in the 1952 Gold Cup, the year that Miss Dorothy Paget's Mont Tremblant won at 8–1 for Fulke Walwyn and Dave Dick from Shaef (Fred Winter).

The money lost by the connections of the Ballydoyle stable through that costly fall was recouped the following year when Knock Hard triumphed at 11–2 – but those with weak hearts and high blood pressure certainly suffered and had reason to be grateful for the brilliant riding of Tim Molony. Nat McNabb considers that it was one of Vincent O'Brien's finest hours at Cheltenham, taking into account the problems he had to overcome with Knock Hard and that the gelding was facing that day a field that included the previous year's winner, Mont Tremblant; also Teal, the 1952 Aintree Grand National winner; E.S.B., who would win at Aintree in 1956; Halloween, the mount of Fred Winter; Mariner's Log; Galloway Braes and Rose Park.

'I viewed the race with Vincent and Jacqueline,' he said. 'There was fog about that day and, as they started down the hill, I could make out Mont Tremblant, Rose Park and Galloway Braes dominating events at the head of the field. Knock Hard had dropped right back. We were mystified. He seemed out of it at that point. Tim was driving him and driving him. Suddenly, the horse started to pick up and came from a seemingly hopeless position to be there with a chance at the last. The odds, however, were still very much against him winning.'

Vincent takes up the story: 'Knock Hard produced his best leap at the last and, seeing that there were no more fences in front of him, decided to put his head down and

117

run. He stormed up the hill and had 5 lengths to spare at the finishing post over Halloween, who had come through beaten horses from a long way back. It was an incredible performance.'

'A victory conjured by Tim Molony from the impossible,' summed up Nat McNabb.

Knock Hard never recaptured the glory of that day in 1953 and failed to win in ten further outings before his retirement, Vincent accepting that there was a sad falling-away in his form. He failed to figure in the first three in the 1954 Gold Cup when starting at 9–4. He passed from the Keoghs to the ownership of Frank More O'Ferrell.

11

Nights At The Adelphi With 'Mincemeat' Joe

The Adelphi Hotel in Liverpool had never seen anything like it before in its history – and nothing since has quite matched for flair and flowing champagne the victory parties thrown by 'Mincemeat' Joe Griffin after Vincent O'Brien had trained Early Mist and Royal Tan to win the 1953 and 1954 Aintree Grand Nationals for him.

'Mincemeat' Joe was one of the most colourful characters ever to hit the racing scene. He was small and stocky with twinkling eyes, the direct opposite of the archtype business tycoon, but with a sharp brain and that native Dublin cunning that made him see a good business opportunity.

In the food shortages that still persisted after the Second World War, the English hankered for 'goodies' that were taken for granted in Ireland. 'Joe, we haven't seen mince pies for years,' an English friend remarked to him. His mind immediately began to tick over.

He bought on 'tick' from the Greek Government a £100,000 shipload of dried fruit, a cancelled order from a British grocery chain. He used the fruit in mince pies and sold the product in jars to the same British grocers for £200,000. It was easy to pay the Greek Government on the resultant profit. Joe was on his way.

When Royal Tan beat Tudor Line by a neck in 1954 to make him the first owner in the history of the National to win the race in successive years with different horses, he danced an Irish jig and threw his hat in the air as the 8–1 winner was being led in. In the unsaddling enclosure, he was joined by his vivacious 30-year-old wife, Peggy, a curly-headed brunette wearing diamonds, pearls and mink stole for the occasion. 'Life's wonderful,' exclaimed Joe, then only 36 and styled the 'Irish Mincemeat King'.

'Bring on the champagne,' he said – and they certainly did. He sent a dozen bottles of champagne into the jockeys' room and that same evening in the Adelphi Hotel in Liverpool over 70 guests sat down to a dinner of Dublin Bay prawns – specially flown in from the Irish capital – smoked salmon, turtle soup, chicken and asparagus, flown in from France.

When Early Mist won the 1953 Grand National, Joe gave up to £10,000 (more than the stake money at the time) in presents to the trainer, jockey and handlers of the horse. And the party in the Adelphi cost £1500.

Joe brought ten of his office staff to the race. And at the racecourse he invited four of them in the aftermath of victory to the champagne dinner party. They rushed from the course into the city to buy evening dresses and managed it just before the shops closed.

All the staff in the factory had been told by Joe to back the horse. Some who were saving up to be married put half of their savings on Early Mist at 33–1. It brought them £330 each. 'Mr Griffin is very kind and generous and gives us a tip whenever he expects one of his horses to win. He has never let us down,' said a 20-year-old girl from Walkinstown, who was a shorthand typist in the office.

It was those kind of spontaneous philanthropic gestures that endeared him to the public and the colour writers alike. Without any effort, he was the maker of headlines and a natural with the quotable quote.

His wife blended in perfectly to the new world that Joe had discovered and every minute of which he was living to the full and relishing as if the tap from which the finance was coming would never run dry. 'When you have, as we had, profits running in the region of £1,000 a day, money doesn't mean anything. It loses its value and you just spend and spend,' he would recall later, looking back on those days when there was never a cloud in the sky. 'Whoever was in the company was welcome to have a good time.

'Money for me is for spending and for making people happy. I have made a lot of people happy – even though I realise now that a lot of them were just hangers-on. I should have chosen my friends more carefully but I have no regrets about spending the money.'

In the period 1950 to 1953 he achieved what members of the aristocracy and money barons had spent their lives and fortunes trying to achieve and yet failed to realise. He won the Grand National not just once but twice in succession and could have had a third if he had taken the advice of Vincent O'Brien and purchased Quare Times when it was offered to him – and granted his fortunes had not taken a plunge in the meantime.

For example, the year that Joe Griffin won with Early Mist, Lord Bicester, owner of some of the finest chasers in the history of National Hunt racing, was then 86 and had been trying unsuccessfully for fourteen years to win the National – and he was still not giving up hope. And, ironically, on the death of Mr J. V. Rank, whose lifetime's ambition it had been to win this race and whose time ran out just too soon, Early Mist was bought at the dispersal sale of the Rank horses by Vincent O'Brien on behalf of Joe Griffin for 5300 guineas.

In three short years, 'Mincemeat' Joe won £65,000 in stake money alone on his horses and winning bets brought that figure well beyond the £100,000 mark. Multiply it by ten and you can quickly calculate that he was in the millionaire class as a successful owner.

On the morning of the 1953 Grand National, Peggy Griffin handed Bryan Marshall a St Christopher medal and said to him, 'Well, if you don't win, at least don't break your neck.' Bryan won by 20 lengths and received a present of £5000 as Joe Griffin netted £35,000 in winning bets.

Joe and Peggy gave a diamond bracelet in platinum, worth £1000 then, to Joe's secretary, Rose O'Duffy. Later it would emerge in the bankruptcy court that Rose pledged the bracelet for £600 and gave a loan from this money to Mrs Griffin.

Joe had perhaps his proudest moment when a civic reception was accorded Early Mist on his return to Dublin. Thousands turned out to watch as the horse was paraded through O'Connell Street to the Mansion House where the Lord Mayor, Andy Clerkin, officiated. It culminated in the gelding receiving a pat on the neck from the Lord Mayor as Joe posed for photographers.

Harry McDonald, later to become head porter at the Adelphi Hotel – a position he still held when I met him on Grand National eve, 1988 – was a junior porter in the heady days. He can still recall as if it was only yesterday the sign writers coming in once the result of the National was known and putting up the name 'Early Mist' and then 'Royal Tan' a year later on a banner flung across the spacious lounge area where the guests at Joe Griffin's fabulous parties would dance after dinner into the early hours to a full orchestra.

The restaurant they now call the Sefton was known then as simply 'The French Restaurant' and it was appropriately enough fitted up in green foliage in honour of victory for the Emerald Isle. The tables set in alcoves overlooked the dance area. There was Guinness aplenty for those who tired of champagne. And Irish whiskey also. Whatever you wanted, in fact.

Harry McDonald remembers the Swiss head chef, called Bruche (or was it Brusche? – what does it matter, he had style) going to tremendous lengths to leave his mark on the celebratory dinners. Harry cannot forget the atmosphere generated by those nights with 'Mincemeat' Joe at the Adelphi.

Later he would see Roy Rogers bringing Trigger into this same lounge – the famous horse mounting the stairs as thousands of kids screamed in welcome. He remembers Gregory Peck and the adulation he engendered. And 'our Harold' (Wilson) smoking a cool pipe as he arrived to talk to his constituents – and how he loved dear old Liverpool town. And Lester Piggott arriving in the days when there was flat racing at Aintree. The old steam train coming into

Central Station before the underground overtook it and the porters going down to meet the train and bring up the bags.

Harry McDonald remembered great occasions also when Liverpool Football Club used the Adelphi for celebratory dinners, and they added to the store of trophies brought back to Merseyside. But somehow in the whirling nostalgia as we chatted in this same lounge area beside the Sefton Restaurant where they shot scenes for the film on the sinking of the Titanic, it was unmistakably clear that the nights created by Joe Griffin had left an imprint on a young porter that could never be erased, especially the memories of that champagne dinner after Early Mist had won 'Mincemeat' Joe his first National in 1953.

The Keoghs, Harry and Moya, owners of triple Champion Hurdle winner, Hatton's Grace, would sell Royal Tan to Joe Griffin to win for him his second National. Moya Keogh recalled the unusual circumstances in which she found herself at the lavish Early Mist victory party in the Adelphi.

'Jacqueline O'Brien was expecting and so did not travel over with Vincent when he left for Liverpool. But as she listened to the commentary on the race, she caught the excitement of Early Mist's 20-lengths win. She rang me immediately and said simply, 'We'll go over, Moya.' Of course, it was all dependent on my being able to arrange two seats on a flight to Liverpool in double-quick time. I told Jacqueline I would ring her back.

'I had to pull strings to get the two seats. Everyone in Aer Lingus was as excited as we were at Early Mist's victory for Ireland and they kindly provided the seats for Jacqueline and myself – on a freight plane, due to leave that evening. Jacqueline rushed by road to Dublin Airport where I was waiting for her – and I had even bought two orchids, one for each of us.

'We sat on two tea-chests with our evening dresses on our laps. We didn't have to go through Customs, as we were probably regarded as 'freight' on that flight.

'We jumped into a taxi at Liverpool Airport and, arriving at the Adelphi, dashed up the steps with our evening dresses ready to put on immediately we got to a room to change. Just as the speeches were commencing, we walked into the lounge looking cool, calm and collected. Vincent O'Brien was never one to show emotion in public but he certainly was surprised to see Jacqueline and myself arriving out of the blue.'

'Tremendous' was the word used by Harry McDonald to describe the first Joe Griffin victory dinner and the one that followed Royal Tan's triumph in 1954.

'No, we shall never see their like again. But then I suppose there was never a character quite like Joe Griffin. I was young, very young at the time; he just seemed to take over the place lock, stock and barrel.'

The parties in the Adelphi were followed by homecoming parties in the Gresham Hotel and in the Kilcoran Lodge Hotel in Cahir, County Tipperary, with bonfires blazing on the hillsides and bands out to lead the victory parades. It seemed that the days of wine and roses would last forever and Joe Griffin cashed in on Early Mist's resounding win by introducing on to the market the 'Early Mist' chocolate.

Joe Griffin's Redbreast Preserving Company was on the crest of the wave for a time, turning over, according to Joe, '£½ million to £2 million a year in exports for three years and that at the time was a lot of money coming into the country for a single exporter.'

But the climax to his career was a tragic one, culminating in the black Friday in July 1954, when he was adjudged a bankrupt.

After the fall, he admitted: 'I had no background training for big business. I had nobody to help me – it was a one-man show. I brought in an accountant who I hoped would have been able to keep everything on a proper legal and financial footing. I had the brains to do things and to sell but I lacked the experience to control the finance.'

Without the necessary control, the 'unorthodox' accounting practices that came to light at the bankruptcy trial, were certain to happen. One of the most bizarre was the disclosure that a cheque drawn on the company for £5565 and entered in the ledger under the heading 'raw materials' was for the purchase of Early Mist.

The bankruptcy hearing was the final humiliation for Joe Griffin, leading to the point where he was forced to promise that he would not go to the Grand National of 1956. His passport had been taken away and it was only given back to him when he gave a categorical assurance that he would not travel to Liverpool.

The nightmare of his two-year legal grilling in the bankruptcy courts would haunt him for years.

Two bailiffs, on the Sheriff's instructions, had gone to Vincent O'Brien's Ballydoyle stables and impounded all Joe's horses, including Grand National winner Royal Tan. Joe looked on helplessly as all his other possessions – even down to his racing binoculars – passed into the hands of the bankruptcy court's official assignee. Subsequently even his two Grand National trophies – gold cups each weighing 50 ounces – were auctioned in Dublin.

In what one newspaper described as 'The Best Show In Town', hundreds thronged to the Royal Dublin Society in Ballsbridge for the sale of the Griffin horses. The newsreel cameras whirred as, in the presence of many leading racing personalities, on that grey November day in 1954, Royal Tan was knocked down to the representative of Prince Aly Khan for 3900 guineas and Early Mist was sold to Vincent O'Brien for 2000 guineas.

Galatian, winner of eleven races, including the Old Newton Cup at Haydock Park, and runner-up twice to Sir Ken in the Champion Hurdle, was also knocked down to Vincent O'Brien for 1900 guineas. 'I like to keep old friends,' said the trainer.

Teapot II, for which Joe Griffin had paid £10,000, fetched a mere 40 guineas. Solar Crown was bought by Mrs E. C. Whitton, Honorary Director of the Irish Branch of the International League for the Prevention of Cruelty to Horses, for 8 guineas.

The eight sold realised 8178 guineas.'Mincemeat' Joe had paid £20,000 for three of them.

Joe dreamed, years later, of winning a third Aintree Grand National – 'to beat Raymond Teasy Weasy and the other owners who had won the race twice. Yes, I am going to win it for a third time.'

He never did make it back to the big-time. But he will be remembered as the one who helped, in his days of wine and roses, to play his part as a 'lucky' owner in Vincent O'Brien's completing the first two legs of a unique treble at Liverpool.

12

'A Master Of His Art'

The night before the 1953 Grand National Vincent O'Brien brought Bryan Marshall up to his suite in the Adelphi Hotel in Liverpool where he had a slow-motion movie projector. He went through a number of previous Grand Nationals and showed Bryan the mistakes that had been made, what to avoid, where to stay, where to go.

'Mincemeat' Joe Griffin was in the room that evening and later he would reflect: 'Yes, I will say one thing about Vincent O'Brien – he is a master of his own art.'

Bryan Marshall, who was 37 the year of his success on Early Mist and in the maturity of an outstanding career as a National Hunt jockey, said of Vincent O'Brien: 'He is very, very thorough and leaves no stone unturned.'

Again that thoroughness reflected itself in the manner in which he asked Marshall to come over to the Ballydoyle stables for a gallop on Early Mist – his first acquaintance with the gelding. Now Early Mist when trained by Tom Dreaper for J. V. Rank was only seven and patently lacking in experience when he challenged for the 1952 Grand National. In the cavalry charge by the field of 47 to the first jump he lost his balance on landing and toppled over. Shrewd race readers noted that it was *after* he had got over the jump that he came down and remembered this when backing him to win the 1953 race.

However, Bryan Marshall would recall 35 years later that 'when other jockeys heard I was going to ride Early

Mist they were all saying to me that he was a "dodgy" fellow. They all thought I'd get crucified. He was a nervous horse all right. He'd shy at a cigarette pack if he saw it on the ground. He'd see things that weren't there and shy away from them. But he was a terrific horse, Gold Cup standard really, but just idle. People have asked me, which was the better of the two, Early Mist or Royal Tan? There was no comparison really. It would always have to be Early Mist for me.'

Vincent O'Brien concurred with Marshall's viewpoint that Early Mist was ahead of Royal Tan on the score of class. In fact, he would view him as the 'classiest' of the three Grand National winners he trained, noting also that he had 'a bit of speed'.

However, while Early Mist ran in the Cheltenham Gold Cup two years after his Aintree triumph, Vincent did not see him as a natural jumper in the mould of Royal Tan. He pointed to the 'several blunders' that Early Mist made in winning the National. In the final analysis, Royal Tan emerges in Vincent's viewpoint as the best of his three National winners.

Early Mist took off a bit far back at Valentine's – though he made it – then hit the second fence from home near the top; the packing parted and he continued on his way without losing ground; finally, he brushed the last but that did not prevent him going right away on the long run-in from the gallant seven-year-old Mont Tremblant (12 stone 5 pounds), who was conceding 17 pounds to the winner and who was dashingly ridden by Dave Dick.

In the Cheltenham Gold Cup Early Mist, with Bryan Marshall up and starting at 5–1 after being well backed by the Irish contingent, could only finish fourth to the shock 33–1 winner, Gay Donald. In fairness to Vincent O'Brien's charge, his training for the Cheltenham race had been interrupted because of trouble with his feet.

Early Mist, by Brumeaux out of Sudden Dawn (by Hurry On), was bred in England by Mr D. J. Wrinch. He had sold Sudden Dawn and her yearling in January 1946 at the Newmarket Sales. The yearling, Early Mist, fetched 250 guineas but when resold at the September Sales of the same year went to Mr H. Bonner for 625 guineas. Mr Rank then acquired him and allowed him to develop slowly until he was put into training with Tom Dreaper. The death of J. V. Rank and the subsequent dispersal sale proved the hinge of fate that resulted in Early Mist moving into the charge of Vincent O'Brien – and becoming his first Grand National winner.

Vincent O'Brien did not want Bryan Marshall to go into the Aintree race without assessing for himself how he should ride Early Mist. Marshall was delighted with the way the eight-year-old went in the gallop at Ballydoyle and seemed happy that his jumping was good enough to see him safely around Aintree. He deliberately rode him at speed into a few fences on the gallops, then pulled back half a length behind the leader at another and Early Mist negotiated the obstacle without trouble and even jumped to the front again.

Marshall expressed his optimism and enthusiasm afterwards to Vincent O'Brien, who, however, showed his customary caution. This caution stemmed not alone from the doubts he still entertained about Early Mist's ability to jump the Liverpool course without serious error but also from the fact that the horse's preparation had been short and hurried. His preference was slightly for Lucky Dome, who had shown himself to be a lion-hearted little horse and of whose well-being there was no doubt. 'A great little horse – a great one to have a gamble on – he would nearly always bring it home. And extremely versatile also,' was the tribute to Lucky Dome by T. P. Burns, who scored some outstanding victories on him on the Flat and over hurdles.

When Early Mist should have been in training for his initial outing of the 1952/53 season, he was sidelined with a splint, which Vincent O'Brien recalled was so bad that 'it went right through his cannon bone, as it were, affecting both the inside and outside of his foreleg'.

Then a decision was taken to fire him for the trouble. The man who did the job was Bob Griffin – 'And a first rate job it was too,' said Vincent, quick to recognise that some of his greatest successes, including those Grand National triumphs, could never have been achieved without the advice, outstanding professionalism and personal dedication of this veterinary surgeon, whose long and close links with Vincent and his family went right back to the time of Dan O'Brien.

Indeed, Bob Griffin, who lived on the Curragh, remembered Dan O'Brien winning the big Irish autumn handicaps with Astrometer and Astrologer. And yet 45 years later Bob played a crucial role when Golden Fleece coughed a number of times in his final work-out at Epsom on the eve of the 1982 Derby.

In January 1953 there seemed no hope of getting Early Mist ready in time for the Grand National but the Griffin magic had worked once again. Vincent O'Brien knew that he was sound enough now to be got ready for a tilt at the Aintree race, though whether he was fit enough to win in a gruelling battle from the last was another matter entirely.

On 7 February he had his first race of the season in the Scalp Handicap Hurdle at Leopardstown but, after the long lay-off, it was not surprising that he finished at the tail-end of the field. A fortnight later Vincent sent him to Baldoyle for the Baldoyle Handicap Chase and again he was unplaced. Then he went for the Newlands Handicap Chase (3 miles 76 yards) at Naas just three weeks before the National and, carrying 12 stone 3 pounds, he obliged at odds of 4–7 – only to be disqualified for taking Southern Coup's ground. In these three races he was ridden by P. J. Doyle.

In plumping for Bryan Marshall as the rider in the National, Vincent had opted for a horseman – one to gain inspiration by the challenge presented to him by the Aintree fences, where another might catch the eye with flash and flourish on park courses. Ten times he would go round Aintree – 'Not ten times in a row and I remember that one year I was in the stands with a broken arm.'

Vincent O'Brien and himself came together again with Pat Taaffe (who rode the third of Vincent's National winners, Quare Times, to victory in 1955) on a day in the 'eighties in Dublin's Westbury Hotel as they were presented with the Kaliber awards in memory of their Aintree triumphs.

Even in his 'seventies, Bryan Marshall still retained the powerful build and rugged looks that had Paul Haigh in a feature in the *Racing Post* in the count-down to the 1988 Grand National likening him to Victor McLaglen, the Hollywood star 'who turned up in about a hundred black-and-whites as the battered tough guy with the heart of gold'.

He was born in County Kilkenny of an American father and Irish mother. He was eleven years old when he went to England in 1927 at the invitation of 'Atty' Persse, then Master of the Limerick Hunt, who admired the way he rode. To Persse, who had actually started training in Ireland in 1902 before moving to Britain four years later, was attributed the immortal comment: 'Good trainers are born, not made. Without natural flair it is better to keep away from racing stables and run a garage.' For around 50 years there was no need for him even to contemplate running a garage, as he was one of the most brilliant of his era. One of the most famous horses to be trained by him was The Tetrarch, owned by his cousin Major Dermot McCalmont and after whom the Tetrarch Stakes at the Curragh was named.

'Atty' Persse's judgement in spotting the emerging talent of Bryan Marshall was to be fully vindicated, for at the age of thirteen Marshall rode his first winner on the Flat. Because of increasing weight he had to switch to the jumps at sixteen and reached one of the high peaks of his career when becoming champion jockey at the age of 31.

His Liverpool triumph on Early Mist left no doubt that he was one of the great riders over the Aintree course. And further proof was forthcoming when he rode Royal Tan to victory for Vincent O'Brien the following year. Pat Taaffe likewise showed himself to be an outstanding National jockey by winning not only on Quare Times but also on Gay Trip (1970).

Marshall had garnered from the experience gained in previous Nationals that the quickest line down to Becher's

131

Brook was near the outside. 'People don't realise that but if you look, there's a slight elbow. You miss a lot of the barging that goes on in the middle of the field if you go that way, too.'

Where there had been 47 runners in 1952, now there were 31, and this made Vincent O'Brien happier as he saw less danger from loose horses.

Mr Alec Marsh got them away to a perfect start at the first attempt. Vincent O'Brien knew quickly that he would be looking to Early Mist rather than Lucky Dome to win him his first National. Lucky Dome, failing to get a clear run, was last to the first fence, where he was squeezed for room and lost another half-dozen lengths. By the time he had reached the third fence he was a dozen lengths behind the last horse, and out of the race. Seldom had a Grand National more quickly become a contest between only a few runners.

After crossing Valentine's Brook the first time, it was reasonably certain that only Ordnance, who had forged a long lead after the first circuit, Mont Tremblant, Little Yid, Early Mist and Armoured Knight had any chance of winning. Ordnance was still in front as they came over the water.

Going into the country Bryan Marshall moved Early Mist forward in front of Mont Tremblant. Armoured Knight was then beaten. Ordnance's lead was well reduced and he fell two fences before Becher's Brook. Now as he trained his glasses on the field Vincent O'Brien saw Early Mist land in front at Becher's second time round.

'I thought for a while the others were being cunning and leaving me there,' said Bryan Marshall, as he recalled for Paul Haigh in the *Racing Post* interview the climactic stage of the race.

'Then I said to myself, "all right, let's go. It's catch as catch can now." ' And no one was going to catch them.

'He won so easily, he was only a split second outside Golden Miller's record,' said Bryan Marshall.

Vincent O'Brien was the first to acknowledge that Bryan Marshall was the right jockey for Early Mist because the gelding had to be 'asked one' at each fence and when Marshall gathered him going into a jump, he responded the right way for him. The National fences took more jumping in those days as they were not as 'sloped' as they are today. Marshall rode Early Mist with almost a full length and it is his firm belief that most National Hunt jockeys today ride too short.

At the time of the Kaliber lunch in Dublin Bryan Marshall was head of Compton Transport and his horseboxes had become an integral part of the racing scene – a jockey who had made it rather than sinking into struggling obscurity when the tumult and the shouting that follows National triumphs no longer rang in the ears.

Vincent O'Brien greeted him with special warmth at that lunch, knowing that Bryan was the man who helped set him on the road to that unique National treble, while Early Mist's success also contributed to Vincent emerging as leading trainer in Britain at the end of the 1952–53 National Hunt season.

There was not a cloud in the sky, it seemed, as Knock Hard had won the Gold Cup at Cheltenham and then Chamier took the Irish Derby at the Curragh.

Twelve months after Early Mist's triumph, however, Vincent O'Brien found himself in trouble with the Stewards of the Irish National Hunt Steeplechase Committee and would be stood down for a period in the most extraordinary circumstances.

13

When Vincent First Lost His Licence

Behind closed doors in the old headquarters of the Irish Turf Club in Merrion Square, Dublin, in March 1954 Pierce Molony, then Chief Steward of the Irish National Hunt Steeplechase Committee, threatened to resign if the drastic action contemplated at one point against Vincent O'Brien was carried through.

It was a moment of crisis outstripping anything the Turf Club had faced in its long and chequered history. There seems little doubt that it was this resignation threat by a man who was a deeply-respected figure in Irish racing at the time that resulted in Vincent O'Brien only losing his licence to train for three calendar months when the penalty imposed could have been far heavier.

At one point the threat hung over Vincent that he might be put out of racing indefinitely. The intervention of the Chief Steward saved him at a crucial juncture in his career. And the members of the O'Brien family have never forgotten their debt of gratitude to Pierce Molony, of The Racecourse, Thurles (father of the late Dr Paddy Molony and grandfather of Pierce Molony, Secretary/Manager of Thurles Racecourse).

It was five days before Royal Tan ran in the 1954 Aintree Grand National that Vincent O'Brien found himself attending an inquiry in Dublin stemming from alleged discrepancy between the English and Irish form of four

134

horses – Royal Tan, Lucky Dome, Early Mist and Knock Hard – trained by him.

Jockeys T. P. Burns, Pat Taaffe, Phonsie O'Brien, P. J. Doyle and Eddie Kennedy were among the witnesses examined at the first hearing along with owners Harry Keogh and Vincent's brother, Dermot. The hearing was adjourned to 31 March to allow Rear Admiral H. B. Jacomb and Lt-Col J. M. Christian, Stewards Secretaries to the English National Hunt Committee, and jockey Bryan Marshall and owner John A. Wood to give evidence.

Afterwards a statement was issued to the effect that 'The Stewards of the INHS Committee could not accept Mr M. V. O'Brien's explanations and when considering what action to take on these findings, the Stewards had before them the fact the Mr M. V. O'Brien had been warned and cautioned on several occasions as to the running of his horses.

'The Stewards under Rules 16(ii) and 104(vii) withdrew his licence to train for three calendar months from 2 April 1954.'

Vincent O'Brien was flabbergasted. In a statement issued to members of the press, he said, 'I am completely in the dark as to what, if any, offence I am alleged to have committed.

'No suggestion was made against the manner in which the horses were ridden in any of their races. In fact, no specific charge of any kind in respect of the running of any of the horses in any of their races has been made.'

Dermot O'Brien, looking back on it 35 years later, said, 'The Stewards first informed Vincent that they were holding an inquiry into *all* the horses under his care for a period of two years. At the inquiry, they said they had reduced it to four horses. But meanwhile Vincent had to look into all the races in which the horses he trained had run in the previous two years. How could you put together a proper defence when in making their announcement of the inquiry in the first place, the Stewards never mentioned any specific race and, more important still, never pinpointed what actually was the discrepancy in form that they were concerned with. That would never happen today.

'Horses are not machines and where particular horses of ours ran badly, perhaps on courses that did not suit them, the Stewards, if we are to take the words "inconsistent running" strictly at their face value, obviously concluded that the horses in question had not been allowed to run on their merits.'

Phonsie O'Brien said that some of the horses did not run well on certain tracks, in fact ran inexplicably badly. 'Baldoyle was a funny track and several good horses got beat there; Tramore was another. Royal Tan and Early Mist, who were essentially National types, could hardly be expected to sparkle at Baldoyle as they did at Aintree. In the case of Lucky Dome and Knock Hard, there were explanations for poor performances they had given before they were successful at Cheltenham. Yet, the Stewards were not happy and seemed to have taken the view that they were deliberately stopped when that was not the case at all.'

Getting down to specifics, Dermot O'Brien said that Lucky Dome's victory in the Spa Hurdle at the 1954 Cheltenham Festival appeared to be one of the races the Stewards had in mind when they referred to discrepancy between English and Irish form, as Lucky Dome had run badly in his two previous races in Ireland.

There was a clear and valid explanation for those failures, said Dermot. First he contested a chase at Baldoyle and had baulked and run through the wing of a fence. He returned to the same course for a second-class hurdle event, a 2-mile handicap, with Bryan Marshall up, as he was to have the ride at Cheltenham and Vincent wanted him to get acquainted with the horse. He was allotted 12 stone 7 pounds that day and for a little horse that was a hell of a burden to be asked to shoulder, even though he was a decent animal. Then, too, the distance of the race was short of his best, as subsequent events would show.

'Any horse we ran that was going on to Cheltenham had to run prominently,' Dermot explained. 'In this case,

Lucky Dome would have had to have a hard race even to be third but the Stewards obviously did not see it that way.

'Lucky Dome clearly remembered his experience at Baldoyle on his previous outing and ran a hopeless race in the handicap hurdle. In fact, Bryan Marshall was very disappointed with him and gave him no chance at Cheltenham. His running was much too bad to be true.

'The question then was: "Would we send him to Cheltenham or not?" On form it did not seem worthwhile but John A. Wood, who loved to have a runner at the Festival meeting, told Vincent to let him take his chance.

'He entered him for the Spa Hurdle (3 miles). Bryan Marshall took a bad fall and was stood down. I said to Vincent, "T. P. Burns has no ride, let's book him," and that was how T.P. came to be on him that day. Lucky Dome won easily and, of course, the Stewards may have felt that they had every reason to ask questions about that unplaced run in the hurdle race at Baldoyle.'

Turning to Knock Hard, Dermot O'Brien said that Harry Keogh had lost a fair bit of money when this most versatile of horses failed so narrowly, with Billy Nevett in the saddle, in the major gamble on the Manchester November Handicap. 'He said to Vincent that he would like to go for the King George VI Chase at Kempton. After training the horse for speed to win the November Handicap, the problem now was to get him settled and relaxed to win a chase of the calibre of the big Kempton Christmas event.

'Tim Molony rode him that day. He jumped off taking a hell of a hold and jumped the first so strong that, as he landed, his forelegs went straight out in front and his hindlegs shot straight out behind along the ground. Tim managed to stay in the saddle. He sat quietly and allowed Knock Hard to get going again. But that first blunder had left its mark, as Knock Hard had got a real fright and he never really jumped throughout the rest of the race. His class, however, carried him into third place, behind Halloween and Mont Tremblant.

'Towards the end of January Vincent ran him in a 3-mile handicap chase at Leopardstown, where he was asked to carry 12 stone 7 pounds, giving no less than 21 pounds to a very good horse in Mariner's Log, owned by Lord Bicester. Pat Doyle, who had not been riding very long for us, had the mount. Mariner's Log and Mr What (9 stone 7 pounds) were ridden by the Taaffe brothers, Pat and "Toss".

'Vincent's instructions to Pat Doyle were that he was on a high-class horse, that he was to ride the best he could, "be there to win if you can, but don't knock him about".

'The Taaffe brothers set a hell of a gallop. Knock Hard had not as yet regained his confidence after the fright he got at Kempton. He could not peg back Mariner's Log and anyway he was conceding too much weight to him that day. He was beaten into fourth place.

'He met Mariner's Log again in the Gold Cup where at levels they jumped the last upsides. So you can see how difficult it was to expect him to give 21 pounds to that horse in the Leopardstown race and win. Nowadays, people won't run their top-class horses with more than 12 stone.'

On his way to winning the Gold Cup, Knock Hard had taken the Great Yorkshire Chase under 11 stone 7 pounds and obviously the Stewards took that victory, along with the subsequent Cheltenham success, into account in their assessment of 'inconsistent running' between Ireland and England.

It would be shown that the key race in the entire affair was Knock Hard finishing only fourth at Leopardstown when starting at 5–2. But, as Dermot O'Brien revealed, Vincent thought there could be something wrong with the horse's heart. 'He got someone down from Trinity College to Ballydoyle and it must have been the first time that a cardiograph was done on a horse in Ireland. Anyway, it was shown that Knock Hard had a murmur and we were given the news by the expert from Trinity that the horse could drop dead at any time. Fortunately, it didn't happen in any of his subsequent races, but he dropped dead one day out hunting after he had been given in retirement to Lady Lily Serena Lumley.'

On the night that Royal Tan, after winning the 1954 Aintree Grand National, came back to a tremendous homecoming victory reception in Cashel, with bonfires blazing on the hillside on the way into town and the Rock floodlit, Mick Davern, local member of Dail Eireann (Irish Parliament) stood on the platform and hit out at the fact that Vincent O'Brien was the subject of a Turf Club inquiry.

He talked of 'green-eyed' individuals and his sentiments echoed the feelings of thousands who believed that Vincent was the victim of jealousy because of his outstanding run of success. Dermot did not hide the fact that he felt that his brother was the victim of 'jealousy' and Phonsie maintained that the sweeping indictment mentioning merely alleged discrepancy between the English and Irish form of four horses without one single specific detail being elaborated would never happen today.

The Turf Club Stewards, including Judge W. E. Wylie, 'sat in' with the National Hunt Stewards during the inquiry. It was Judge Wylie who introduced the 'sit in' as it enabled him to be present at all inquiries. As he was retired as a judge, he had ample time on his hands and with his experience on the bench, he tended to dominate the meetings. While ostensibly Pierce Molony as Chief Steward of the Irish National Hunt Steeplechase Committee was chairing the inquiry into the running of the Vincent O'Brien-trained horses, Judge Wylie may as well have been in the chair as he just took over.

Vincent O'Brien has never forgotten a remark he passed to him one evening in the St Stephen's Green Club (both Vincent and the judge were members). It was at the very time when the Stewards of the Irish Turf Club had met to decide whether they would follow through on a decision of the English Stewards in relation to what became known as 'The Blue Sail Affair'.

'Mincemeat' Joe Griffin provided a link between Vincent O'Brien and Blue Sail, trained by P. J. 'Darkie' Prendergast. Paddy Prendergast had purchased Blue Sail as a yearling for Joe Griffin for 3000 guineas. Rae Johnstone had the mount when the colt was unplaced to subsequent

Irish 2000 Guineas winner Tale of Two Cities in the Railway Plate (over 6 furlongs 63 yards) at the Curragh in September 1954. The following month Tommy Gosling rode him in the Cornwallis Stakes (1 mile) at Ascot and he was gambled on down to 5–2 favouritism, only to lose by a neck to Plainsong.

Despite the defeat, the Local Stewards still held an inquiry into what they saw as a discrepancy in form and referred the matter to the Stewards of the English Jockey Club. Their verdict was not to warn Paddy Prendergast off but to tell him that 'horses trained by him would not be allowed to run under their Rules and that no entries would be accepted from him'.

In normal fashion, such a penalty would have been acted upon right away by the Irish Turf Club but they held their own inquiry on 23 October and, on the basis of the difference in distance between the two events, came to the conclusion that Paddy Prendergast had no case to answer (this, incidentally, created a historic precedent and one that earned much public support for the Irish Stewards).

Vincent, knowing that Judge Wylie was present at the meeting of the Irish Stewards, asked him if he could give him any news on how Paddy Prendergast had fared (Paddy Prendergast had actually been called to appear before the inquiry).

'We could find no discrepancy there,' replied the Judge and then made the remark which left Vincent deeply shaken and which he could never forget: 'If it had been me, I'd have warned you off over Knock Hard last January at Leopardstown. He ran like a hairy dog.'

Dermot O'Brien has often pondered over the past 35 years – when he reflects on the three months' suspension imposed on his brother – why Judge Wylie seemed so deeply concerned about the running of a chaser in an individual race at Leopardstown, why too a man whose principal concern and area of control as a Steward of the Turf Club was the Flat should be so inordinately interested in performances in the National Hunt sector that he should say what he did to Vincent.

Dermot has come to his own conclusions but he prefers to keep these to himself – and will carry them with him to the grave. On the broader plane, he contends that it was only natural and human that there should be jealousy of Vincent's success, extending right across the board, even to owners who did not have horses in the stable and to trainers who could not match his strike rate. And as Vincent, at that point, was still winning his biggest prizes in the National Hunt arena, especially in Britain, one could expect that in a country where racing over the jumps meant so much, trainers of National Hunt horses had to be envious.

Nat McNabb was coming back from Cheltenham one year with Vincent O'Brien when Vincent said to him, 'Look out, Nat, for a horse that might win the National Hunt Chase like Castledermot.'

Now Castledermot had triumphed in this testing event for amateur riders in 1949 with Lord Mildmay in the saddle and Vincent O'Brien knew that Harry and Moya Keogh were very anxious to get their hands on another horse like him. Of course, it would have to be a maiden.

'Naturally, I kept my eyes open at every jump meeting I attended, running the rule over horses running in maiden chases,' said Nat. 'One afternoon I saw this horse in a chase at Naas. He was one hell of a jumper. He finished nowhere but I could not get his jumping out of my mind all that evening.

'I rang Vincent immediately I got home from Naas. I said, "I think I have got the horse you are looking for." I told him what I had seen. He was down to run at Leopardstown next. I asked Vincent to come and judge for himself. "Come and have a look at him anyway." '

Vincent said he did not think he could make it to Leopardstown that day but would get Dermot to have a look. Dermot duly arrived for the Leopardstown meeting. Dermot O'Brien and Nat McNabb went out to the parade ring to have a closer look. After watching the horse walking around, Dermot remarked, 'I don't like *that*,' meaning that he was not entirely happy about the hind legs.

Nat said, 'Wait, Dermot, until you see him jump, before passing final judgement.'

They went up into the stand together to watch the race. 'God, Nat, I have never seen such a jumper for a maiden,' said Dermot as he put down his race glasses. The horse was Royal Tan.

A big chestnut, he had close Tipperary connections and with the Ballydoyle area at that, for his sire Tartan, belonging to the Carroll family, was standing not far from Cashel. He was actually bred by the Tophams from Tullamaine, less than 2 miles from Ballydoyle and this family was renowned in hunting circles.

Vincent O'Brien bought Royal Tan for the Keoghs from the late Ben Dunne of Dunnes Stores. There was a lot of confidence behind the horse to win the 1950 National Hunt Chase (4 miles), often styled the 'amateur's Grand National' and he was backed down to 9–2. Phonsie O'Brien had the mount.

Royal Tan overjumped and fell at the very first fence to a loud groan from a big Irish contingent, who had backed him as if he was a certainty. Phonsie was almost in tears when he came in and the Keoghs were sorry for him as he was very young at the time. When it came to the Aintree Grand National the following year, Harry Keogh remembered Phonsie's discomfiture at Cheltenham and said to Vincent O'Brien that he should give the mount to his brother.

Now Vincent had in mind a top professional rider and all his instincts told him that the National was not really a race for amateur riders, though they would always be attracted by the challenge and it was not unknown for the race to be won by an amateur. (Indeed, from the day that Capt Josie Little became the first amateur to win on The Chandler in 1848, this race has always had a magnetic attraction for 'gentlemen jockeys'. Fulke Walwyn prevailed in a battle royal with another amateur, Anthony Mildmay – later Lord Mildmay of Flete – on Davy Jones, to win the 1936 National on Reynoldstown, and among other memorable 'amateur' successes were those of Mr Tommy Smith on Jay Trump in 1965, Mr Charlie Fenwick on Ben Nevis in 1980, Mr Dick Saunders on Grittar in 1982 and, of course, Mr Marcus Armytage on Mr Frisk triumphing in an adrenalin-pumping battle from the last with Durham Edition and the luckless Chris Grant in the 1990 renewal.)

But the Keoghs were among his most loyal owners and Phonsie had won the Kilcoole Handicap chase (2 miles 5 furlongs) on Royal Tan at Leopardstown on 28 February, before finishing second in the Irish Grand National at Fairyhouse in the count-down to Aintree. In the final analysis, Vincent went against his better judgement and allowed his brother to take the ride.

Royal Tan was only seven when he contested the National for the first time in 1951 – the year of Nickel Coin's triumph at 40–1. Vincent's charge started at 22–1 in a field of 36 – and 34 of the runners would fail to complete the course after a disastrous and highly-controversial start that led to havoc at the first fence.

On a spring day in 1989 in the sitting-room of his home, set in the most picturesque surroundings imaginable, beside the River Suir at the edge of the little village of Kilsheelan where, on his appropriately-named Landscape Stud, he today successfully combines breeding with pin-hooking (buying foals and selling them as yearlings), Phonsie O'Brien recalled the moment 38 years earlier when he looked to have the 1951 National at his mercy.

'There I was approaching the second-last with Johnny Bullock and we were the only two still standing, so bar a fall we had to finish first and second. The question was: which of us would be first past the post? "What's that you're riding?" I called across to Johnny. "Nickel Coin," he shouted back. "Your goose is cooked, Johnny," I said across to him and I was going so easily that there was no way I could see us getting beat.

'We strode on to the last fence. I knew I could go on ahead of him at that point if I wished but I remembered Vincent's instructions – "Don't jump the last in front if you can avoid it." Vincent's theory was that with that long run-in at Aintree, you would be in front for too long if you took the lead before the last. Later events would prove that Royal Tan was a horse that hated to be dictated to, though he was very clever, highly intelligent, in fact. In retrospect, I believe now that if I had kicked on and let him do his own thing, it might have been all so different.

'He just made a goddam mistake at the last, after jumping all the earlier fences without trouble. That was it in a nutshell, nothing less, nothing more.'

But a lot of ink has been used since 1951 in probing the whys and wherefores of Royal Tan's so-near-and-yet-so-far failure to lift the 1951 National. Vincent's own view of that fatal last-fence blunder is that when Phonsie gave Royal Tan a kick with his heels going into the jump, the horse seemed to resent it. He hit the top of the fence and came right down on his nose. Amazingly he did not topple over and Phonsie, at the same time, managed to stay in the saddle. Meanwhile, Nickel Coin and Johnny Bullock, having safely negotiated the last, galloped home to a bloodless victory. But it shows how far superior Royal Tan was that, despite being almost on the floor, he still got within 6 lengths of the winner at the finish. How much would he have won by if he had jumped the last as he did in 1954?

Phonsie revealed that Royal Tan was so intelligent that he never forgot the experience of what happened to him at that last fence. 'In November of that year Vincent decided to send him over to Cheltenham for the Cowley Hurdle, a 3-mile event for novices. The boat trip was from Waterford to Fishguard and, as he had gone by boat for his first tilt at the National, he thought he was being brought back to Liverpool. He refused to get off the boat and the travelling lad, Dave Manning, had a hell of a job in inducing him to comply with his efforts. Eventually, after an hour and a half, Dave succeeded in getting him to step off the boat.'

Royal Tan, backed down to 11–10, landed a gamble in that event and was then sent to Listowel for the Festival meeting in October to contest the Newcastlewest Plate (amateur riders) with Phonsie up.

Again, the memory of Liverpool haunted him. The sad-

144

dling stall at Listowel then was an exact replica of Liverpool and Royal Tan would not walk out. Again it was only with extreme difficulty that he was induced out. Gambled on down to 1–3, he further recouped losses suffered at Liverpool – 'But it was a close thing as we only got home by a neck,' recalled Phonsie.

In 1954 – the year of Royal Tan's triumph at last at Aintree – Vincent O'Brien, conscious that he had to protect the horse against the mental block he had about Liverpool, sent him to Haydock Park to be stabled. 'That was twenty miles away from Aintree and Royal Tan was fooled in the lead-up to the big race into thinking that it wasn't the National he had been sent to contest,' said Phonsie. Again Vincent's attention to the details that matter paid off handsomely.

Royal Tan endured a lot of trauma from the time he contested that first National as a seven-year-old in 1951 until he finally won it as a ten-year-old. In 1952, with Phonsie O'Brien again riding, he came to the last in third position and having every chance. But he made a blunder that was almost a replay of 1951. The picture shows Royal Tan (number 7) with his head right down on the ground and one of his feet has come back level with his tail. As was the case the previous year, he struggled back to his feet – but this time Phonsie was pitched out of the saddle. So Royal Tan is recorded as a faller in the 1952 race, which was won by Teal at 100–7 from Legal Joy and Wot No Sun.

After Bryan Marshall won the 1953 Grand National on Early Mist, it was inevitable that both Vincent O'Brien and 'Mincemeat' Joe Griffin, the owner, would contemplate no one else for Royal Tan in 1954 but Bryan Marshall, especially in view of the fact that injury had ruled Early Mist out of the race.

Marshall rode Royal Tan in 'prep' races at Naas and Leopardstown, finishing unplaced in both, before being sent to Gowran Park for the Thyestes Chase. Vincent was concerned that man and horse were not hitting it off. And his anxiety and fears on this score were further heightened by what happened in the Thyestes Chase itself.

On the second circuit, as Royal Tan went into the open ditch, Bryan Marshall gave him a couple of kicks and the horse clearly did not like it – just as he resented it when Phonsie had given him a kick with his heels going into the last in the 1951 National. Marshall ended up on the floor.

'It was a week before the 1954 Grand National that I discovered the correct way to ride Royal Tan,' recalled Bryan Marshall. 'It was to leave him alone.'

Again, with that thoroughness, that meticulous attention to details that others might overlook, Vincent O'Brien had decided on one last effort to try and achieve the combination between Royal Tan and Bryan Marshall that he knew could win him his second National – if he pulled it off, especially as there was no question of the horse not being able to jump the Aintree fences.

Vincent arranged a school at Gowran Park after racing at the Kilkenny track. He phoned Bryan Marshall and told him to come over. In the meantime in a tactical discussion between Phonsie, Dermot and himself, Phonsie made the point to Vincent that he should impress upon Bryan Marshall that he must not adopt forceful tactics but leave Royal Tan to do his own thing. Vincent conveyed this to the jockey before he took the horse out for the Gowran Park school.

However, a number of Bryan's Kilkenny friends had come along to watch the school. 'Right, I'll show them how Marshall can ride,' Bryan said to himself as he passed them and really drove Royal Tan into one of the fences. Not only did he make a mess of it but, as his head came up, he smacked Marshall in the face with his head with the result that he was left with a bloody nose. But that bloody nose was the key to the winning of the National, as Bryan admitted later. For the rest of the school he left Royal Tan to do his own thing and found that he jumped perfectly.

'What he objected to was being driven,' he summed up. 'I decided there and then to take Vincent's advice and leave him alone in the National. I kept that promise until we came on to the racecourse itself and there were only four in front of me. Momentarily, I found myself falling into the fatal trap of riding and punching but I could see that these tactics were entirely wrong.

'So I sat still from that point on. He quickened and, as I let him go on, he cut down those in front of him (20 fell in the field of 29) and I knew I was within sight of victory at the last, if he didn't blunder as on previous occasions at this fence. By allowing him to jump it rather than kicking him into it, he sailed over and I sighed with relief – no more fences to go, so I really got down to riding him then.'

It was Tudor Line who blundered at the last. He recovered, however, to come from the elbow with a sustained challenge and it was to develop into one of the most memorable and pulsating finishes in the history of the race. Tudor Line (10 stone 7 pounds) had exactly a stone advantage over Royal Tan and was also a year younger and it seemed that George Slack on the outside would get the better of the dramatic struggle to the line. However, Bryan Marshall held on to win by a neck, with the favourite, Lord Sefton's Irish Lizard, ridden by Michael Scudamore (father of Peter), a further 10 lengths away third.

Vincent O'Brien had sent a record five challengers for the 1954 National and had the pleasure of seeing Churchtown (Toss Taaffe), whom he had given as a gift to Jacqueline, finish fourth despite bursting a blood vessel between the last two fences. Jacqueline had put £5 each-way at 40–1 on Churchtown.

It was a wonderful Liverpool and National day for Vincent O'Brien, who was the toast of the Irish. Not only did he win the big race, but Stroller had also scored on the Friday and Galatian on the Saturday. So 'Mincemeat' Joe Griffin, who owned all three, had reason to let the champagne flow.

At a victory party Jacqueline O'Brien wore a heart-shaped necklace pendant of diamonds and platinum – Vincent's gift to her on the birth of Susan, their second child.

The 1954 Grand National was run on 27 March, four days before the Stewards of the Irish National Hunt Steeplechase Committee took Vincent O'Brien's licence away for three months.

All the horses were dispersed from the Ballydoyle stables and Dermot said that Joe Osborne (father of Paddy Osborne and of Vera, who was to become wife of Liam Cosgrave, Taoiseach over the Coalition Government of 1973–1977) proved himself a tremendous friend at the time. 'He took some of the horses, specifically to ensure that Vincent would have them back fit to run for their lives when his licence was restored; other fellows would be far less scrupulous in such circumstances and would take horses from you with the intention of never giving them back.'

A short notice in the *Irish Racing Calendar* provided the official announcement that Vincent O'Brien was back in business: 'M. V. O'Brien has been granted licences to train under the Irish Rules of Racing and the Irish National Hunt Rules. These licences were withdrawn by the Irish Stewards last March for three calendar months from 2 April 1954.'

But a darker hour lay ahead for Vincent O'Brien when he would lose his licence again, this time for a year over the alleged doping of Chamour. Five years before that fateful landmark in his life, he would win a third successive National and set the seal on his conquest of Liverpool as he had conquered Cheltenham.

14

Vincent Offers National Winner For £2500

After the fall, 'Mincemeat' Joe Griffin always regretted one missed opportunity in his life – the moment when Vincent O'Brien came to him after Royal Tan had won the 1954 Aintree Grand National and said, 'I'll sell you the winner of next year's Grand National for £2500.'

The horse that 'Mincemeat' was being offered was Quare Times, who in 1955 became Vincent O'Brien's third successive National winner.

'What a marvellous trainer this man was that he could tell me within a couple of hours of winning one National that he would sell me the winner of the following year's race,' said Joe Griffin twenty years later.

P. B. (Teasy Weasy) Raymond won the race in 1963 with the 66-1 outsider Ayala and again in 1976 with Rag Trade. Noel Le Mare emulated Joe Griffin's two-in-a-row feat (Early Mist and Royal Tan in 1953 and 1954) when Red Rum won for him in successive years, 1973 and 1974 – but Joe Griffin's feat was unique in that it was achieved with different horses. (Red Rum took a third National for Noel Le Mare in 1977.)

'Mincemeat' Joe, however, if he had acquired Quare Times and had not been declared a bankrupt, would have had the distinction of being the only owner in racing history to have won the National three years running. And making it more remarkable still, he would have done it with three different horses.

149

In the euphoria following Early Mist's triumph in 1953, 'Mincemeat' Joe paid £10,000 for Teapot II, who had finished third behind Sir Ken (Tim Molony) and Joe's own Galatian (Bryan Marshall) in the Champion Hurdle of that same season, beaten 3½ lengths. Teapot II was then owned by Mrs Clem Magnier and trained by her husband. He went on to Liverpool and won a handicap, the Liverpool Hurdle, with 12 stone 7 pounds. That was his eleventh win over hurdles. The merit of that weight-carrying performance probably convinced Joe Griffin that Teapot II could turn the tables on Sir Ken in the Champion Hurdle the following season under the master touch of Vincent O'Brien and with his own lucky star riding so high in the sky. But he overlooked the fact that Clem Magnier's charge was eight years old when he paid £10,000 for him, whereas Sir Ken would be a seven-year-old in 1954.

Teapot II started 11–10 favourite under 12 stone 7 pounds for the Tostal Free Handicap Hurdle at Baldoyle on April 15, 1953. Ridden by Pat Taaffe, he failed to give 3 stone to Olave (Aubrey Brabazon), who won by 3½ lengths. He ran twice on the Flat after that, winning the Melitta Handicap at the Curragh in the Joe Griffin colours and then broke down.

The reason that 'Mincemeat' Joe did not accept Vincent O'Brien's offer was that he must have known deep down that he had a rush of blood to the head when he purchased Teapot II at Liverpool out of the prize money and successful bets he had netted through Early Mist's triumph. Anyway, his fortunes were now in decline and he was in the middle of bankruptcy proceedings.

Yes, there would be a victory party at the Adelphi Hotel in Liverpool on Saturday night, 26 March 1955 after Quare Times had completed that fabulous Grand National hat-trick for Vincent O'Brien, but nothing like what it would have been if Joe Griffin had owned the winner and had been riding the crest of the wave.

'Hurrah for Ireland and Vincent O'Brien' read the introduction to the page one lead story in the *Sunday Independent*. Inside, on the sports pages, Michael O'Hehir, then the highly-regarded Racing Correspondent of Independent Newspapers and later an internationally-renowned commentator and Head of Sports with Radio Telefis Eireann (Irish Television), who always brought a unique touch of heightened drama to his description on radio of the National field thundering towards Becher's Brook, wrote how Vincent O'Brien had made history by completing a feat never before accomplished in the annals of this great race. In winning his third successive Grand National, he had become the first trainer to scale the Everest peak of what had seemed the impossible – and he had done it with three different horses. No trainer has equalled that feat in the 34 years that have elapsed since that afternoon of overflowing emotion and excitement among the big Irish contingent at Liverpool – and it seems unlikely that the record will ever be broken, just as Vincent O'Brien's singular achievements at Cheltenham will never be surpassed.

On the eve of the race Vincent O'Brien gathered his four National jockeys in his suite in the Adelphi Hotel. 'What an amazing man,' said Pat Taaffe. 'Once he knew what horses he would be entering, he had already lined up three of the best jump jockeys in Britain. Bryan Marshall was automatically earmarked for Early Mist, which he had ridden to victory in the 1953 National and which had missed the 1954 race because of injury. Dave Dick was engaged for the 1954 winner, Royal Tan, while Fred Winter was chosen for Oriental Way.'

Pat Taaffe, a born horseman, who had been riding Quare Times since the outset of the 1954–1955 season and knew the horse perfectly, had the mount on Vincent's fourth challenger.

'Yes, Vincent was exceptional in the way he planned things,' said Pat. 'He left absolutely nothing to chance. As I've said, he went after three of the top riders in Britain. But not alone that. He would always have a spare rider standing by for each of his chosen jockeys in case any of them got injured or had to cry off at the last moment for some other reason.'

Vincent played the films of the two previous Nationals.

151

'As Bryan Marshall had won on Early Mist and Royal Tan, it was only natural that Vincent should ask Fred Winter, Dave Dick and myself to study closely the tactics employed by Bryan in victory and use these tactics as our guidelines,' Pat continued. 'He ran through those films again and again, pointing out what he felt we should avoid and indicating the best route to take, especially in the very tricky run to Becher's Brook. At that stage it looked as if the going was going to be goodish. But it rained all night, a torrential downpour. Next morning at 10.30 Vincent got on to me and asked me up to his suite to discuss new tactics in the light of the changed going.

'I suggested to Vincent that he should get Bryan Marshall to ride Quare Times and I would take the mount on Early Mist. But he wouldn't hear of that. His approach to the riding of Quare Times was that I should go on a mile from home to utilise the stamina which he had shown in winning the National Hunt Chase over 4 miles at Cheltenham the previous year. But I had already made up my mind that I would wait as long as possible. T. P. Burns, Vincent's jockey on the Flat, had told me that Quare Times was leading the two-year-olds at home on the gallops and that proved to me that he wouldn't be beaten for a turn of foot in the long run in, if it came to a battle from the last.

'I left Vincent's suite without telling him how I planned to ride Quare Times. I believed that Quare Times had the ability to win the race bar the accidents that can happen to any runner in the National. I was quite confident.'

In that 1955 Grand National, Pat's brother, 'Toss', was on Carey's Cottage, trained by his father, Tom J. Taaffe at Rathcoole, County Dublin. When they both jumped Becher's Brook safely the second time round and were right there with the leaders, with the odds favouring one of them to win, Pat, glancing across at 'Toss', said to himself: 'What will the public say if *both* of us fall now!'

They didn't fall. And what a thrill they gave their parents and other members of the family who had travelled over, by finishing first and third. And Pat's fiancee (Molly Lyons) was in the stand to cheer him to victory.

Early Mist, despite the fact that he was shouldering 12 stone 3 pounds in the mud, started 9–1 second favourite to the 7–1 shot Copp (10 stone 8 pounds), an eleven-year-old ridden by Tim Molony. Tudor Line (11 stone 3 pounds), who had figured in that dramatic finish with Royal Tan the previous year, was third favourite at 10–1. Quare Times, a nine-year-old carrying 11 stone, was 100–9. Royal Tan, now an eleven-year-old and owned by Prince Aly Khan, was set to carry 12 stone 4 pounds and he went off at 28–1.

Conditions were so bad that the water jump was cut out. In fact, it was thought at one stage around midday that the race would have to be abandoned, as the rain continued to pour down. And to make matters worse, the complete outsider, Wild Wisdom, got fractious at the start, which was delayed for six minutes.

Copp and Tim Molony fell at the fence after Becher's Brook first time. Passing the stands for the second circuit, Sundew (P. J. Doyle), who would win the race two years later in the hands of Fred Winter, was in the lead, with Carey's Cottage and Quare Times both going extremely well and Tudor Line moving into a menacing position. Sundew fell four out. The Royally-owned M'as-Tu-Vu also went at this fence.

Three out Tudor Line jumped into the lead, making a death or glory bid to wear down the easily-running Quare Times but, as Michael O'Hehir reported in the *Sunday Independent*, 'the one who appeared to be worn down was Tudor Line himself'.

As his rider George Slack put it afterwards: 'I thought I would get Quare Times off his feet but when I moved up I saw that Pat Taaffe was not in the least worried – and I knew that was that.'

Once over the last fence, Quare Times raced away to a 12-length victory. While there were those who argued that Tudor Line would have been nearer but for repeating the previous year's jump to the right at the final obstacle, there was no question whatsoever of this costing him the race. Carey's Cottage ran the greatest race of his career in taking third place, four lengths behind Tudor Line.

Apart from the immense thrill of seeing Quare Times complete the historic hat-trick for him, Vincent O'Brien had the satisfaction of watching his two previous Grand National winners get round unscathed, Early Mist finishing ninth and Royal Tan twelfth. His fourth challenger, Oriental Way, was brought down at the eleventh fence, falling over the prostrate No Response.

Quare Times was bred in County Tipperary by the late Phil Sweeney at his Orwell Stud, near Thurles. By Artist's Son out of the Flamenco mare, Lavenco, Quare Times got his name from the famous greyhound owned by Bill Quinn of Killenaule, County Tipperary. He was sent as a yearling by Phil Sweeney to the 1947 Ballsbridge Sales, where he was bought for 300 guineas by Mrs Cecily Welman of Mullingar, a very good judge of horseflesh.

'I picked the horse out myself and thought of him as a likely Cheltenham winner,' she revealed after her Liverpool triumph. 'I never thought of him as a National candidate at that time.'

Widow of the late Major Robert Smyth, whose eighteenth century ancestral home was 'Gaybrook', Mullingar, she married Major W. H. E. Welman three months before the 1955 Aintree Grand National. They returned from their honeymoon in Madeira a few weeks before the actual day of the race. In January they had placed a bet of £50 each way on Quare Times at 100–8 and without knowing it had already won the cost of the honeymoon before leaving for Madeira.

Incidentally, Pat Taaffe's tallness in the saddle – he stood six feet – deceived the British public during that Grand National week-end. With 'Toss', who was also quite tall as jockeys go, he was invited to the BBC to appear on the Sunday night television programme, 'Guess My Story'.

Pat and Toss travelled to London direct from Liverpool immediately after the victory party in the Adelphi Hotel. Because of an industrial dispute, there were no Sunday papers in Britain. When the members of the panel were asked to guess the area of sport the two brothers were involved in, they immediately plumped for two oarsmen who had taken part in the Oxford v Cambridge Boat Race the previous day!

Of course, if there had been Sunday papers that mistake would never have been made – as Pat Taaffe's face would have been leaping out of the sports pages, if not the front pages.

Later in his career when Pat Taaffe became associated with the peerless Arkle, he regretted after winning three successive Gold Cups (1964–66) on this superb jumper that Anne, Duchess of Westminster would not allow the gelding to take his chance in the Aintree Grand National. She was so devoted to Arkle that she was terrified of him being injured through no fault of his own (the hazards presented by loose horses, for example).

Taaffe felt that Arkle would have had no problem adapting to the Aintree fences and was certain he would have triumphed in the National.

Tom Dreaper, Arkle's trainer, found it hard for a long time, according to Pat Taaffe, to bring himself to concede that there could be any horse better than Prince Regent. 'In the end, however, he remarked to me quietly one day: "I suppose, Pat, I have to admit that I have trained none greater than Arkle".'

And some really great chasers had been trained at his Greenogue stable.

Thirty-three years on from the day at Aintree when a broadly-smiling Pat Taaffe dismounted from Quare Times, his son Tom rode Monanore into third place behind Rhyme 'N' Reason and Durham Edition.

The torch had been fittingly handed on.

When Vincent O'Brien, Pat Taaffe and Bryan Marshall came together again in Dublin's Westbury Hotel on 26 March 1987 at the Kaliber Lager Anniversary Lunch, Vincent and Pat each received a replica of page one of the *Sunday Independent* published the day after Quare Times took the 1955 National. Bryan Marshall also received a fitting memento of his two triumphs for Vincent.

Vincent took the microphone in thanking Kaliber for the 'great honour' that had been bestowed on him that day. 'It's nice to know that those victories in the fifties are not forgotten,' he said.

He then went on to grip his audience by the authoritative manner in which he spoke about his three winning National horses and the men who rode them. He did not conceal his admiration for Bryan Marshall as a horseman and added that, similarly with Pat Taaffe, 'I found him to be a wonderful man and a wonderful rider'.

'It wasn't possible for me to have Pat as my stable jockey, because his services were acquired by Tom Dreaper – but I had him the day I needed him most, when I was going for the third in a row with Quare Times.'

He stressed that Early Mist was never a natural jumper – 'and that is why he had to have a master on his back like Bryan Marshall'.

'Quare Times was a free-running, free-jumping horse and he suited Pat Taaffe to perfection. Pat for a tall man rode very short. His father told him before Aintree to let down his leathers a couple of notches but Pat wouldn't change and sat up his neck. It paid off, as he never made a mistake that day at Liverpool. They were an ideal partnership together.'

Then Vincent delivered his judgement on which of his three National winners he thought was the best of all and, unhesitatingly, he came out in favour of Royal Tan. 'For me Royal Tan was the best jumper I ever had,' he said with emphasis. 'A really clever horse – so smart, in fact, that he would never allow anyone to dictate to him. Early Mist had to be asked, Royal Tan was just a natural when it came to jumping fences and he took to them like a cat. If you ask me which was the classier of the two, I would have to say Early Mist but again, let me repeat, there was no comparison between them in the pure art of jumping. Royal Tan had it there over Early Mist – by a clear margin.'

If Royal Tan had got over the last fence without mishap in the 1951 and 1952 Aintree Grand Nationals, he would almost certainly have been acclaimed the winner and would not have had to wait until 1954 for his first triumph. As we have seen already, he jumped the course to take twelfth place under 12 stone 4 pounds in 1955 in 'impossible' conditions of mud and rain and the following year, when a twelve-year-old, he carried 12 stone 1 pound into third place behind E.S.B., with 'Toss' Taaffe in the saddle.

In all the discussion of the might-have-beens since those early seasons in the 'fifties, one fact emerges crystal clear – Royal Tan's Aintree record should have been far more impressive than the record books show it to be. In fact, we should be assessing his final achievements side by side with Red Rum's. Leaving aside how weight can become the great leveller, he could easily have won three in his prime and there was a distinct possibility of three in a row. But again that's racing.

Talking about the genius that Vincent O'Brien revealed in preparing Quare Times for that National success in 1955, Pat Taaffe recalled, 'The uncanny way he brought him out five weeks after Aintree fresh enough to win a Maiden Hurdle over 2 miles at Leopardstown. I don't think anyone else could have emulated that achievement.

'I rode Quare Times in the National Trial Handicap Chase (3 miles 5 furlongs) at Haydock and in the National Hunt Handicap Chase (3 miles) at Cheltenham on the way to Liverpool. I finished fourth at Haydock Park and second at Cheltenham. Looking back now, I feel that Vincent had timed things so that Quare Times would reach his absolute peak on the day that dwarfed everything else for him that season – the target of taking a third successive Grand National.'

For many racing aficionados, Vincent's brilliant record of achievement on the Flat – not even the winning of six Epsom Derbys – could not quite surpass Cheltenham and Aintree. Cheltenham and Aintree in a way presaged and laid the foundations of all that was to follow.

Churchtown will always be linked with Cottage Rake and Hatton's Grace and the start of the golden days at Cheltenham. Ballydoyle was irrevocably bound up with the three successive Aintree Grand National triumphs, though strangely enough, in the minds of the racing public, it came to be linked more and more, with the passing years, with success on the Flat.

Now we look at how Vincent made the move to Bally-doyle, how he met and married Jacqueline and how Lark-spur won for him the first of his six Epsom Derbys. It is a story of new peaks scaled that Vincent and Dermot could never have imagined when first they set their eyes on the rolling acres in the shadow of majestic Slievenamon that would become world-famous Ballydoyle.

PART TWO

IN THE SHADOW
OF SLIEVENAMON

15

The Move To Ballydoyle

When Hatton's Grace returned to Ireland after winning his third successive Champion Hurdle on Tuesday, 6 March 1951 he did not go back to the Churchtown stables in County Cork, which had set Vincent O'Brien firmly on the road to becoming a household name. While Vincent was at the Festival meeting, the training establishment was being moved to new quarters at Ballydoyle, Cashel, County Tipperary.

Jimmy Gordon, one of Vincent's most trusted employees in that era, remembers coming back from Cheltenham with Hatton's Grace to Ballydoyle. 'Vincent made me a very generous offer to start anew with him in the new stables. It was very difficult to refuse but Mai, the girl that I would marry, had a grocery shop-cum-drapery in Churchtown and I was also thinking at that stage of setting up as a trainer myself. "So you won't come?" Vincent said. "I'm afraid I have to say no," I replied.

'It was the hardest thing I ever had to say in my life. I had known very happy times working with Vincent in Churchtown and I knew I could never repay him for all the knowledge I acquired in those years.'

The marriage settlement had decreed the inevitability of the move to Ballydoyle. Vincent was renting the gallops and boxes from Donal and had rented extra land from the Lynch family of Cregane. The only way that he could have remained on in Churchtown was if Donal had sold the family homestead and lands to him and bought another farm. But in the Irish way of things, it is extremely difficult for an eldest son to sell his birthright. Donal could not bring himself to do it. Vincent understood his feelings.

Jimmy Gordon sees the irony of Vincent O'Brien moving on a year too soon. Jimmy himself was able to acquire the land – around 100 acres – that allowed him to set up as a trainer. 'Look, within twelve months of Vincent's departure, enough land became available in the area that would have made it totally unnecessary for him to leave – if he had really wanted to stay. One 700-acre estate came on the market and soon afterwards another large estate. Indeed, there was far more land available than what Vincent initially acquired in County Tipperary. When subsequently we realised this, it made us all the sadder.'

Dermot, Vincent's assistant, Maurice O'Callaghan, the faithful headman for 30 years, Danny O'Sullivan, an outstanding schooling rider – they all moved to Ballydoyle. The kernel of the team that had known such success already under Vincent's inspired captaincy remained together.

That, too, made the wrench even tougher for Jimmy Gordon. There were facets of the Churchtown operation that he remembers as special. 'We had a thing called "Betting money". You see, money was put on for us on horses that Vincent really expected to win and on which the stable would be really having a cut. That meant that you always got a nice Christmas box. If you were going on holidays, or had become engaged, or some crisis arose in the family, then you could ask to see Vincent and request something from the "betting money" to tide you over. If you were someone he had really come to trust and if you had built an understanding with him, then he never refused you.

'We had this sense of community in Churchtown that was very real – a whole village and parish caught up in the fortunes of one stable, one trainer. A lot of people depended directly, or indirectly, on the stable and its success. You could never have had that if Vincent had been training from the outset at the Curragh, for example.'

But for Vincent O'Brien new horizons beckoned. He wanted to explore unchartered territory that he knew deep down would put him on a new plane if he was equal to the challenge. He had taken horses that were given to him when the concentration was more on jumping than on the Flat. Now he wanted the resources at his back that would allow him to go to the sales and pick and choose.

More important still, he no longer wanted to gamble to survive. That meant that he would have to attract millionaire owners to his stable who were 'not in a hurry'.

When he turned exclusively to the Flat, he wanted the operation at Ballydoyle to be on his own terms and that meant, in turn, putting things on an entirely new plane.

Dermot O'Brien said that as Vincent and he went scouting, they must have looked at something like twenty-four different places before they finally opted for the house and land that would become Ballydoyle. 'I remember so vividly the day we came up the avenue and saw the old Georgian farmhouse and the 180 to 200 acres going with it. We both looked at each other and we knew without a word being exchanged: "This is it."

'There was an immediate feeling about the place that captured us. I know we were both looking for the same thing. We had seen so many places that disappointed in one way or another. It wasn't possible to say exactly in so many words the moment we reached our silent decision but, even before the bulldozers got to work to prepare the gallops, we could picture it as it would be – the place of our dreams with the Knockmealdowns, the Comeraghs and Slievenamon forming the ideal backdrop to close on 200 acres in Ireland's Golden Vale.'

It has been written that at one point Vincent tossed about in his mind the idea of moving to the Curragh from Churchtown, that he sought the advice of veteran Headquarters' trainers Hubert Hartigan and Bob Featherstonhaugh and that they both advised: 'Keep away from this place. There is no variety in these wide open spaces.'

However, Dermot made it clear that a move to the

Curragh was never on, was never a serious option in Vincent's or, indeed, his own mind.

'No, I can tell you truthfully that Vincent never wanted to go to the Curragh. As he put it to me at the time – there was too much light. By that he meant that it was too open, too flat. Like riding a bicycle on a straight road that seemed to go on for ever, or across a desert like the Sahara into nothingness. Vincent would like a few bends on the road, or put another way, he couldn't contemplate public gallops that had no undulations and neither could he contemplate living in an area where you couldn't see hills around you,' said Dermot.

In the final analysis then, the main reason Vincent wanted to have his own place was that he could make the gallops he wanted for his horses and not be forced to use inferior working ground at someone else's direction. At public training grounds you are told what ground to use and when. With private training grounds you can keep the best ground for the best horses, open special pieces, etc. It was for this reason that Vincent would not train at a public training place. And this was much more important than privacy from a betting point of view. There cannot be total privacy about trials whether in public or private as people may talk intentionally or otherwise.

So Vincent decided to open his own gallops to his own vision of things. He would fence in the area under his control. He would have an operation that carried on from Churchtown, expanding on what he had created there and yet not losing that sense of distinct individuality that was a hallmark of his whole approach from the beginning. In time Ballydoyle would become a model of everyone's idea of what a modern stable should be.

I stood with him on the gallops on a mild, overcast late March Monday morning in 1987, four days before he celebrated his 70th birthday, as he supervised his string of about 60 thoroughbreds, his son Charles beside him.

Vincent instantly recognised every horse on the gallop – even before it had topped the rising ground – and reeled off, professionally and authoritatively, the pros and cons of each of them, right down to a lead horse. He talked about their breeding, about the way the three-year-olds of this 1987 season had performed as two-year-olds, whether he was satisfied or disappointed and his hopes in each individual case for the season ahead. 'That's a Kris . . . that's a Northern Dancer . . . that's a Be My Guest, the best looker he bred so far . . . that's a Nijinsky two-year-old looking very well . . . that's a filly called Music and Dance . . . we paid five million for the mare when she was carrying her . . .'

He mentions 'five million' in as matter-a-fact way as a man in the foreign exchange department of some bank might refer to that sum being transferred from one businessman's account to another. But then when you have put colts like Nijinsky and Alleged through your hands – colts whose stud value reached astronomical figures – you are no longer surprised at the mention of a million or even five million.

What stirs you is Classic potential suddenly revealed on the gallops and maybe when the sophisticated electric timing apparatus of the modern era confirms what your eye has told you.

This morning his daughter, Susan, wife of Coolmore's John Magnier, has come over to 'ride work'. There is no mistaking the close kinship between father and daughter. Susan comes up the gallop with her horse in perfect control. A mother of five, she rides to hounds twice a week during the hunting season. And the professional manner in which she talks to her father reveals that she knows her horses. Charles does too.

First, the horses are exercised in lots of around 23 in the circular covered ride. Brian Moloney, from Mallow, one of the assistant trainers, is supervising this particular lot. The lads arrive at 8 a.m. and get down to business at 8.30 a.m.

Vincent O'Brien has always been an innovator. And he has set standards that make him the envy of others worldwide. All his boxes are lined with rubber – so that no valuable colt or filly can get cast in its box. The padding in each box has an aero material in it to protect the horses.

165

He has plumped for shavings in the boxes rather than straw. 'I think horses find the shavings more comfortable,' he said. 'But they are difficult enough to get.'

It is obvious that the blue bloods in the stable are treated in a manner that 'royalty' deserves. But the totally professional approach does not end there. Even in these days of high security, he does not believe in closing off the world outside completely to his charges. The half doors allow the horses to look out and Vincent O'Brien believes it enables them to satisfy their curiosity. 'You may not believe it but I know from my experience with horses that they want to know what's going on outside their own box.' The boxes are very spacious by any modern standards. This was achieved by converting three into two to make them more comfortable and luxurious.

There are many other ways in which the total attention to detail manifests itself. In a tour of the stables, your eye will immediately be caught by the starting stalls in the big barn where the two-year-olds are given plenty of practice at coming out smoothly – and there is even background music to soothe the nerves of the highly-strung fretting ones. Was I correct in hearing that they normally prefer classical to pop?

Nothing is left to chance in what must be one of the most efficiently-run stables in the world.

The Ballydoyle set-up that has inspired so many laudatory articles lay a long way ahead on the day that Vincent walked into the Munster and Leinster Bank (now absorbed into Allied Irish Banks) in Cork and asked for a substantial loan to buy the house and land that was to comprise his new training establishment in County Tipperary. The same bank had facilitated him when he was getting going on his own in far more modest circumstances in Churchtown after the death of his father in 1943. He has never forgotten the help he received when he needed it most and to this day has kept an account in the same Cork branch.

The house and land at Ballydoyle were acquired from the Sadlier family, who had owned a lot of land in the

Cashel area at the turn of the century. The member of the family with whom Vincent concluded the deal was Miss Daisy Sadlier who was living then on the farm with her invalid mother. She was finding it too much to look after the farm and wanted out.

The money garnered from successful gambles, in particular the ante-post coups on Cottage Rake and Hatton's Grace, and Alberoni with Aubrey Brabazon up winning the Leopardstown Handicap Hurdle under 10 stone 2 pounds in July 1950, plus the loan from the bank, enabled Ballydoyle to be purchased for £17,000. The 280 acres would, in time, be expanded to over 600 and the boxes that had housed champions such as Cottage Rake and Hatton's Grace absorbed into new offices. The staff had grown to 85 by the end of the 'eighties and the special features that could not have been contemplated in the spring of 1951, when Vincent and Dermot first set eyes on the place, included a complete veterinary station, a computerised health system for the horses, gallops that were not put out of action by inclement weather and an isolation area where thoroughbreds aimed at big prizes could be isolated from those that might be suddenly hit by a virus.

Before Vincent actually made the move from Churchtown, Phonsie had spent months helping to supervise the task of preparing the new gallops. It was back-breaking work. Vincent remembers that it was simply a case of transforming ordinary farm land, which up to then had been used for tillage or grazing, into gallops. 'You have got to imagine thick hedges that, in quite a number of cases, had stone wall-facings and initially we made gaps in the hedges for the horses to work, before eventually achieving the kind of gallops that people see nowadays when they come to Ballydoyle,' he recalled. 'It was a long haul, a terribly long one and I wouldn't like to be starting out on it again.'

He was fortunate to have the dedicated support of Dermot and Phonsie, which allowed him to maintain the winning momentum where otherwise he might have got bogged down through having to shoulder a welter of work himself. The affinity between the three is something that has never emerged fully, I believe, in all that has been written about Vincent O'Brien. Without that affinity, without the total loyalty forthcoming from Dermot and Phonsie, I do not think that Vincent could have made the transition so successfully from Churchtown to Ballydoyle and neither could he have survived the crises that would hit him, especially the trauma of 'The Chamour Affair', which is dealt with in detail in Chapters 18 and 19.

Phonsie was a successful trainer in his own right, not on the scale, of course, that Vincent achieved, but he had triumphs to his name that would have represented the high plains of success to many a small man in Munster. As, for example, when he won the prestigious Galway Plate four years running (1962–1965) – first with Mrs Miles Valentine's aptly-named Carraroe with Fred Winter in the saddle, next with Lord Fermoy's Blunts Cross (H. Beasley) and then in successive years with Mrs G. Buchanan's Ross Sea, with Stan Mellor the successful jockey on both occasions. Other important races that fell to him were the Benson & Hedges Handicap Hurdle with Beau Chapeau (1967), the Power Gold Cup with Bold Fencer (1968), the Irish Cesarewitch with Polar Fox (1972) and the Fingal Hurdle with Ribosaint (1974).

Vincent was fortunate that Phonsie was in a position to take over at Ballydoyle during the days of suspension as a result of 'The Chamour Affair', ensuring continuity where otherwise there might have been a complete shut-down.

Dermot was also an invaluable cog in the Ballydoyle machine. In fact, it could never have operated as smoothly as it did without his self-effacing but cool, authoritative presence. The fact that he had served in the Irish Army had enabled him to acquire the ability to handle men.

It did not matter one iota to Dermot if the writers put the spotlight on Vincent. A lesser man might have become jealous of his brother. Not so Dermot. They represented a powerful duo together, the perfect foils for each other – just as Phonsie, with his outgoing personality, complimented them both.

Eventually, Dermot decided to get out of the heat of

the kitchen, having borne intense pressure at the very highest level for close on three decades. It was a mutual parting with Vincent as he set up on his own in the Derrygrath Stud, near Cahir, County Tipperary. Bringing all the knowledge that he had acquired over the years to the breeding of horses, he has enjoyed some singular successes. From his outstanding mare, Driella, he bred Seskin Bridge, Commeragh King and two other winners. Another daughter, Derrynaflan got injured and did not win but bred Suir Run, for whom Dermot got 43,000 guineas at Goffs Derby Sale in 1987. Unfortunately, he was killed in England in a hurdle race when there was a tremendous amount of money on him. In 1988 Dermot got 135,000 guineas for a Thatching colt.

16

The Chemistry Of Love

The hinge of destiny decreed that in the very year that Vincent O'Brien started a new life in Ballydoyle he would, at the age of 34, be smitten by the chemistry of love – on an evening in Dublin when the last thought in his mind was that he would meet the girl he would marry before the year was out.

Vincent had travelled to Dublin on that Friday afternoon with the intention of going racing the following day at the Curragh. An early meal and early to bed was his intention – and some essential work in the morning before going to the races.

The Russell Hotel on St Stephen's Green was then one of Dublin's most famous hotels – more famous in some respects than the Shelbourne (sited on the other side of the Green). If you did not meet some of your racing friends in one of them, then it was odds-on that they could be in the other. The Russell, just down from Iveagh House, which today accommodates the Department of Foreign Affairs, got swallowed up in development as, sadly, the Hibernian Hotel also did. Look today for the site of where the Russell stood and you will find the offices of Diners Club International occupying that prestigious corner of the Green.

Vincent decided on a quiet drink before dinner. Then in walked a long-standing friend in Waring Willis, who was to be an usher at his wedding. He was accompanied by Gerry Annesley. And with the two was a girl, who did not immediately make any particular impression on Vincent. Drinks were ordered all round. Vincent's idea of eating on his own was soon lost in the general conversation about racing.

He joined Waring Willis and Gerry Annesley and the girl for dinner. 'During dinner I just started to look at this girl,' he would recall, looking back on that evening 38 years later.

The girl was Jacqueline Wittenoom, from Perth, Western Australia, where her father, the Hon. C. H. Wittenoom, was a Member of Parliament and had been Mayor of Albany for almost twenty years. In fact, the Wittenooms were one of the most prominent and oldest families in Western Australia. Jacqueline is fifth generation Australian and can trace her roots to the time when her great-great-grandfather, the Rev. J. B. Wittenoom, brought the first settlers out to Western Australia just after the Napoleonic Wars.

'After his wife died suddenly, my great-great-grandfather, who had been a Don at Brasenose College, Oxford, then Headmaster of Newark Grammar School, decided to emigrate with his five sons and a sister to Australia,' Jacqueline said. 'His wife's death had affected him deeply, so deeply that he wanted to start a completely new life.

'He applied for the post of Chaplain to the new colony, which was not a convict settlement as were other parts of Australia. He combined the duties of Chaplain with teaching the children of the settlers. He had to build a church and a school – the first in that part of Australia, laying the bricks himself with the help of his sister.'

He was one of the pioneers who built Australia and the legacy of service he left was marked by the places named after him in Western Australia. His son Charles, incidentally, was an artist and his paintings are the earliest of Perth (no mere coincidence then that Vincent and Jacqueline should name their second son Charles).

Jacqueline's grandfather, Sir Edward Wittenoom, was an explorer in the truest sense of the term and helped open up Central Australia. His brother, Frank and he travelled around on horseback developing big tracts of land in the Murchison district for sheep grazing. Frank Wittenoom started racing in this area in 1880, while Jacqueline recalled that she had a cousin, Langlois Lefroy, who was the President of the Western Australia Turf Club for many years.

Jacqueline caught something of the spirit of the outback during what she described as 'a wonderful childhood'.

'We lived for half the year on a sheep station – 250,000 acres of dry red earth where the sheep ate mulga and salt bush. There was no green grass, but the wool was the finest merino produced. Our nearest neighbours were 30 miles away. My mother had been a school teacher and she saw to it that we were studious and committed to our lessons.' Something of the away-from-it-all call of those childhood days and their special quality can be gleaned as Jacqueline relates that school-work had to be mailed to Perth each fortnight for correction. During the summer, the sheep station was too hot. 'We lived then in Albany, a town on the south coast.'

Once she went to boarding school in Perth, she entered an entirely different world – an academic life that would lead on to university and a Degree in Economics and then to two years of research followed by a post in the Economics Department of the Central Bank in Sydney.

She confesses: 'I was an academic person in those days, very interested in books. I am afraid the horse world didn't mean very much to me, though, as I have said already, my cousin was very prominent in Western Australian racing circles.'

Most Australians feel the urge to make a trip to Europe and Jacqueline was no exception, as she sought to broaden her education. When she decided that Ireland would be part of her itinerary, she could never have guessed that it would change her life.

It was not surprising that Vincent should be captivated and eventually captured by the girl sitting across the table from him at the dinner in the Russell Hotel. Jacqueline does not like to put any emphasis on it herself nowadays,

172

Above left: T. B. Burns and (*above right*) Tim Molony, two jockeys associated with memorable triumphs for the Vincent O'Brien stable. *Below*: Vincent O'Brien's three Grand National winners: Royal Tan (1954), Early Mist (1953) and Quare Times (1955).

The Piggott magic . . . Lester (at left) taking the 1970 Epsom Derby (*above left*) on the brilliant Nijinsky, and (*below left*) sweeping round Tattenham Corner on Nijinsky (wearing a noseband, at left) with Gyr (W. Williamson up) immediately behind. Gyr finished second and Stintino (G. Thiboeuf up) third, tracking Gyr on the outside. *Above*: Lester being led in on The Minstrel after winning the 1977 Irish Derby.

Above: Lester Piggott's triumph on Alleged over Balmarino (R. Hutchinson up) in the 1977 Prix de l'Arc de Triomphe. Alleged emulated the mighty Ribot (1955–6) by winning again the following year. *Left*: Golden Fleece (Pat Eddery up), showing quite phenomenal acceleration, comes from an 'impossible' position rounding Tattenham Corner to win the 1982 Epsom Derby with consummate ease. Lester Piggott believes he 'could have been the best horse Vincent O'Brien ever trained'.

Below: The 'wonder colt', El Gran Senor, cuts down Chief Singer (R. Cochrane up) and Lear Fan (B. Rouse up) with an amazing burst of speed in the 1984 English 2,000 Guineas, but in the Epsom Derby finishes second amid pulsating drama (*right*) as Secreto (C. Roche up) on the left wins by a short head in a photo finish.

Ballydoyle House, Cashel, Co. Tipperary, home of Vincent and Jacqueline O'Brien, and (*below*) the imposing sweep of the stables area and magnificent gallops, photographed by Jacqueline from Vincent's helicopter.

ustralian Scobie Breasley (*above left*), who scored memorable victories on Ballymoss in the
958 season, and Pat Eddery (*above right*), who succeeded Lester Piggott as first jockey to the
allydoyle stable. Eddery says he will always remember 'those five years riding for a marvellous
ainer'. *Below*: The close association between Vincent O'Brien and Robert Sangster (at left) has
een a rewarding one for Ballydoyle in Classic and big-race successes.

Below: The Keeneland battleground . . . the sales auditorium where the Vincent O'Brien/Robert Sangster Syndicate created a new world record in 1985 when going to $13.1 million to secure the Nijinsky colt, later named Seattle Dancer. More recently, Sheikh Mohammed (*above left*), pictured with his pet falcon against a desert background, and American trainer, D. Wayne Lukas (*above right*) have been two of the most dominant figures at the sales.

but research revealed that she was a university beauty queen in Western Australia and some of the photos taken at Ballydoyle in the immediate aftermath of her wedding bear out the striking quality of her looks.

Strangely enough, Jacqueline was not initially swept off her feet. It was Vincent who made the running. After dinner he accompanied Jacqueline and Waring Willis and Gerry Annesley across the Green to the Shelbourne Hotel. Waring Willis and Gerry Annesley went to bed early – by the standards of the racing set in those days.

Vincent was left alone with Jacqueline – 'and then we got talking'. He asked her to accompany him to the races the next day. She agreed and he fixed the time that he would call round from the Russell to collect her. After the last race, they joined Aubrey Brabazon for drinks. Aubrey was to be another of the ushers at the wedding.

It could easily have ended with the trip to the Curragh on that day in May 1951. Jacqueline's leave of absence from her job was up in July when she was due back in Australia. 'I didn't think then that the friendship would come to anything. The time was very short and I was leaving by boat from Southampton. There was no flying in those days, and berths on ships were very scarce – you couldn't cancel and expect to get another berth later so that you could pursue a friendship with a man you had met. So I really thought it would end once I got on the boat.'

But Vincent was persistent and insistent. He knew he had met the girl he wanted to marry and as Jacqueline put it: 'By the time I was due to take the boat we had decided to be married and Vincent gave me an engagement ring in Jammet's Restaurant over strawberries and cream. My stay in Australia was to be a short holiday to say "goodbye" to my family and friends there.'

Vincent's brothers, Dermot and Phonsie, were best man and groomsman, respectively, at the wedding on Saturday, 29 December 1951 in the University Church in Dublin.

Jacqueline, the academic, would in time find herself in a

world where the books that dominated were the books on breeding rather than economics – a world in which there was no escape from people and she had in a way to become Vincent's protector. 'You take the calls, you meet the people,' was his approach, she said smilingly – and she did not mind. It was a perfect marriage of contrasting personalities, of opposites.

How did a girl who had not really been involved in racing fit so easily into this new world at Ballydoyle? 'Because my father was always involved in politics, my two brothers (one was to become a doctor and the other an engineer) and myself were accustomed to a public life. I found people in Ireland were very kind and friendly and tolerant of my ignorance of horses and racing. I had to learn about horses quickly as we did not have much staff and I filled in as assistant, telephonist, secretary – wherever there was work to do. In the early days most communication with owners was done by letter and Vincent and I did most of this together.'

Vincent is the first to admit that Jacqueline has been a tremendous influence in his life. She is his protection from the many people who would not give him a moment to himself if he was willing to meet the constant demands on his time and energy. She knows what is important and what is not – and what demands his personal attention. 'I think that better be left to Vincent himself,' she will say if you are giving her something you think she can deal with and trying to avoid at the same time troubling The Master.

There is a deep mutual respect between them, a silent communication and understanding that does not always need to be put into words and which is the hallmark of growth in marriages that stand the test of time, at the time of writing the celebration of their 40th wedding anniversary is not all that far away. She is not only a wife but a confidante and for someone who knew little or nothing about the Sport of Kings when she first came up the avenue of Ballydoyle, she has certainly come a long way in knowledge and in what is demanded at the very top in the racing world.

She is recognised today as an outstanding photographer in her own right – one with a professional's ability and with an eye also for the unusual, as in the case of her beautiful shot of the main yard at Ballydoyle, taken from the house on a rare day of snow, reproduced with other outstanding colour prints in the book, *Vincent O'Brien's Great Horses*, which she produced with Ivor Herbert.

There was also the unique picture she took of Sheikh Mohammed against a desert background in Dubai, holding his falcon perched on his right hand. When that was reproduced in colour in the 1985–86 *Irish Racing Annual*, the impact it made was immense. The picture has been reprinted again and again in different newspapers and magazines, and is included here (facing p. 173).

On press mornings at Ballydoyle, when members of the Irish racing press gather, maybe in advance of the opening of a new Flat season, to run the rule over leading prospects and discuss the pros and cons with Vincent, Jacqueline will oblige by having photographs, taken on the gallops that morning, ready for them before their departure. Yes, she knows all about deadlines.

She is happiest when she is busiest and the children will tell you that she has hardly one major project finished but she goes head first into another; indeed, sometimes the projects overlap and she is overwhelmed with her own photographic work and all that she does in other fields, including her quiet, unobtrusive work for charity.

Jacqueline showed her resilience, her courage – a resilience and courage worthy of her pioneer ancestors in the aftermath of 'The Chamour Affair'. 'They were our darkest days,' she said. 'That's when I think I was the greatest help to Vincent,' and she still remembers the deep wound and the fierce wrench it represented for them having to leave house and home for the period of suspension.

Vincent and Jacqueline have five children – Elizabeth, Susan, Jane, David and Charles – and at the time of completing this book in the summer of 1989, they delighted in thirteen grandchildren.

Elizabeth (Liz) married James Bond film producer Kevin

McClory. Susan (Sue) became the wife of John Magnier of the Coolmore Stud, while Jane married Philip Myerscough of Ballysheehan Stud, Cashel. David's wife, Catherine, is Australian-born like Jacqueline and actually comes from the same Perth area.

Vincent and Jacqueline are particularly happy that their children live so near Ballydoyle, for it means that they can enjoy the grandchildren all the more. 'Vincent is wonderful, simply wonderful with children,' is the unanimous verdict.

17

Days Of Gladness And Ballymoss

It was early November 1958 when the announcement came that Vincent O'Brien was to give up training 'over the sticks'. While he was in America supervising Ballymoss's preparation for the Washington International at Laurel Park, his brother and assistant, Dermot, confirmed at Liverpool the 'no more jumpers' decision.

Quick Approach, trained by Vincent, had won the November Hurdle by 8 lengths. 'I don't expect we shall have a runner under these rules at Aintree again,' said Dermot. 'Quick Approach and Fine Point come up for sale at Newmarket in December. After Cheltenham in March I expect Vincent will give up the jumpers altogether.'

True to what Dermot had predicted, Vincent had his last Cheltenham runners at the 1959 Festival meeting. York Fair won Division One of the Gloucestershire Hurdle and Courts Appeal was second to Albergo in Division Two. Both were ridden by T. P. Burns.

By now, however, Ballymoss has proved himself a champion colt, taking a spate of major prizes as a four-year-old, including the Coronation Cup, the Eclipse Stakes, the King George VI and Queen Elizabeth Stakes and the Prix de l'Arc de Triomphe, to supplement his Irish Derby and English St Leger wins as a three-year-old. The brilliant mare, Gladness, won no less than eight races in the 1956–59 seasons, including the Sunninghill Park

Stakes, the Irish Champion Stakes, the Ascot Gold Cup, the Goodwood Cup and the Ebor Handicap.

It was only natural that Vincent should want to get his hands on more top-class flat horses. He realised that he could not give the Flat the totality of attention it required if he were still caught up aiming at targets at Liverpool and Cheltenham, especially as it had come to be expected that certain Cheltenham events, such as the Gloucestershire Hurdle, would be the medium of major gambles.

He would never really forget what National Hunt racing had meant to him – and the success it had brought him. He personally won a lot of kudos from the racing public in Ireland and Britain for his generous gesture in sponsoring the Vincent O'Brien Irish Gold Cup at Leopardstown, the inaugural running of which was on Saturday, 14 February 1987. It was a marvellous race. Forgive 'N' Forget, trained by Tipperary-born Jimmy Fitzgerald, triumphed from Very Promising and Barrow Line.

T. P. Burns, popularly known in his riding days as 'Young Tommy' to distinguish him from his famous father, Tommy 'The Scotsman' Burns, played a key role in the surging success that Vincent O'Brien knew in the 'fifties both 'over the sticks' and on the Flat. His name will always be linked, too, with Ballymoss and Gladness.

When he retired at the end of 1975 at the age of 50 after 37 years in the saddle, T.P. had seven Classic triumphs to his credit: an Irish Derby and English St Leger (Ballymoss), two Irish St Legers (Vimadee and Pidget), two Irish 2000 Guineas (El Toro and Padeh) and an Irish 1000 Guineas (Shandon Bell); and he was placed on no fewer than 25 others. He was twice short-headed in the Irish Oaks. He lost count of the number of winners he rode on the Flat and over hurdles.

While he mixed hurdling and chasing, it was really as a superb hurdles jockey that many will prefer to remember him in the National Hunt sphere. The race that left him with the proudest memory of all was in defeat on Stroller for Vincent O'Brien against the Ryan Price-trained, Clair Soleil in the 1955 Champion Hurdle.

French-bred Clair Soleil, unbeaten over hurdles in England (having won twice in France), started favourite at 5–2 but there was a great stable confidence behind Stroller, heavy support seeing him start at 7–2 second favourite.

The two fought out a truly magnificent duel to the third last hurdle after the flattering Prince Charlemagne (Bryan Marshall) had cracked. T.P. brought Stroller upsides of the favourite. Fred Winter, however, riding like a man possessed, responded by getting a superb leap out of Clair Soleil. Burns was almost level again going into the second last. Again Clair Soleil came away in front and was a half a length to a length in front as they came to the ultimate flight. Now T.P., calling upon all his experience, settled Stroller for the supreme effort and got back some of the lost ground. But it was Clair Soleil that landed first on the Flat.

The Cotswolds echoed to the sustained roar of the crowd. Sixty yards from the post T.P. had brought Stroller level and the odds then were on Vincent O'Brien's charge coming out on top. However, the superior stamina of Clair Soleil proved the deciding factor and he held on to win – but only by a head, with Cruachan third.

On the Flat T.P.'s judgement was such that Vincent O'Brien had no qualms in putting him up on Ballymoss in the 1957 English Derby and St Leger and there is no doubt that the association would have continued through the following season but for the crashing fall he suffered on Boys Hurrah at Clonmel in May, when a horse fell in front of him and his mount could not avoid it. For ten weeks he lay in a hospital bed with serious back injuries (twice previously he had suffered damage to some vertebrae in racecourse falls) and a broken breastbone and the accident could not have come at a more inopportune time, as Scobie Breasley took over on Ballymoss and Lester Piggott on Gladness. During the long painful weeks of recovery he had to lie on his back; by July he was fit enough to be able to nip into the television room – just in time to see Ballymoss score his biggest English triumph of the season in the King George VI and Queen Elizabeth Stakes at Ascot.

It would be hard to estimate exactly how much his injuries cost T.P. in financial terms. At least a sizeable five-figure sum by the money levels of the 'fifties. Any regrets he had, however, about his unfortunate accident had nothing to do with money. No, they came down to missing out on being part of further golden triumphs with Ballymoss, the horse he admired so much, and also with the gallant mare Gladness.

Although he was back in the saddle by the time Ballymoss contested the 1958 Prix de l'Arc de Triomphe, he was philosophical enough to accept that it would have been difficult at that point for Vincent O'Brien to have changed the winning combination forged between the colt and Scobie Breasley in the Coronation Cup, the Eclipse Stakes and the King George VI and Queen Elizabeth Stakes. He accepted also that it would have been placing a very heavy responsibility on him to ask him to ride Ballymoss in such an important race so soon after coming back from serious injury. 'All sorts of things can happen,' T.P. summed up.

We have seen how Jackie O'Brien of Fermoy was the instrument of fate who put Vincent O'Brien in contact with Frank Vickerman, whose business originally was in Yorkshire. Now a similar link was again to work in Vincent's favour. An English lawyer, Hedley Nicholson from Yorkshire, set the wheels in motion for Vincent to meet the American millionaire, John McShain, who was to exercise as big an influence on his progress up the ladder to achieving real international fame as a Flat trainer as Frank Vickerman did in the National Hunt sphere.

John McShain provided the financial backing that resulted in Vincent buying a batch of yearlings at the 1955 Tattersalls September Sales, which at the time were staged at Doncaster during the St Leger meeting. Among the batch were York Fair (who won as a two-year-old at Mallow but, of course, is best remembered as the winner of Division One of the Gloucestershire Hurdle at Cheltenham in 1959) and Ballymoss. John McShain sent some of the batch to America, where he had 35 horses in training.

Hedley Nicholson, a great racing enthusiast and a lover of National Hunt racing in particular, had become a keen admirer of Vincent O'Brien. That admiration extended to the point where he got an introduction to Vincent and formed an immediate friendship with him. As destiny would have it, Nicholson was prevailed upon by a friend of his, James Turner (later Lord Turner), President of the National Farmers' Union in Britain, to look after John McShain when he came over for the Tattersalls September Sales (Turner had met McShain in the States when leading a visiting group of farmers and was anxious to repay the hospitality shown the group in a hotel in Philadelphia owned by McShain).

John McShain was no ordinary American millionaire categorised as of Irish descent (no less than 40 million Americans claim Irish blood in their veins). He became one of the biggest and most-respected building contractors in the States, and was responsible for building the Pentagon and restoring the White House.

He passed away at 90 years of age in September 1989 at his residence, Killarney House, Killarney. Some 28 years earlier he began using Killarney House as a summer home. For the years immediately preceding his death, however, he lived there permanently with his wife, Mary, to whom he was married for 63 years. A keen golfer, he loved to play the famous Killarney course up to the time his health began to fail and equally he loved to fish the famous lakes. He invariably attended the Killarney July Festival race meeting and sponsored the John McShain Handicap. For racing enthusiasts around the globe, this American multi-millionaire has gone into the history books as the owner of Ballymoss and the man who acquired Gladness on the advice of Vincent O'Brien.

Vincent bought Ballymoss for 4500 guineas from Richard Ball, who had a small stud farm in County Dublin. Known affectionately as 'The Poet', as he once published a book of poetry, he had the distinction of breeding dual Aintree Grand National winner Reynoldstown, as well as

Lincolnshire winner Babur and Star King, who, renamed Star Kingdom, became a top sire in Australia.

He secured one of the greatest bargains in racing history when paying only 15 guineas for Indian Call, the dam of Ballymoss, at the Newmarket Sales in the early days of the Second World War. It is difficult to understand how anyone should wish to part with a mare so superbly bred (she was by Singapore, ridden to victory in the St Leger by Sir Gordon Richards), but perhaps it could be explained by the fact that she only ran twice and the only winner bred by her dam, Flittermere, was successful abroad. However, Flittermere, who was by Buchan, won three races, including the Yorkshire Oaks for the late Lord Derby, and was second in the Newmarket Oaks and Knowsley Dinner Stakes. The next dam was the great mare Keysoe, winner of the St Leger, Newmarket Oaks and the Gratwicke and Nassau Stakes at Goodwood.

Ballymoss's sire, Mossborough, was bred by Lord Derby, by Nearco out of Hyperion's half-sister All Moonshine by Bobsleigh. Mossborough was a good handicapper, who as a sire had the ability to get horses better than himself.

Anyone who was at the Curragh on Saturday, 6 April 1957 and saw how Ballymoss performed in the Madrid Free Handicap (7 furlongs) – his first race as a three-year-old – could never have imagined what a horse he would turn out to be later that same season and more especially the following season.

Ballymoss had been unplaced in his first outing as a two-year-old at the Curragh in July of the previous year, then finished second in a Maiden Plate at Mallow (5 furlongs) before winning over 7 furlongs at Leopardstown, but he could only finish second at the Curragh over the same distance in October when starting at 5–4.

Nat McNabb was in the stand watching the Madrid Free Handicap. He recalled turning to Vincent, as Ballymoss finished in the ruck, and pondering aloud if the Mossborough colt was actually ungenuine (shrewd experts on breeding were asking questions about Mossborough's off-

182

spring both in Ireland and Britain at that point). In fact, one man even posed the question to Vincent whether he would consider gelding Ballymoss.

However T. P. Burns was able to tell Vincent O'Brien after the Madrid that Ballymoss did not act at all in the heavy going. Still, Ballymoss was allowed off at 20–1 in the Trigo Stakes (12 furlongs) a month later with John Power in the saddle. Gladness (T. P. Burns) was the stable hotpot that day at 11–10 after shouldering 10 stone into second place in the Irish Lincolnshire Handicap. But the top-of-the-ground conditions were all against the mare, whereas Ballymoss at last got the going that would reveal him in an entirely new light.

He had been bred to win a Derby and had been entered for Epsom. But, unfortunately, he suffered a stone bruise in his foot which curtailed his preparation for the Classic at the crucial stage. However, after the colt had turned in an amazing performance in a mixed gallop at the Curragh over a distance 1 furlong short of the Epsom 12 furlongs – and with some very good horses from 'Darkie' Prendergast's stable taking part – Vincent concluded that he had to let him take his chance, though all his knowledge and professionalism told him that Ballymoss would not be at his peak. Both Vincent O'Brien and T. P. Burns are convinced that if it was at the Curragh that Ballymoss had been meeting Crepello, he would have beaten him. Epsom came three weeks too soon.

In the Epsom race T. P. Burns took up the running with a quarter of a mile to go but then up went the roar: 'Here Comes Crepello'. And, yes, there was Lester Piggott on the magnificent-looking chestnut, trained by Sir Noel Murless, ranging alongside battling Ballymoss. In a few strides he was more than 2 lengths in front, heading apparently for the easiest of victories.

However, with T.P. riding a tremendous race, Ballymoss came again to such an extent that a once-confident Piggott was at work on his mount. Crepello responded like a really good colt and in the last 50 yards went on to win by a 1½ lengths. The winner's time was the fastest recorded, up to that time, since Mahmoud in 1936.

On then to the Irish Derby, in which Ballymoss at 4–9 was the hottest winning favourite since The Phoenix in 1943 (Orby had won at odds of 1–10 in 1907).

Thirty-three-year-old T. P. Burns, in slamming Hindu Festival and Rae Johnstone by 4 lengths, with Valentine Slipper (Paddy Powell) a further length away third in a field of eight, was emulating his father who had won this race on Raeburn in 1936.

Ballymoss went on to become Ireland's first-ever winner of the English St Leger at rain-soaked Doncaster, after finishing second in heavy going in the Great Voltigeur at York to Brioche. Explaining that York defeat, T. P. Burns said, 'At York the going was far more like a wet peat moss gallop than the going at Doncaster. And you know as well as I do, when you get wet peat moss – which was applied to the turf at York – it is a very cloggy surface.'

The second explanation for Ballymoss's failure in the Great Voltigeur (when he started at 7–4) was that he had to travel by boat and train to York as Aer Lingus had discontinued its horse transport service and this arduous journey seemed to have taken a lot out of him. For the St Leger Vincent O'Brien sent him over by chartered plane.

In the St Leger Ballymoss became the horse that no one wanted to back because of the changed going, his starting price drifting out to 8–1 as he was judged to be a top-of-the-ground specialist. But the big chestnut, after being restrained by T. P. Burns throughout the slowly-run first 1½ miles, pulled to the front 2½ furlongs out, with all the power and determination of a colt at his peak, and won with considerable ease from Court Harwell (Scobie Breasley), with Brioche (Edward Hide) third.

Mrs Mary McShain warmly congratulated T. P. Burns on the cool manner of his victory while her husband, John, when asked about future plans, said simply, 'The horse is Vincent O'Brien's – to do with as he likes.' Vincent already was looking ahead to 1958 – and there was one target pencilled in in his mind, the Prix de l'Arc de Triomphe, which he knew would set the seal on the career of Ballymoss. And there were other major prizes also, including the King George VI and Queen Elizabeth

Stakes, which he was confident could be won on the way to Longchamp.

'A hell of a horse,' is how Vincent O'Brien's brother, Dermot, described Ballymoss. 'It was as a four-year-old that he really came into his own.' In fact, Ballymoss failed only once in five outings and that was when he finished second in the Ormonde Stakes at Chester. Scobie Breasley had the rides in his four major victories that season.

Meanwhile, Gladness was also carrying all before her during the 1957 season, winning three out of five. Lester Piggott was engaged to ride her in the Ascot Gold Cup. Vincent gave Lester really detailed instructions on how to ride the mare in the race. But then when a jockey had not ridden a charge of his before, Vincent believed in giving instructions. Later the professional relationship between Vincent and Lester would develop into something completely different – Vincent trusting Lester's judgement when he knew the animal he was riding. There was no better example of this than Lester impressing upon Vincent that he was convinced The Minstrel would get the Epsom Derby distance – even after the colt had failed to win the English and Irish 2000 Guineas.

Gladness (by Sayajirao out of Bright Lady) is mentioned in the record books as having been bred by one S. McGregor and also T. Venn. Fifteen years before Gladness won the 1958 Ascot Gold Cup in the hands of Lester Piggott, the 'S. McGregor' – Sidney McGregor – had stepped into Vincent's life at the most opportune moment imaginable. Vincent, then 27, had gone to the 1943 Newmarket Sales with a masterful eye for picking out a good one, but with no financial backing worth talking about. He got a real bargain in Drybob.

And then he was introduced to Sidney McGregor, from Warwickshire, a great racing man who could proudly claim the distinction of having bred April The Fifth (Craig an Eran out of Sold Again by Call o' the Wild), who did not win a race as a two-year-old but came out as a three-year-old to win the Lingfield Derby Trial by 2 lengths and then went on to take the Epsom Derby.

185

Lady Fortune was certainly smiling on Vincent that day at Newmarket for not only did Sidney McGregor get someone to take 50 per cent of Drybob for Vincent but he also told him that he would send him a horse called Good Days to train. Good Days was to win the Irish Cesarewitch in 1944, while Drybob dead-heated for the Irish Cambridgeshire. But, even more significantly, Bright Lady, the dam of Gladness, was an own sister of Good Days, for whom Vincent always retained a special affection. Little wonder when he looked at Gladness's breeding that he should press John McShain to buy her in mid-career.

Ballymoss and Gladness were both sent to Ascot for the 1958 King George VI and Queen Elizabeth Stakes. 'I had my mind made up that I would challenge for the prize with Ballymoss if he got the conditions to his liking – that is firm going – but Gladness would run if it came up soft,' recalled Vincent. The going was not just firm but quite hard. Vincent did not have to think twice before deciding that Ballymoss would be the challenger from Ballydoyle. And his judgement was vindicated in the ease with which Ballymoss justified 7–4 favouritism.

Gladness, having followed up her Ascot Gold Cup triumph by landing the odds of 1–2 in the Goodwood Cup, again with Lester in the saddle, was sent for the Ebor Handicap at York. The going was soft – ideal for the mare.

Gladness shouldered 9 stone 7 pounds in victory and Vincent agrees that it was her 'finest hour' – certainly one of the greatest performances that a mare carrying that weight could give in a competitive handicap race of this kind. And, of course, Lester was seen at his scintillating best.

That memorable Ebor performance set the seal on the career of Gladness, for although she was kept in training the following season as a six-year-old, she had only one victory to her credit and that was in her first race of the season, the modest Glendalough Stakes (9 furlongs) worth £411. 10s at the Phoenix Park. Carrying 10 stone 1 pounds she landed the odds of 1–2 with Lester Piggott in the saddle. She developed tendon trouble, and this on top of the fact that her fetlocks had been fired. She was unplaced in the Prix du Cadran at Longchamp on 10 May and Vincent knew from his trusted vet, Bob Griffin, that the King George VI and Queen Elizabeth Stakes in July would have to be her last race.

Even though she could not be given the kind of preparation that Vincent would really have liked if she had not begun to develop leg ailments, she ran the gamest of races in taking runner-up position behind Alcide, the Alycidon colt who, after being 'nobbled' before the 1958 Epsom Derby from which he had to be withdrawn, duly won the St Leger in smashing style by 8 lengths and failed by inches at the Ascot Gold Cup the following season before success in the King George. So Gladness, after all, did not achieve the supreme accolade by winning the King George, as Ballymoss had done in 1958.

On being retired to stud, Ballymoss sired one outstanding colt in Royal Palace, who won the English 2000 Guineas and Epsom Derby in 1967 and only missed the St Leger because of a mishap, and the following season took the Coronation Cup, Eclipse Stakes and King George VI and Queen Elizabeth Stakes. He was also the sire of two winners of the Irish Oaks, Ancasta (1964) and Merry Mate (1966).

Gladness bred four winners, including Glad One, runner-up to La Lagune in the 1968 English Oaks and third the same season to Celina in the Irish Oaks. Merry Mate was the produce of Gladness's mating with Ballymoss (a mating which also produced another useful horse in Ballyjoy).

The mating of a dual Classic winner with a mare commanding Gladness's record might seem the perfect 'match'; but just as the mating of an Epsom Derby winner with an Oaks winner has seldom proved the ideal combination, so the Ballymoss/Gladness matings did not produce the super champion some might have anticipated.

Vincent O'Brien, with the accumulative knowledge of breeding he has gathered since, and with his knowledge, too, of what is demanded in an ideal mating, might well advise now against mating Ballymoss with Gladness and might go for a different stallion entirely from a son of Mossborough.

But undoubtedly the temptation at the time to mate the two horses more than once was very strong and even breeding purists would have found it difficult to run against the tide.

These achievements of the two horses on the racecourse stand the test of time and are part of the early years of greatness of Vincent O'Brien as a trainer who was still on the 'dual mandate', so to speak, mixing the Flat with National Hunt. The statistics speak for themselves. Ballymoss won a total of £107,165 in stake money – a record in his day – while Gladness in eight successes added a further £27,000, making a grand total of £134,165.

18

The Day It All Turned Sour

Vincent O'Brien's brother, Phonsie, looked out of the window of his home beside the village of Kilsheelan in South Tipperary one afternoon in February 1989 and, turning around suddenly, said, 'You know, one ten thousandth of a grain of something resembling methylamphetamine cost Vincent his licence to train for twelve months.'

Almost 30 years had elapsed since the most traumatic event in Vincent O'Brien's life – the happening that left him so shell-shocked and shattered that he turned his back on racing altogether for the period of his suspension. In the words of Phonsie, 'he wanted to hear nothing about racing and for months and months wouldn't even talk about it.'

It meant exile for him and his wife, Jacqueline, and his young family from their home, Ballydoyle House, Cashel. They moved to Phonsie's home, South Lodge, near Carrick-on-Suir, County Tipperary, while Phonsie and his wife and family moved to Ballydoyle. Phonsie took over the training of Vincent's string in addition to his own.

It seemed at one point that Vincent might emigrate to the States, as John McShain, one of his millionaire owners, announced: 'Vincent O'Brien is a genius in the world of racing. I feel this so strongly that I would be prepared to take him back to the States with me and set him up there.'

The most amazing aspect of the whole affair was that Vincent O'Brien was the victim of a doping certificate which should never have been accepted by the Stewards of the Irish Turf Club. There was, in fact, no positive identification of the drug alleged to have been administered to Chamour when he won the 4.30 p.m. event on the Curragh card on Wednesday, 20 April 1960 – the £202 Ballysax Plate, a 10-furlong race for maidens for which the Vincent O'Brien-trained colt started at 4–6.

The certificate that resulted in the trainer losing his licence for twelve months simply stated that the sample of saliva received from the Irish Turf Club by the analysts, Herd and Mundy, at their headquarters building in Weymouth Street, London, by registered parcel post, gave the following result on analysis: 'The sample contained approximately 1/10,000th grain of an Amphetamine derivative resembling Methylamphetamine.'

The sweat sample gave 1/5000th (approx.) on analysis.

Eminent veterinary scientist Dr Brendan Farrelly of University College, Dublin, later drew this conclusion in an article in the *Irish Veterinary Journal*:

'It is regrettable that a Committee of laymen should adjudge a horse to have been "doped" and a trainer to merit deprivation of the means of practising his art on the evidence of a certificate which, to the writer, appears to be misleading and entirely negative in the sense that no specifically-named drug was mentioned. It is even more regrettable, and in fact deplorable, that veterinary opinion had failed to refute adequately its implications.'

Vincent O'Brien was originally suspended for eighteen months on the strength of this certificate. The suspension was later reduced to a year. He was prepared to pursue the matter to the very limits to clear his name – both with the Stewards of the Irish Turf Club, and also through the courts. Indeed, prior to bringing a High Court action against the Irish Turf Club, he was told privately that if he resorted to legal action, he would never be given a training licence again. As Jacqueline recalled: 'Vincent's view was that he didn't care. It was more important to him to have the record put straight. In those days, remember, no one could question a decision by the Stewards. And even if you had lost your livelihood when you felt you had been wrongly accused of doping a horse in your stable, it was still the position that you must not, under any circumstances, contemplate legal proceedings.'

'Vincent, however, felt so strongly about wanting to clear his name that he was determined to go right to the brink and over it, if necessary. So he went ahead with his Court action – regardless of the consequences.'

Jacqueline explained that when Vincent first saw the certificate he was completely taken aback, as he had never heard of a derivative resembling Methylamphetamine and he did not know how to go about refuting the certificate. The Stewards, for their part, were in the same boat in the knowledge stakes about Methylamphetamine, as drug testing had only just been introduced. Only samples of sweat and saliva were taken – not urine. And no second sample was taken for testing against.

Yorkshire businessman F. W. (Walter) Burmann, owner of Chamour, showed the certificate to a scientist friend of his in Glaxo, who expressed surprise that any action could have been taken on such a vague statement. So now, Vincent O'Brien and a group of friends, including Tim Vigors, the famous fighter pilot during the Battle of Britain and an internationally-respected figure in the bloodstock and breeding industry, set the wheels in motion for the assembly of one of the most formidable bodies of scientific opinion. Judge Lavery was one of Vincent's closest friends and guided him in the presentation of this material. He was a brilliant counsel and had no time for injustice.

The findings of this body of international experts stated categorically that:

(1) No identification of a drug was made.
(2) Only approximate amounts of a derivative resembling something were found.
(3) It appeared that the amounts purported to have been found were outside the scientific limits available then with the most up-to-date techniques.

The body of scientific opinion was presented to the Stewards of the Irish Turf Club in printed form by Vincent

191

O'Brien as he lodged an appeal for reconsideration of the case. The extraordinary response he received – and this is now only being revealed for the first time, roughly 30 years after the event – was that if they went back and admitted a mistake, the whole fabric of racing would be damaged. As one of the Stewards put it to Vincent: 'The captain must go down with his ship.'

And as Jacqueline said: 'The Stewards appeared not to know how they could admit the possibility that they were wrong and, therefore, face the blame for their action. So, while they reduced the original suspension of eighteen months to a year, they failed, in face of the body of expert international opinion presented to them, to clear Vincent's name.' They felt that the perception of authority in racing was more important than the fate of one person.

Before dealing in more detail with the events leading up to 'Black Friday', 13 May 1960 – the day Vincent O'Brien learned that he was being put out of racing for a period – and with the aftermath to that day, let us look at the powerful case Vincent presented to the Stewards of the Irish Turf Club.

Nothing in the body of expert opinion he garnered from Britain, France and Germany was as incisive and clear-cut as the report from L. C. Nicholls, Director of the Metropolitan Police Laboratory at Scotland Yard. He noted that secretions of animals, including horses, contain a very large number of substances, many of which are known but the nature of some of which are not fully understood. Some of these are basic substances related chemically to materials of the nature of amphetamine. 'It is common to obtain traces of basic substances from horses' secretion. These basic substances are natural in origin,' he stated.

Then he stressed: 'Before it is possible to be dogmatic in saying that there is a foreign substance present which is characteristic of a horse-dope, it is essential, in my opinion, that the substance should be identified *beyond reasonable doubt*. It is obvious from the certificates supplied that the analyst has not done this in this case and, in fact, says so in the report which implies that an unidentified drug resembling methylamphetamine has been found.'

He concluded: 'As one constantly giving evidence in criminal cases, I am satisfied that the information given in the certificate might be valuable to an officer investigating a possible crime, but it is *valueless as definite proof of that crime.*'

Dr W. A. Menne, a Director and leading Executive of the Board of one of the largest German firms producing veterinary and other products and a past President of the German Chemical Industry, pointed out in his report that proof of a dope in sweat and saliva alone was not recognised in Germany as conclusive – an exact analysis of urine and blood *must* be presented.

'According to our knowledge, it is not possible with the method applied in England to differentiate exactly amphetamine and its derivatives from natural substances produced by the body. It is, therefore, very doubtful whether it was actually a matter of amphetamine or a derivative, respectively.

'In conclusion, it is my opinion that the analyses mentioned are not proof that the horse, Chamour, had received amphetamine or some of its derivatives.'

The French view, expressed by J. J. Pocidalo of the Laboratory of the Claude Bernard Hospital in Paris and Director of Researches at the National Hygiene Institute, was that the quantities found by the English experts in the sweat and saliva samples taken from Chamour were so small that it was perfectly admissible that the derivative in question 'may well not be the result of medicinal administration to the horse but the result of some physiological excretion of a product normally secreted by the organism.'

Finally, the British Home Office Pathologist, Dr Francis E. Camps, a recognised expert in Forensic Medicine, flatly rejected the certificate on the basis that there was no evidence that Chamour had ever ingested any drug because:

(1) The drug had never been properly identified (i.e. it is simply reported as a derivative resembling).

(2) The mere fact that it resembles the derivative of a drug does *not* – when other substances can be present which were not derived from the drug – *prove the presence of a drug*.

(3) The absence of any reference to the method used makes any opinion by even the most skilled chemist impossible, far less does it make it impossible for lay persons to arrive at any conclusion. It may well be that the technique employed is subject to error.

(4) Basically, the position appears to be that it has, in my opinion, been assumed that the certificate contained evidence of the presence of a drug when, in fact, it did not.

It is obvious from the conclusion of the British Home Office Pathologist that if a judge was about to direct a jury in a murder case on the certificate that resulted in a 'guilty' verdict being brought in against Vincent O'Brien, he would there and then have found that there was no case to answer on the evidence before him.

You cannot have approximate amounts of a substance *resembling* a drug. Either there is a drug in the system or there is not. If no drug had been properly identified, then the certificate itself cannot be accepted as a *certificate of dope*. To bring in a 'guilty' verdict on such a certificate must rank as a grave miscarriage of justice.

The most damning indictment of all against the verdict imposed on Vincent O'Brien came from the Director of the Metropolitan Police Laboratory at Scotland Yard, who as we have seen concluded that the information given on the certificate would be valueless as 'definite proof' of the alleged crime.

So, in all the circumstances, Vincent O'Brien has even more reason now, looking back across a span of 30 years, to feel deeply aggrieved at the wrong wrought on him at the time. He has kept his thoughts about it mostly to himself. It wounded him so deeply that he does not like even to discuss it. That, of itself, only re-opens the wounds, causing them to fester again. He leaves it to

Jacqueline to elaborate on the facts, to pinpoint the blatant weaknesses in the certificate on which his whole career as a trainer rested in the final analysis.

Jacqueline, as a result of the 'Chamour Affair', admits to being deeply sympathetic to anyone who has been charged or found guilty in the wrong.

'You have to go through such an experience to understand,' she said. Vincent and she certainly understand.

The 'Chamour Affair' evolved from a race at the Curragh which Vincent O'Brien could never have used as the medium of a major gamble – even if the stable was tilting at the ring then as it did in the old days. 'My personal gain from Chamour's victory was £20 – 10 per cent of the stake,' Vincent would say subsequently as he went to see his solicitors on receiving the news of his suspension.

Vincent O'Brien sent eleven horses to the Curragh for that particular meeting, four of them entered for the one race. He had supervised them as they left the Ballydoyle stables the previous day.

On his way with Jacqueline to keep a luncheon appointment with Roderic More O'Ferrall at Kildangan before racing on the Wednesday, he made time, in his usual meticulous fashion, to call to the rececourse stables at the Curragh to enquire from the stable-lads how the horses had travelled.

In subsequent police investigations, it was established beyond any shadow of doubt that the trainer did not see any of the horses individually, and certainly was not at any stage in the stable with Chamour.

Chamour's target was the Irish Derby that same season and it would have been sheer madness to have administered a drug to him in order to ensure that he would win a maiden race that was not going to make one iota of difference to his value. Die Hard was the colt earmarked for the Epsom Derby.

Dope testing had only recently been introduced by the Irish Turf Club. It commenced with the practice of picking 'out of the hat' the name of one winner on each day's card who would be tested for dope. No second sample for checking was taken, so once the single samples of saliva and sweat were sent to London, that was that. The findings sent back from London to the Irish Turf Club were accepted, with no basis available to the Stewards, for cross-checking with another source before handing down sentence.

Chamour, a classy chestnut colt, duly justified favouritism in the Ballysax Plate and fate decreed that he would be the winner selected by lot that day.

Vincent O'Brien and Jacqueline went home from the Curragh never for one moment contemplating the dramatic days that lay ahead for them.

It was on Friday, May 13 1960 – subsequently to be imprinted in Vincent's mind as "Black Friday" – that the whole world seemed to fall apart in an instant for the Master of Ballydoyle.

Ironically, it was on the same day that Vincent O'Brien lost his licence that Prince Aly Khan was killed in a car accident. Six years previously he had paid 3900 guineas to secure Royal Tan in the 40-minute auction in Dublin of the string of racehorses owned by 'Mincemeat' Joe Griffin.

Vincent O'Brien and his brother, Dermot, and stable-jockey, the Australian Garnie Bougoure, gathered in the Shelbourne Hotel on the afternoon of the Turf Club inquiry. The Turf Club headquarters, now at the Curragh, across the road from the racecourse, were centred then in Merrion Square, Dublin.

The inquiry was conducted by the following Stewards: Joe McGrath; Sir Cecil Stafford-King-Harman and Major Victor McCalmont, then in his 'forties and later to become Senior Steward. As always with inquiries of this nature, it was held behind closed doors. Only the verdict was made public.

In the official terminology, the Stewards were meeting 'to hear Mr M.V. O'Brien's explanation of the presence of a drug and stimulant in the samples of saliva and sweat taken from Chamour.'

The evidence of 21 witnesses was heard, including veterinary surgeons and a Garda Sergeant. Publication of the

Irish Racing Calendar was held back so that the result could be announced without delay. It was rushed to the printers within minutes of the Stewards' decision.

In the official statement, as carried in the *Irish Racing Calendar*, the Stewards expressed themselves 'satisfied that a drug or stimulant had been administered to Chamour for the purpose of affecting his speed and/or stamina in the race.'

The statement added: 'The Stewards of the Turf Club accordingly withdrew Mr O'Brien's licence to train under Rule 102(v), Rules of Racing and declared him a disqualified person under that Rule and under Rule 178 from 13 May 1960 until 30 November 1961.

'They also disqualified Chamour for the Ballysax Maiden Plate at the Curragh and ordered the Stakes to be forfeited under Rule 178 and ordered that Timobriol be placed first and Cassieme second (on the disqualification of Dillyear): no third place.'

Timobriol, incidentally, was a stable-companion of Chamour – so Vincent O'Brien still got his £20 as his cut of the prize money. But it was poor consolation as the real effect of the Stewards' announcement sank home. The fact that he had been declared a disqualified person meant that he was not allowed to 'enter, run, train or ride a horse in any race at any recognised meeting or enter any racecourse, stand or enclosure'.

Though subsequently the Stewards would make it clear in a statement in the *Irish Racing Calendar* that they did not find that Vincent O'Brien 'had administered the drug or stimulant or knew of its administration', the fact remained that, as the Rules operated then, he was held responsible as the trainer of Chamour. There and then, the Stewards summarily withdrew his licence to train and disqualified him.

The rules are different now and a forbidden substance can show up after a test without the axe coming down to deprive a trainer of his livelihood. Of vital importance is the fact that a trainer has the right to have the sample checked.

The other great change brought about by the 'Chamour

Affair' was that the Irish Turf Club appointed their own analyst and no longer left themselves totally dependent on the doping certificate sent back to them from Britain from the sample they had forwarded across the Irish Sea. Every Irish winner would be automatically tested in Ireland.

Most important of all, however, was the decision not to rely solely on analyses of saliva and sweat. The Irish Stewards decided that a sample both of urine and saliva would be taken. Top veterinary experts on both sides of the Irish Sea had come out strongly in favour of this, arguing that it was impossible to decide beyond any shadow of doubt whether a horse had been doped from an analysis of saliva and sweat alone. This did not take cognisance of dilution in the system, whereas in the blood and urine of a horse a drug was secreted and excreted in its entirety.

The changes wrought by the furore caused by his suspension were in the future and Vincent O'Brien, then only 43, looked suddenly visibly older as the news reached him that evening in the Shelbourne Hotel.

To the media representatives who crowded into the hotel, he issued the following statement: 'The Stewards have withdrawn my trainer's licence and declared me to be a disqualified person on the grounds that they found evidence of drugs in a routine sweat and saliva test taken from Chamour on April 20, a test to which I knew the horse was liable to be subjected.

'This horse won a £200 maiden race at the Curragh and neither I nor any person associated with the horse had a bet. My personal gain was £20 – ten per cent of the stake.

'I did not drug this or any other horse. I trust my staff and I have placed the matter in the hands of my solicitors.'

Events accelerated quickly. Vincent O'Brien asked the Garda authorities to help in trying to find the person or persons who doped Chamour. At the same time it was announced by his solicitors that he had decided to postpone any further action until the result of this investigation was known. It was reported in the media that

Scotland Yard inquiries were being pursued in Ireland 'concerning an alleged "drug ring" in England' and that the same ring might have "got at" Chamour. Walter Burmann, as the owner of Chamour, offered a £5000 reward for information leading to the identification or conviction of the persons responsible for doping the colt.

Then on 19 May the Stewards of the English Jockey Club announced that the ban imposed on Vincent O'Brien had been extended to Britain and would also cover National Hunt Racing.

The Irish Stewards stopped short of ordering that Vincent O'Brien remove all the horses trained by him from the Ballydoyle stables. This allowed his younger brother, Phonsie, to take over the training of the 70-strong string. 'He knows my methods, so it will make no difference to the horses,' said Vincent. To make the change-over operate as smoothly as possible, Phonsie soon moved the twenty horses he was training at the time from Carrick-on-Suir to Ballydoyle.

The Irish Turf Club permitted Chamour to continue racing, which surprised some English commentators, who pointed out that in England a horse found to be doped would be automatically barred for life. Chamour impressed when finishing fourth to stable-companion Die Hard, in the strongly contested Trigo Stakes and then won the Gallinule Stakes, his final preparation race before the Irish Derby.

The most amazing consequence of all of the Irish Stewards allowing him to continue to race resulted in the wrath of the racing public being brought down publicly about the heads of the Irish Turf Club the day the colt won the Irish Derby. It was, perhaps, one of the most significant and extraordinary demonstrations ever witnessed on the occasion of an Irish Classic race at the Curragh . . .

19

Curragh Crowds Chant 'We Want Vincent'

'We want Vincent, We want Vincent.'

This was the chant that went up from thousands of throats at the Curragh on the Wednesday afternoon in June, 1960 when Chamour, in the hands of the artistic Australian jockey, Garnie Bougoure, won the Irish Derby.

As Chamour passed the post a length in front of Alcaeus (Ron Hutchinson), runner-up to St Paddy in the Epsom Derby, with Mrs Frank Vickerman's Prince Chamier (T. P. Burns) staying on to take third place, the crowd of 10,000 who had watched the race in sweltering heat, gave vent to their feelings, in no uncertain fashion. They made it clear in the ensuing scenes, first wildly enthusiastic and then very tense, that they were concerned primarily with the injustice of the suspension imposed on Vincent O'Brien.

'We want Vincent, We want Vincent.' It echoed from the packed enclosures out over the wide expanse of the Curragh plain and it carried on the radio waves to Vincent who, at that moment, was fishing along his favourite stretch of the Blackwater, a portable radio at his side.

Now hundreds burst across the course from the infield area to the reserved enclosure and joined the swelling throng already congregated outside the Stewards' room. 'Give Vincent back his licence, give it back,' they shouted. It was the roar of an angry crowd, the eruption of deep-felt feelings. Men in shirt sleeves in the sun, who had swept across from the 'popular' area of the racecourse, mingled in the swaying crowd with those who had dressed more sedately for a Classic occasion. But all, who had come to idolise Vincent O'Brien for his momentous achievements at Cheltenham and Liverpool, could no longer conceal their disappointment at the fact that he was so cruelly denied the honour of being there to see Chamour win a second Irish Derby for him. These race-goers knew that instead of 'Trained A. S. O'Brien', the entry in the racecard should have read 'Trained M. V. O'Brien'.

The crowd surged towards the Stewards' room and, for one terrible and very frightening moment, it seemed that they would burst into its hallowed precincts. The unthinkable was fortunately avoided.

However, this became the day when the Stewards of the Irish Turf Club came to realise the mood that had been stirred among the Irish racing public. The overwhelming demonstration of the people's will was to contribute in no small way to the reduction of the term of suspension from eighteen months to a year.

Another major contributory factor was the spotlight put in the media on a report that Vincent O'Brien was going to test the Turf Club decision in the Courts.

In taking away Vincent O'Brien's licence, the Stewards in their haste to meet the printing deadline of the *Irish Racing Calendar* on Friday, 13 May 1960 had not only mentioned Rule 102(v) but also Rule 178. It would have sufficed for them to have mentioned Rule 102(v), which held the trainer responsible and liable to disqualification – if a drug was found to have been administered.

However, Rule 178 goes much further. It opens: 'No person shall administer or cause to be administered . . .' Therefore, once Vincent O'Brien was convicted under rule 178 he was deemed to have personal involvement in administering the drug.

A statement from the Stewards published in the *Irish Racing Calendar* on Friday, 22 July 1960 was viewed as complete exoneration for Vincent O'Brien. The statement read:

'The Stewards of the Irish Turf Club have been informed by members of the Turf Club that there are doubts as to what the Stewards actually decided in their finding published in the *Irish Racing Calendar* dated 13th May with regard to the disqualification of Mr Vincent O'Brien.

'The Stewards gladly publish the following statement: 1. That a drug or stimulant had been administered to Chamour; 2. That Mr Vincent O'Brien was the trainer of Chamour; 3. That, as trainer, he was responsible under the Rules of Racing, and was consequently deprived of his licence; 4. The Stewards did not find that Mr Vincent O'Brien had administered the drug or stimulant, or knew of its administration. Any other impression given by the wording of their previous decision is incorrect.'

The reaction of the media was that any suggestion that Vincent O'Brien had administered a drug or stimulant or connived at this had been shown to be entirely without foundation. The statement offered a measure of justice but, yet, he was still a disqualified person, unable to pursue his livelihood and unable to set foot on any racecourse in Ireland or Britain.

He was forced to apply to the Stewards of the Irish Turf Club to have the suspension reconsidered. On foot of this application, a special meeting of the Stewards was held on 25 November 1960 and it was decided to cut the suspension from eighteen months to twelve.

But why did they not lift the suspension entirely from him? Why did he have to wait until mid-May, 1961 to have his licence to train restored to him?

The strain of those months of waiting were well-nigh intolerable. At last, his period in the wilderness ended, on Saturday, 13 May 1961. He was free to go racing again and to watch his runners perform in public.

But the trauma of 'The Chamour Affair' was still not ended for him. There was one final act to be played out in this long drawn-out drama.

In the period before his suspension was due to end Vincent O'Brien had sued the Stewards of the Irish Turf Club for libel. His action was based on the Turf Club making the extraordinary bloomer of repeating, in the *Races Past Plus Calendar* Volume (Bound) for 1960, mention of the fact that Vincent O'Brien had been declared a disqualified person under Rule 178.

The Stewards admitted publication but claimed that it was not libellous and, further, that it was privileged.

The libel case was due for hearing in the High Court in Dublin on Wednesday, 5 July 1961. As Mr Justice Murnaghan was about to swear in a jury, Mr John A. Costello, S.C. for Vincent O'Brien, said that a settlement had been reached. He read an apology from the Stewards in which they said that it was never their intention to blame Mr O'Brien personally during the doping inquiry. They acknowledged that there was no evidence before them upon which such findings could be made.

The statement went on: 'The Stewards now disclaim having had any intention of imputing to Mr O'Brien any such responsibility and unreservedly withdraw any imputation of that kind. The Stewards recognise that Mr O'Brien's object in bringing these actions was to clear his reputation of such imputations.

'Mr O'Brien recognises that there was scientific evidence given at the inquiry on 13 May 1960 upon which the Stewards would have been entitled to hold that a drug had been administered to the horse and that they thought fit, in the exercise of their discretion under rule 102 of the rules of Racing, to impose penalties on him which, in fact, it was.

'Mr O'Brien maintains the horse was not drugged and he has furnished the Stewards scientific opinions and reports which were not available at the inquiry in support of this. It is not necessary that this issue should be pursued further.'

The final humiliating admission from the Stewards came in the conclusion to the statement read in Court:

'The Stewards admit that the publication in the Calendar also imputes personal responsibility to Mr O'Brien. Such publication was negligent on the part of the Turf Club and the Stewards accept responsibility, apologise and express regret to Mr O'Brien for any suffering and injury that may have been caused to him or his family as a consequence of such publication.'

Vincent O'Brien accepted the statement from the Stewards as amends and agreed to forego any claim for damages. The Stewards had to pay all legal costs. As he left the Court, he told reporters: 'My only aim was to clear my name. I had no interest in damages. The matter is now closed.'

Subsequent to the settlement, the Turf Club faced the embarrassment of having to call in all the Bound Volumes of *Races Past* (1960) and erase from page 350 mention of Rule 178. For anyone holding one of these volumes, it has become something of a prized collector's item.

Derby winner Chamour never went to stud. He died suddenly in his box at the Ballydoyle stables and a post-mortem examination was carried out to try and ascertain the cause of death. The finding of the post-mortem was that Chamour got cast in his box and while struggling to right himself the buckle in front of his rug paralysed a nerve close to his windpipe and caused him to suffocate.

Walter Burmann, his owner, was sitting down to dinner in Monte Carlo that same evening with Vincent O'Brien, who was on holidays there, and Bob Griffin, the Ballydoyle vet. There were thirteen to dinner – including the people most closely associated with Chamour. Vincent was loath to sit after that at a table of thirteen.

20

Picking Up The Threads

Vincent O'Brien stepped on to a racecourse for the first time in twelve months as a spectator at the evening meeting at Leopardstown on Wednesday, 17 May 1961. In a way it was like the homecoming of an exile as he was warmly applauded by fellow trainers and literally mobbed by hundreds of ordinary racing enthusiasts wishing to shake his hand. Vincent saw Roi Des Monts, trained by Phonsie, justify 4–7 favouritism in the feature race, the Dargle Stakes. By a strange coincidence the winner was owned by Walter Burmann, owner of the ill-fated Chamour.

Vincent quickly picked up the threads after his period in the wilderness. He had his first winner at Limerick Junction (now Tipperary) racecourse on Thursday, 25 May 1961 when, in a driving finish to a Maiden Plate (3–y–o), Garnie Bougoure won on Mister Moss by a head and a neck.

Bougoure had proved himself a tremendous servant to the Ballydoyle stable in the twelve months that Phonsie was at the helm there. Phonsie ended up in 1960 as Champion Irish Trainer with 32 horses winning 42 races to a total value of £19,215 and Walter Burmann, principally through the Irish Derby win and other victories by Chamour, was Top Owner, winning a total of £11,216 in stake money. Bougoure's association with Ballydoyle continued successfully during 1961 and he rode Light Year to a 6–1 triumph in the Irish 2000 Guineas in a field of 17. In the records Light Year is given as 'Trained A. S. O'Brien' and that is correct, as it was after this race that Vincent resumed training.

The same season, as Vincent became fully operational again, Bougoure was successful on the domestic front on John McShain's Silver Moon, the 7–1 favourite in the Blandford Stakes at the Curragh; won the Philips Electrical Rockingham Stakes (Handicap 5 furlongs) on Sea Fever at 7–1 and then took the Irish Cambridgeshire on the three-year-old Travel Light (8st 12lbs) at 10–1. In Britain Die Hard, now a four-year-old, who had been sold by John McShain during the winter for £25,000 to Major Laurie Gardner, won the Ebor Handicap carrying 8 stone 9 pounds in the hands of Lester Piggott, who was engaged to ride after the withdrawal of St Paddy.

This was the era when Irish trainers tended to tap the brilliance of Australian riding talent and racing followers thrilled to the artistry of Garnie Bougoure, Ron Hutchinson, Bill Williamson and visiting stylists Scobie Breasley and George Moore in some of the Classic events. For example, the 1960 Irish Oaks saw five top Australian jockeys in contention against one another with three of them – Bill Williamson (Lynchris), Scobie Breasley (Sunny Cove), and George Moore (Nubena) – occupying the first three places while at an earlier Curragh meeting Garnie Bougoure, Ron Hutchinson and Bill Williamson shared in five wins out of six races open to them. Vincent O'Brien was not the only Irish trainer to rely in this era on the skill of Australian jockeys – that was, of course, before the association he had with Scobie Breasley gave way to the finest partnership of all, that with Lester Piggott.

Seamus McGrath utilised Bill Williamson ('the best of the Australians to ride in Europe', in his view) to win the Prix du Cadran, Ascot Gold Cup and Prix de l'Arc de Triomphe on Levmoss, though controversy rages to this day over his short head defeat by Tambourine II (Roger Poincelet) on the John Oxx Sen.-trained Arctic Storm in the inaugural Irish Sweeps Derby in 1962.

Paddy ('Darkie') Prendergast could only entice the great

Sydney champion, Jack Thompson, to stay in Ireland for one season but he won the 1950 Irish Derby for him on Frank More O'Ferrall's Dark Warrior. It was on the specific recommendation of Thompson that Ron Hutchinson came to ride for Paddy Prendergast and immediately made his mark by winning both the 1960 Irish and English 2000 Guineas for Prendergast with Kythnos and Martial while the same season he won on Typhoon and Floribunda at Royal Ascot.

The 1962 season would see Garnie Bougoure riding for 'Darkie' Prendergast while Vincent O'Brien engaged another Australian in T. P. ('Pat') Glennon. During that 1962 season Bougoure rode Tender Annie and Display to victory for Prendergast at Royal Ascot, but 1963 would be his most memorable year. He was victorious on Ragusa in the English St Leger and Irish Derby, rode Noblesse to victory in the English Oaks and won the Irish St Leger on Christmas Island – all for 'Darkie' Prendergast. And then in 1964 he took the English 2000 Guineas on Pourparler for the same trainer.

Vincent O'Brien would later bring over Jack Purtell, who won the Melbourne Cup three times, and 19 races on that Australian 'colossus', Comic Court. Purtell, who was greatly admired by both Vincent O'Brien and John Oxx Sen. for his superb jockeyship, made a lasting impression on knowledgeable Irish race readers and he was to win the 1965 English Oaks for the Ballydoyle stable on the 100–7 chance, Long Look, owned by J. Cox-Brady. He also won the 1964 Queen Mary Stakes at Royal Ascot on Brassia.

It is a tribute to Vincent O'Brien's extraordinary resilience that twelve months plus twenty-three days after the Irish Turf Club's suspension on him was lifted, he won the Epsom Derby for the first time with Mr Raymond Guest's Larkspur.

Scobie Breasley, who had ridden Ballymoss in the Coronation Cup at Epsom and other big races in 1958, could not take the mount on Larkspur as he was retained by Sir Gordon Richards. However, he recommended fellow Australian Neville Sellwood. It was the Derby in which seven horses fell – six of them streaming riderless into the straight well behind the leaders. King Canute II was the only one who did not appear, as he was so badly injured in the pile-up that he was put down. Nine other horses in the field of 28 had their chances ruined through being impeded.

The fall of the seven happened on the downhill descent to Tattenham Corner. The fading Romulus struck into Crossan and both went down. Then the favourite Hethersett, Persian Fantasy, Changing Times, Pindaric and King Canute II were all brought down. Larkspur's amazing good fortune in avoiding the pile-up was revealed when Neville Sellwood said that the colt 'passed between the upturned legs of Hethersett'. If he had been a big, gangling horse he would almost certainly have toppled over.

Larkspur took the lead 2 furlongs out pursued by the French horse Le Cantilien, ridden by Yves Saint-Martin. A second French challenger, the 40–1 outsider Arcor (Roger Poincelet) ran on strongly in the last furlong to pass Le Cantilien but could not get in a telling blow at Larkspur, who had 2 lengths to spare at the winning post. Le Cantilien was a further half length away third.

The winner, a small (15.2½ h.h.), neat, compact colt, started at 22–1 and Sellwood won without having to show him the whip. Sebring, the more fancied of the two O'Brien runners in the betting and chosen by stable jockey Pat Glennon as his mount in the race, was fifth.

Neville Sellwood maintained afterwards that he would have won the race even if there had been no pile-up. However, the weight of informed and detached opinion contends that Hethersett, trained by Dick Hern, would almost definitely have triumphed if he had not been brought down. The bay colt by Hugh Lupus (out of Bride Elect by Big Game) proved his class by subsequently winning the St Leger from Monterrico and Miralgo, with Larkspur unplaced.

The time of the race even though the going was firm, was 2 minutes 37.6 seconds, the slowest since the last Irish-trained winner, Hard Ridden (1958) – another reason why Larkspur's victory tended to be down-graded.

However, there were certain extenuating circumstances to explain why the colt failed to win in his three subsequent outings after the Epsom Derby.

He was actually under a cloud in the count-down to Epsom, developing a swelling on his near-hind leg nine days before the race. He was laid off work for two days on the advice of the vet, Bob Griffin, and there was doubt as to whether he would run in the Derby. However, when Bob returned to Ballydoyle six days before the Classic, he said that Larkspur could resume work – and that he could be sent to Epsom, even though the swelling on his leg was still visible.

Vincent O'Brien is convinced in retrospect that racing downhill on the Epsom gradients on firm going certainly left a lasting mark on the colt's limbs, which were never the soundest anyway.

In the final analysis, Larkspur does not rate with the three most brilliant of Vincent O'Brien's Epsom Derby winners – Sir Ivor, Nijinsky and Golden Fleece – and he cannot be put in the same league either with dual Prix de l'Arc winner Alleged or El Gran Senor.

Nevertheless, after Larkspur's Epsom victory Vincent found that the world was his oyster. All doors were opened to him when it came to expanding the list of owners attached to the stable. The Americans saw the Epsom Derby as the equivalent in British terms of the Kentucky Derby and the significance of winning it was certainly not lost on them. And when someone as prominent as Raymond Guest, the United States Ambassador to Ireland, landed the prize, the impact on the other side of the Atlantic was all the greater. Greek shipping tycoon Stavros Niarchos was another who would be attracted by the Ballydoyle strike rate – though he did not stay the course like Robert Sangster.

We tend today to think of Vincent O'Brien making his first onslaught on Keeneland in the mid-seventies because so much evolved from 'The Syndicate' hitting Lexington for the first time in 1975. In reality, however, Vincent had been a visitor to the Bluegrass country of Kentucky and the Keeneland Sales since 1958. It was at the behest of

John McShain, owner of Ballymoss and Gladness that he first went there – and really got to know Raymond Guest.

The pieces of the jig-saw that had begun to fall so neatly into place in 1943, when Jackie O'Brien introduced Vincent to Frank Vickerman at Limerick Junction Races, were now, fifteen years later, coming together again in perfect fashion. For it was not so much that Raymond Guest would become the owner of Larkspur but that he would own Sir Ivor, the brilliant 1968 Epsom Derby winner. After Sir Ivor came Nijinsky, Roberto, The Minstrel, Golden Fleece, Alleged and El Gran Senor.

Sir Ivor was special to the career of Vincent O'Brien as he not only won on this side of the Atlantic but also took the Washington DC International at Laurel Park – the very place where Vincent had first been introduced to Raymond Guest. He was special, too, in another way in that he was the first of Vincent's Epsom Derby winners to be ridden by Lester Piggott.

It was an O'Brien-trained filly called Valoris who precipitated the events that led to the break, in 1966, between Lester and Sir Noel Murless, for whom he had been number one jockey for twelve years.

Lester had known great days with Noel Murless. There were the Epsom Derby triumphs on Crepello (1957) and St Paddy (1960), the Oaks victories on Carrozza (1957) and Petite Etoile (1959), the St Leger wins on St Paddy (1960) and Aurelius (1961). However, after 1961 the stable hit a lean period at the highest Classic level.

While he was champion jockey once again in 1965, Lester hankered for rides on horses in the Classics that he knew had a real chance of victory. And that, of course, meant he must be free of the shackles that tied him to one stable.

Noel Murless's hand in the 1966 Oaks was a filly called Varinia. Naturally he expected Lester to take the ride. But Lester informed him that he wished to ride the Vincent O'Brien-trained Valoris, owned by Charles Clore. He wanted the right of choice, whereas the Master of Warren Place wanted a first jockey under contract to him on whom he knew he could count on in every eventuality. Noel Murless informed the media that his partnership with Lester Piggott was at an end. Lester duly rode Valoris to victory. Varinia was third.

Lester that same season won the Eclipse Stakes for Vincent on Pieces of Eight, turning down the ride on the Noel Murless-trained Hill Rise – and his judgement was shown to be right once again. Those who were privileged to be at Sandown on that July day can never forget the tremendous power and incredible will-to-win that Lester showed as he fought back from seeming defeat against Ballyciptic in a pulsating duel literally to snatch victory on the line.

Strangely enough, he continued to take mounts for Noel Murless, but on his own terms. Before 1966 was out, he had twice ridden a colt called Royal Palace. Sir Noel saw the potential but Lester, who was rarely wrong in these matters, did not rate him out of the ordinary. If he had opted to ride Royal Palace in 1967, when the horse won both the English 2000 Guineas and the Epsom Derby, he might never have ridden Sir Ivor in the Grand Criterium at Longchamp. Sir Ivor had been unbeaten in four races, with Liam Ward in the saddle, on the way to the Grand Criterium. After triumphing in the prestigious Paris event, Lester said in the hearing of Christy Stack, travelling lad for the Ballydoyle stable, 'I'll stick with this one.'

He was true to his word. And the 'Sir Ivor Chapter' became one of the most glorious of all in the Vincent O'Brien story and in the unique relationship Vincent forged with Lester, The Maestro Supreme.

21

'I Put Sir Ivor Before Nijinsky'

When asked to choose between the relative merits of Sir Ivor and Mr Charles Engelhard's Nijinsky, Lester Piggott paused perceptibly. Obviously it was not an easy question to answer. 'I know Nijinsky was a brilliant horse, probably on his day one of the most brilliant I have ever ridden. But in the end if you push me on the point, I would have to put Sir Ivor before him'.

'Nijinsky's season as a three-year-old was not, to my mind, a good year. The horses racing against him were not as good as those that opposed Sir Ivor. And lasting judgements can only be made on the calibre of the opposition a colt or filly beats.

'I have always felt that Sir Ivor beat a super colt in Petingo in the Guineas. In the Derby he mastered Remand and Laureate in a few strides and then when I asked him the question, he produced a brilliant surge of finishing speed to leave Connaught literally standing and, remember, Connaught that same season won the King Edward VII Stakes and then the Prince of Wales Stakes two years running (1969 and 1970) and the Eclipse as a five-year-old in 1970.

'In the Eclipse Stakes at Sandown the very firm going was all against Sir Ivor, yet he kept on up the hill to be only narrowly beaten by Royal Palace and Taj Dewan. Royal Palace had won the Derby the previous year and

212

took the King George VI and Queen Elizabeth Stakes in 1968.

'In the Champion Stakes at Newmarket, over his best distance of 10 furlongs, Sir Ivor was much too good for Taj Dewan, which had run within a pound of Royal Palace in the Eclipse, so again on a comparison of form, Sir Ivor comes very well out of that race.

'In the Prix de l'Arc de Triomphe, Sir Ivor was beaten into second place by a really outstanding colt in Vaguely Noble, who had too much staying power for him over the Longchamp 12 furlongs in soft going.

'I knew after the Champion Stakes that Sir Ivor would win the Washington International and I said so to Vincent. It looked at one point that snow might cause a postponement of the race but it cleared, leaving the going very heavy. The ground was terrible. Hock deep, in fact. I had to save him as much as possible. I knew that was the only way he would get the trip in that going. My tactics were to get him as relaxed as possible, conserving everything for a sharp, late run.

'As we swung into the short straight, still lying fourth behind the leader, many people must have thought that it was impossible for Sir Ivor to win from that position. I did not go for the race until the last possible moment and when I pressed the button, it was all over in a few strides. I feel certain that I would have won by 100 yards if the ground had not been soft.

'Behind Sir Ivor that day were two high-class American-trained horses in Czar Alexander and Fort Marcy, second and third respectively, with the French-trained Carmarthen fourth, while the English Oaks winner of that season, La Laguna (trained by Francois Boutin in France), was fifth and Azincourt from the Argentine seventh.'

Lester added, surprisingly, that a horse he did not ride might well have been the best to have passed through Vincent O'Brien's hands.

'I believe that Golden Fleece could have been the best horse that Vincent ever trained – better even than Nijinsky and Sir Ivor. Few horses win the Epsom Derby from the position he won it from. Yet, although he was last coming down Tattenham Hill and had only three horses behind him as they rounded the Corner, he showed such phenomenal acceleration in the straight that he won unchallenged in the end.

'You cannot overlook, either, the time he recorded that day. It was the fastest by a Derby winner since electrical timing was introduced in 1964. Though Mahmoud's Derby winning time in 1936 was slightly better, they had to rely on hand-timing then. There has to be a question mark, therefore, over that record holding up to modern scrutiny.'

Lester said that Golden Fleece had not really been extended in winning any of his four races. 'If he had not been forced into early retirement after winning the Derby, he could – if we are to go on the speed he showed at Epsom – have been capable of anything.'

Where does Vincent O'Brien himself stand in the debate on the comparative merits of Sir Ivor, Nijinsky and Golden Fleece?

There was a stage – before Golden Fleece's Epsom Derby triumph in 1982 – when he placed Sir Ivor and Nijinsky firmly at the top of his Derby winners. He found it extremely difficult to separate the pair of them. He inclined towards Nijinsky on the score of sheer brilliance on the days of his greatest successes as a three-year-old, in particular the Epsom Derby win and also the victory in the King George VI and Queen Elizabeth Stakes. And yet for the acceleration he showed on Epsom Derby day and his courage in the mud in the Washington International at the end of a terribly long and exacting season, that took in nine races in all, Vincent had to put Sir Ivor right up there with Nijinsky – on the score of durability as much as any other quality.

However, walking back to the house from the gallops one morning in 1987, he stopped at the box which used to accommodate Golden Fleece and I vividly recall hearing him remark aloud to himself just two words: 'What speed.' And he said it in a tone of total admiration. He was referring, of course, to the ground-devouring burst

214

of speed that Golden Fleece had produced in taking the 1982 Epsom Derby. He acknowledged there and then that on his performance that day, there was none faster than this Nijinsky colt.

So in the final analysis Vincent coupled Golden Fleece with Sir Ivor and Nijinsky – the 'Magnificent Three' in a hand of six Epsom Derby winners in the twenty-year period 1962–82. Few would cavil with that. It is deciding in what order the three would finish if contesting the same Derby under ideal conditions that must undoubtedly bring sharply-differing opinions from racing enthusiasts.

Sir Ivor was a big handsome bay colt bred in the United States by Mrs Alice Headley Bell, a descendent of the famous hunter, Daniel Boone. By Sir Gaylord, he was out of a good winning mare in Attica (by Mr Trouble), who traced back to the Aga Khan's Mahmoud, while his grand-dam was second in the Kentucky Derby and had excellent winning form to her credit.

Raymond Guest was in the American Embassy in Dublin and, in a quiet moment, he flicked through the catalogue of the forthcoming Keeneland Sale. There were 600 lots and he fancied two of them. He put a call through to Kentucky to his friend 'Bull' Hancock of Claiborne Farm, one of America's best judges of horseflesh. He instructed 'Bull' to buy whichever of the two horses he thought was the better. Thus 'Bull' Hancock secured Sir Ivor for $42,000.

He ran thirteen races in all, four of them as a two-year-old. He won eight times, was second three times and third once. The only time he failed to reach the frame was in his very first outing as a two-year-old in the Tyros Stakes (6 furlongs) at the Curragh. However, after he had finished fourth, Liam Ward was able to predict confidently to Vincent O'Brien that those that had finished ahead of him that July day would never do so again.

Sir Ivor, with Liam again in the saddle, went on to win the Probationers Stakes and the prestigious National Stakes, both at the Curragh, and then in the hands of Lester Piggott showed the brilliant acceleration in taking the Grand Criterium (8 furlongs) at Longchamp in October that convinced both Vincent O'Brien and Lester that this colt was something else entirely.

Sir Ivor's owner, Raymond Guest, went for a real old-fashioned 'touch' on the Epsom Derby. He struck a bet with William Hill of £500 each-way at odds of 100–1. It was amazing that a bookmaker who was one of the pioneers in ante-post betting and whose judgement of odds was legendary should be caught to the extent that he stood to lose £62,500 on one single bet.

'Even before Sir Ivor ran in the National Stakes, I knew I had a pretty good colt on my hands,' said Raymond Guest as he recalled for Richard Baerlein of *The Observer* and *The Guardian* how he came to strike that famous bet. 'I expected Sir Ivor to win the National Stakes so it was essential to get in before that race if I was to get the best odds going at that point on him for the Derby.

'I did not know William Hill at the time, so I asked a friend of mine who knew him well to ring him up. I told him I had three horses entered for the 1968 Derby and I wanted a price about each of them. They were all quoted at 100–1. No sooner had I made the bet than Sir Ivor won the National Stakes and then the Grand Criterium at Longchamp. Owing to the American tax laws, I only kept about £16,000 out of total winnings of £62,500.

'Before the Derby, William Hill approached me and wanted me to lay off my bet. This was impossible because I would have had to pay tax on the total winnings to the American Treasury and would have had to pay in full any price I laid to Hill. I told him that if he paid me £20,000 I would call the bet off. Out of this sum I would be able to keep about £15,000 and would be about as well off as if my horse won the Derby.

'It would have saved William Hill £42,500 but he would not do the deal. "You are a hard man to do business with," he said to me. I replied that I was in the business to make money.'

The bookmakers never recovered their money from Raymond Guest over Larkspur and Sir Ivor. He announced in June 1968 that he did not intend to have another bet.

Sir Ivor wintered in Italy with seven other horses from Ballydoyle. The mild weather in the area around Pisa seems to have been of marked benefit to the colt, for in his first outing as a three-year-old he won the Ascot 2000 Guineas Trial (7 furlongs) despite the very heavy going. After he had beaten Petingo, the Gimcrack and Middle Park Stakes winner, in the 2000 Guineas on 1 May, he was immediately installed favourite for the 1968 Derby, though breeding purists doubted whether he would really get beyond 10 furlongs.

But Sir Ivor, winner now of five races off the reel and unbeaten as a three-year-old, had really caught the imagination of the public and was down to even-money favourite on the Saturday before the Epsom Classic. On the day of the race itself he dropped to 4–5, and would become the shortest-priced winner since Cicero (4–11) in 1905.

Raymond Guest, in his capacity as American Ambassador to Ireland, could not be at Epsom as he was in Wexford that day for the official opening of a memorial park for President Kennedy. A television set was strategically placed at a point beside the VIP stand where he made his speech. It enabled him to see the telecast of the race.

Michael Phillips reported the race thus in *The Times:* 'It was a privilege to have been at Epsom to see a great horse, ridden by a great jockey and trained by an absolute master, win the Derby. I refer to Sir Ivor, Lester Piggott and Vincent O'Brien. What a combination! For sheer brilliance, their great victory will not be matched for many a day.

'When Piggott gathered Sir Ivor for his effort one furlong and a half from the finish, the response was instant, and had to be seen to be believed. "He did it," Piggott said later, "in a few strides." This the camera patrol film bore out. In those last 300 yards, Sir Ivor dramatically cut down Connaught's advantage. From a position four lengths behind Connaught one moment, Sir Ivor was soon on level terms and was on his way to victory.

'Connaught was glorious in defeat and was ridden with fine judgement by young Sandy Barclay, who ruefully said later: "It was just our fellow's misfortune to be foaled in the same year as Sir Ivor." In his quiet unassuming way, Barclay paid high tribute to Sir Ivor when he said that all the way up the straight Connaught was really running for him; yet when Sir Ivor passed him, it was as though he had just jumped in!'

The late Maurice O'Callaghan, who had been with Vincent O'Brien 33 years on the day of Sir Ivor's triumph, went down to the start with the colt and then, despite his 56 years, sprinted back across the Downs to the finish – and was there on hand as Raymond Guest's wife, Caroline, led him in.

In addition to the £62,500 cheque for the winning bet with William Hill, Raymond Guest won £58,525 prizemoney – a total of £121,025. Not long after the Derby, he retired as American Ambassador to Ireland. He made a fine parting gesture to the Irish people by saying 'thank you' for three wonderful years in the most fitting way possible. He decided to stand Sir Ivor at his stud, Ballygoran Park, near Maynooth, County Kildare, for one year before the horse was sent to Claiborne.

When it became known that Sir Ivor was going to stand in Europe – if only for a limited time – requests for nominations came pouring in. There were only 30 available, ten of which the owner was retaining himself. The fee was £4,000 per nomination – the previous highest in Ireland and Britain being about £3,000.

Sir Ivor had two crops while standing in Ireland and these produced Cavo Doro, second to Morston in the 1973 Epsom Derby, and Imperial Prince, runner-up to Snow Knight in the Epsom Classic the following season. Moving to America, he produced horses of the highest calibre, Classic winners among them, including Ivanjica, winner of the French 1000 Guineas and Prix de l'Arc de Triomphe; Lady Capulet, winner of the Irish 1000 Guineas, and Godetia, winner of the Irish 1000 Guineas and Irish Oaks, and he also sired Malinowski, Bates Motel and St Hilarion. Breeding experts have continually made the point that Sir Ivor's daughters have enjoyed more pronounced success than his sons.

Nijinsky has without any question completely overshadowed Sir Ivor, not only as a sire but also as a sire of sires. In 1988 eight of his sons sired group/graded winners. In 1984 a nomination to Nijinsky cost $450,000 dollars. That shows how much he was in demand.

Lester Piggott was 31 the day Sir Ivor won the Derby in 1968 and Sandy Barclay, the 'boy wonder' of the decade, was only 19. Twenty-one years later I met Sandy Barclay on 2000 Guineas Day 1989 in Newmarket – he is now a work rider, the glory days but a cherished memory – and he had no hesitation in putting Sir Ivor ahead of Nijinsky. None whatsoever. The veil was lifted and we went back to that moment at Epsom in 1968 as he talked to the racing writers in the aftermath of a so-galling defeat after doing everything right.

'I thought Sir Ivor wouldn't stay, but when I saw him there half a furlong out, although my chap was running on, I knew that we'd had it.' And then he came up with the immortal quote: 'He is the most brilliant horse I have ever seen – in all my nineteen years!'

He still remains the most brilliant for Sandy.

22

Piggott On Nijinsky's Arc Failure

Lester Piggott did not flinch when he recalled his most controversial defeat while riding for Vincent O'Brien: Nijinsky's failure by a short head in the 1970 Prix de l'Arc de Triomphe.

He was not in the least perturbed by the theories advanced in previously published books that (1) he asked Nijinsky to do too much by forcing the colt to make his run from too far back; (2) he lost the race through over-confidence as he assumed that Nijinsky, with his great turn of pace, could pick up those in front of him immediately the button was pressed and (3) when he hit Nijinsky with his whip, the horse swerved left with fatal consequences.

Now Lester Piggott, a professional to his finger-tips, had always this communion of minds with Vincent O'Brien. Vincent did not have to give him instructions as he would some apprentice or a young jockey making his way up the ladder. The two invariably discussed things on a basis of equality, man-to-man, before and after each race and no one valued Lester's opinion more than Vincent.

'Once Vincent was satisfied that I knew a horse, especially after I had ridden it, he would not bother me with instructions. Yes, we would of course discuss things in a general way. When he had a jockey riding for him all the time and had built up a special relationship with that rider, it wasn't his way to give too many orders. And that was the way I liked it.'

In the discussion they had over the phone in the countdown to the Prix de l'Arc, it was agreed that Lester should 'lie up', Vincent making the point that few horses left with a deal of ground to make up in the short straight at Longchamp went on to triumph in the Arc.

Vincent feared also that in a race like the Arc, in which the field really 'goes' all the way, beaten horses would be coming back on Nijinsky and there was a distinct possibility that he might be obstructed by a sudden wall in front of him when making his run.

Looking back without emotion to that first Sunday in October 1970, Lester discounted all the theories that had made him seem to be the villain of the piece.

'Nijinsky did not really go in the first part of the race,' he said. 'I could not lay up as I had done in previous races. The pace was reasonable enough. There was nothing crazy about it. But I could feel Nijinsky struggling a bit under me in those early stages.

'I decided then not to rush him, to let him settle in order to see if he would come to himself and at the crucial stage of the race give me that "feel" I had always got from him on his great days. When we turned into the straight he was further behind than I would have wished. I had the choice of going in for the rails or else I could eliminate any danger of getting boxed in by moving to the outside. With horses in front of me on the inside, I switched outside.

'Now Nijinsky was moving at last and I reckoned we had a chance of winning, even though we had a deal of ground to make up. I was certainly not as far off the leaders as was inferred by some commentators later. Nijinsky in his Epsom Derby form would have easily cut down any of those in front of him. As it was I got in front of Sassafras and Yves Saint-Martin about one hundred and fifty yards from the finish. I felt then I was going to win, though Nijinsky didn't go away as he had done at Epsom.

'Just about thirty yards from the post, Nijinsky swerved

to his left for no reason at all. It was not because I showed him the whip, as some have claimed. He had never done it before in all the races in which I had ridden him.

'I did not have time to change my whip to the other hand. He only had to keep a straight line to win it. That sudden swerve cost him the race – but only by the narrowest of margins.

'I know beyond any shadow of doubt that I would have won it but for Nijinsky reacting as he did with the post within sight and the race at his mercy. Everything else does not matter. The fact that I got in front of Sassafras one hundred and fifty yards from the post proves that Nijinsky had the beating of the French colt – even though patently not at his best that day.'

Lester is convinced now in retrospect that the bout of ringworm, which resulted in Nijinsky going for the St Leger on a rather rushed preparation, was the root cause of the fatal swerve that ultimately lost him his unbeaten record and led in turn to the disastrous decision to go for the Champion Stakes to try and erase the Longchamp defeat.

As Phonsie O'Brien put it: 'Charlie Engelhard knew his time in this life was limited and he wanted to see Nijinsky complete the Triple Crown by winning the Leger. Vincent wanted to give the colt all the time he needed after the bout of ringworm before going for the primary objective, the Arc de Triomphe, but Engelhard wanted to have his way.'

Nijinsky completed the Triple Crown by taking the Leger – the first horse to win the three colts' Classics since Bahram in 1935 – but Lester Piggott said unhesitatingly; 'Frankly, I was disappointed with his running in the Doncaster Classic. Perhaps afterwards we may have thought that he needed the race, but certainly I wasn't too happy with him. Looking back on it now, there seems little doubt that the ringworm had left its mark and that race, instead of bringing him on, saw him unable to go through with it at the critical point through no fault of his own in the Arc.'

Vincent O'Brien revealed that Nijinsky lost close on 30

pounds after the St Leger (Nashwan, in contrast, lost only four pounds for his exertions in adding the Coral-Eclipse Stakes to the English 2000 Guineas and Epsom Derby triumphs in 1989. His trainer, Major Dick Hern, reported that you would not be surprised if a horse lost up to 20 pounds after such a race. But certainly not 30 pounds).

In hindsight Nijinsky should *never* have run at Doncaster, even though the temptation to see him complete the Triple Crown was very great, especially for his owner.

Lester described Nijinsky as 'an exceptional colt from the time I started to ride him on the gallops at Ballydoyle.

'Because he was a big horse, you noticed him more than the others. When he galloped beside other horses, he made them look like selling platers. Yes, I knew he was special from the very outset. He ran more times as a two-year-old than you would find with many horses of his class.'

In fact, he had five races, winning all of them, including the Railway, Anglesey, Beresford and Dewhurst Stakes.

'But he had a problem with his insides – he got colic very easily. Because of that, it was necessary to really keep him going all the time.'

Lester recalled how this colic problem reared its head 24 hours before the Epsom Derby and it looked odds-on for most of one long agonising day that he would have to be withdrawn.

'As Vincent told it to me, Johnny Brabston, his regular work rider, had worked him on the course and it was when he was back in his stable at the racecourse that they noticed he had started to sweat up. It got worse. Vincent rang his vet, Bob Griffin, and reported the symptoms to him, expressing his own view from long experience that it seemed to him that the colt had a slight touch of colic. Both Bob and Vincent agreed that there was no way he could be injected so close to the race. The Epsom vet, who had meanwhile been contacted, confirmed that Nijinsky actually had a twinge of colic. All Vincent could do was hope – and pray.'

The prayers were answered – for late that same evening

Nijinsky was eating tentatively and soon a very relieved trainer, who had stayed with him throughout the crisis, was able to breathe easily again, knowing that the colt was back to himself.

After easily justifying odds of 4–7 (the shortest odds-on favourite since Colombo in 1934) when mastering Yellow God by two and a half lengths in the English 2000 Guineas, Nijinsky started 11–8 for the Epsom Derby.

If Vincent had issued a statement to the media immediately Nijinsky contracted that twinge of colic and it had hit the evening papers, it would have thrown the ante-post market into total confusion. The big bookmakers had very heavy liabilities. Betting would have been suspended automatically. In the circumstances Vincent would have been on a hiding to nothing. Supposing then, on the attack of colic being overcome, he had been forced to retract his earlier statement, it might well have been construed in a totally wrong manner, especially if Nijinsky won – as he did. In hindsight, it can be seen that he was very wise not to rush his fences but to hold fire until he was absolutely certain as to whether Nijinsky could take his place in the field or not.

As in the case of Sir Ivor, there were breeding purists who contended that Nijinsky might be shown to have stamina limitations for the final 2 furlongs of the Derby distance. Gyr had a lot of admirers. Etienne Pollet had put off retiring for a year in the hope that this impressive-looking chestnut colt would give him a second Epsom Derby triumph to supplement that of the peerless Sea Bird II in 1965. And Stintino was not without his supporters either.

But in the fast going prevailing on that June afternoon at Epsom, there was no withstanding Lester's final surge as he brought Charles Engelhard's colt with an irresistible run to beat Gyr by 2½ lengths, with Stintino a further 3 lengths away third. The form was franked when Gyr went on to an easy victory in the Grand Prix de St Cloud.

Nijinsky would never again start at odds against. He was 4–11 when Liam Ward rode him to win the Irish Derby and 40–85 when taking the King George VI and

Queen Elizabeth Stakes – with Lester back in the saddle – in sweeping fashion by 2 lengths, beating two previous Derby winners in the process.

In thirteen races over two seasons, he was never out of the frame. The final record would read: won, eleven; second, two.

Nijinsky can best be remembered as the colt that helped really to put Northern Dancer on the map as a sire, and in the process changed the face of breeding on both sides of the Atlantic. He was from Northern Dancer's second crop, being out of Canadian Oaks winner, Flaming Page by Bull Page. As related earlier, once Vincent saw the colt at E. P. Taylor's Windfields Farm in Canada, he advised Charles Engelhard to buy him. Charles Engelhard – simply Charlie to his friends in the racing world – had the resources to pay $84,000 easily for him, even though it was a record for a Canadian sale at the time.

Born in New York in 1917, he was a classic member of the American Establishment, having graduated from Princeton University and seen service as a bomber pilot, ranked Captain, with the U.S. Army Air Corps during the Second World War. His immense wealth was made out of minerals. He was Chairman of Engelhard Minerals and Chemicals Corporation, Engelhard Hanovia Incorporated and of the American South African Investment Company Ltd. He represented the American President at the Independence Day ceremonies in Gabon in 1962 and again at the Coronation of Pope Paul VI in 1963 after the death of Pope John XXIII. The right clubs, the right restaurants, the right hotels were his natural milieus, and yet he had that easy zest for life, that *joie de vivre* that made him love the funny side of things. Phonsie O'Brien, who doesn't suffer shams easily – even if they have millions in the bank and a private jet – could talk with affection about 'my friend Charlie' as he recalled the fabulous 'Nijinsky days'.

On the day that Nijinsky won the Irish Sweeps Derby at the Curragh, Charlie Engelhard's wide frame almost filled one end of the VIP presentation stand. The rains came down as Anna McGrath, wife of Paddy McGrath,

225

was presenting him with the winning owner's trophy in the form of a chalice and Charlie Engelhard came up with the classic throwaway remark: 'If this goes on much longer, the water in this chalice will turn into wine!'

His racing interests stretched from the United States to Ireland and Britain and South Africa. He had his own manager in David McCall to look after his interests in Europe. Before the Arab sheikhs engaged a plethora of trainers to train their horses, he had five trainers training his charges in Britain and Ireland; Vincent O'Brien, of course, being the trainer he relied upon in Ireland. Apart from Nijinsky, his familiar colours of green, yellow sleeves and scarlet cap were carried with distinction over a decade – the 'seventies – by Classic winners like Indiana, winner of the 1964 English St Leger; Ribocco, winner of the 1967 Irish Derby and English St Leger; Ribero, winner of the 1968 Irish Derby and English St Leger, and other good horses of the calibre of Ribofilio (runner-up in the Irish Derby to Prince Regent in 1969), Romulus and Habitat. Another owner would have had the champagne corks popping if he had owned Ribocco and Ribero in successive seasons, but when you command centre-stage with a Triple Crown winner like Nijinsky all the lesser actors – irrespective of how good they are – tend to be dwarfed in the scale of things.

Charles Engelhard was only 54 when he died in 1971, having battled unsuccessfully with a weight problem (because of the injuries he had suffered to his legs in a crash-landing while in the U.S. Airforce he was unable to take exercise and was constantly in pain). But then he was the owner in his time of a colt called Nijinsky – named after the Russian ballet dancer, Vaslav Nijinsky, who won a supreme place among male dancers when brought by Diaghilev to Paris and London before the First World War, especially for his spell-binding performance in *Les Sylphides, Spectre de la Rose* and *L'Après-midi d'un Faune.*

Enough.

How many have outlived him by twenty, yes thirty years and have dreamed their dream of success in the Blue Riband of racing on the Epsom Downs on a day in

June and seen it unfulfilled – when even a moderate winner by the ultimate standards would have satisfied that ambition. And failed too to merit – as he naturally did – a mention in *Who's Who*. Not, mark you, as a minerals 'King' primarily, but because he came to be known on both sides of the Atlantic through a champion of champions carrying his colours; and the videos that Nijinsky created outlive the mundane question, which might interest some, of how much Charlie left when he passed on and his widow, June, dispersed the once-proud racing empire.

If racing horses was a hobby for Nijinsky's owner, Charlie Engelhard, and investing in minerals the source of his wealth, it was far different in the case of John Galbreath, who was deeply involved in bloodstock and sport generally, being the owner of the Darby Dan Stud Farm in Kentucky and also of the Pittsburgh Pirates. He prided himself on his knowledge of sports injuries, which was to become a very important factor in the fierce controversy that developed through the jocking-off of Bill Williamson from his colt Roberto on the eve of 1972's Epsom Derby.

Owners of baseball or football clubs in America are not noted as out-and-out philanthropists, who simply want their names up in lights. They can be generous, yes, but at the same time take ruthless decisions; you would hardly survive long in what some might describe as shark-infested waters if you adopted the softly-softly approach every day.

John Galbreath had been introduced to Vincent at the Saratoga Sales, an introduction that led to the American asking the Master of Ballydoyle to train for him and in due course sending him Roberto, whom he had bred himself.

The Derby was due to be run on 7 June. Bill ('Weary Willie') Williamson took a heavy fall on 27 May at Kempton when riding a horse called The Broker. He injured his shoulder. He immediately went for treatment, and was in the expert hands of Bill Tucker, a physiotherapist, who had a big clientele among sportsmen. Bill told the Australian that he would be fit to ride

Roberto in the Derby and actually gave him the green light to go ahead and resume riding in advance of Derby Day itself.

But, significantly, Vincent O'Brien, with his exactness for detail, made contact himself with Bill Tucker and, while getting confirmation that Bill Williamson should be fit enough to ride Roberto, was informed that the only way it would be revealed that he was 100 per cent perfect was when he actually got back in the saddle.

Vincent was naturally worried. From long experience he realised only too well that it was one thing to give a two-year-old or an experienced handicapper a gentle ride in a race at Salisbury or some other track. It represented a far greater test of an injured shoulder if it came to a do-or-die battle up the hill at Epsom in the hurly-burly of the Derby. And, furthermore, he realised that Roberto, unlike Sir Ivor or Nijinsky, would probably need to be driven with power at the finish.

If Williamson was not going to be 100 per cent fit, then Vincent was convinced that Lester was the man for the job. John Galbreath knew from bitter experience how a player 80 per cent fit – no matter how good – could let you down in the crunch.

It did not help 'Weary Willie's' cause either that he was judged by experienced race readers to have left Roberto with too much to do in the 2000 Guineas, failing by a diminishing ½ length to the 85–40 favourite High Top and Willie Carson. Lester, who rode Grey Mirage in the Newmarket race after Crowned Prince was retired with a soft palate, was quite forthright in expressing the opinion to Vincent O'Brien afterwards that he would have won the race if he had had the mount on Roberto. Inherent in that comment was the clear hint that he could do a Sir Ivor or a Nijinsky at Epsom.

However, it was not clear initially that Roberto would actually be Vincent O'Brien's number-one choice for the Derby. Boucher and Manitoulon (owned incidentally by John Galbreath's wife, Dorothy) were both being mentioned very favourably in dispatches and it resulted in Roberto being on offer immediately after the Guineas at the amazing odds – in hindsight – of 8–1, though he started at 3–1 on Derby Day.

Lester actually went over to Ballydoyle to ride Manitoulon, and Roberto was involved in the same piece of work. Roberto came out best but idled when in front – a fact that Lester was not aware of until Vincent told him afterwards. It immediately altered his opinion at the end of the work that Roberto would not win the Derby.

Lester's uncanny 'inner eye' had spotted a quality in Roberto as he went by Manitoulon, and later he quizzed Vincent about the colt. As the Master elaborated, Lester dismissed Manitoulon, whom he had originally preferred as a possible Derby mount, from his Epsom calculations. He came to such conclusions coldly and without sentiment. He would be ready to ride Roberto – if the call came.

The crucial point in the 'Roberto Affair' was that Bill Williamson was due to ride out for an Epsom trainer on the Tuesday morning – the eve of the Derby. Vincent O'Brien and John Galbreath waited most anxiously to hear how his shoulder had stood up to the test.

They were told that Bill had not turned up to ride work because he had overslept. John Galbreath took a very poor view of this and it was then that he made up his mind to put up Lester on Roberto. Vincent agreed with the owner's decision.

The Australian was asked to meet Roberto's owner and trainer in Claridge's on the Tuesday night. When Vincent arrived at the hotel John Galbreath had already conveyed the message to Williamson. At the same time Williamson was informed that he would receive exactly the same percentage (that is 10 per cent of £63,735) as Lester in the event of Roberto winning the race.

Naturally, Williamson was shocked and very upset at being 'jocked off' and took the decision very badly. The fact that he was promised the same percentage as Piggott did not change his mood one iota. His resentment was all the deeper when on Derby Day itself he rode two winners, Captive Dream in the Woodcote and Capistrano in the

Craven Stakes. Those in sympathy with his lot cheered him in resounding fashion as he passed the winning post each time.

When the dust had settled, however, one fact over-shadowed all else – Lester Piggott had done the job he was detailed to do by bringing Roberto home a winner by the tip of a nostril in one of the most dramatic finishes ever to an Epsom Derby.

The verdict was a short head in favour of the Vincent O'Brien-trained colt in a photo finish with Rheingold (Ernie Johnson). And Roberto had to survive a lengthy Stewards' Enquiry before keeping the race. Had Roberto edged away from the rails? Was it Piggott's fault that Johnson could not use his whip?

Hotspur (Peter Scott) in the *Daily Telegraph* wrote next day that Rheingold had bumped Roberto as they passed the pacemaking Pentland Firth a furlong and a half out. 'Roberto was knocked on to Pentland Firth, who had just come away from the rails. Ernie Johnson, whose only previous Derby mount was the 1969 winner, Blakeney, found Rheingold so unbalanced on this course that he had to ride out the colt with hands and heels in case the whip would cause Rheingold to create further trouble!' He concluded that 'disqualification might have followed a victory for Rheingold'.

There is no need to dwell on the controversy that stemmed from Lester's alleged liberal use of the whip to get Roberto home. Vincent was not complaining and neither was John Galbreath. They both saw the colt in the stables shortly after the race and reported that he was in excellent form, without a mark on him.

Lester's admirers were unanimous that he had never ridden a more powerful or stronger finish and that it was his strength that actually lifted Roberto to victory when the Barry Hills-trained Rheingold, the better stayer (he would win the Prix de l'Arc de Triomphe the following year with Lester in the saddle) seemed to have the race in his grasp.

Vincent O'Brien himself said unhesitatingly that Lester had ridden 'a wonderful race' and he doubted whether

Bill Williamson could have powered Roberto home in the same fashion.

The admirers of Williamson, remembering his brilliant Prix de l'Arc de Triomphe triumphs on Vaguely Noble (1968) and Levmoss (1969) – beating Lester on both occasions – would contend that he would have got Roberto to run for him in that special quiet, unflurried way of his and would have won without having to go for the whip.

One could go on for ever discussing this question. The fact remains that Roberto became locked in a desperate battle with Rheingold and Lester came out best in that battle, so that Roberto went into the record books as Vincent's fourth Derby winner.

Roberto's time of 2 minutes 36.09 seconds had been bettered only by Nijinsky in the ten previous Derbys.

The rest of the Roberto story does not bear comparison with the Nijinsky or Sir Ivor stories. He could only finish fourth in a very hot Grand Criterium and was unplaced in the Irish Derby and in the Prix de l'Arc de Triomphe. Kept in training as a four-year-old, he won the Coronation Cup but was unplaced in the King George VI and Queen Elizabeth Stakes.

Legitimate arguments can be advanced to uphold the assumption that his record could have been much better. Lester had deserted Roberto in favour of Rheingold for the Benson & Hedges Gold Cup and John Galbreath was not at all pleased. Vincent flew in the American-based Panamanian rider, Braulio Baeza. He had every reason to be happy with the ride that Baeza gave Roberto that day at York, for not only did he beat Rheingold but he swamped the up-to-then-unbeaten Brigadier Gerard. However, he does not conceal his belief that the same pillar-to-post tactics – dead against instructions – at Longchamp, when Roberto had an outstanding chance of victory on the fast going that was all in his favour, killed any prospect of success even before the straight was reached.

The trainer was also running Boucher, who was ridden

by the star American Lafitte Pincay. One would have thought that Pincay would have ridden the English St Leger winner of that season for stamina rather than speed but, to Vincent's astonishment, the American jockey set out to make it all to 'the wire' and got involved in a cut-throat sprint with Roberto from the moment the tapes went up. Roberto finished seventh.

Roberto ran best on left-hand tracks, nearly breaking the course record when winning the Coronation Cup as a four-year-old at Epsom. It cannot be overlooked either that he was obviously a true 10-furlong horse.

A Hail to Reason colt out of eight-times winner in the States, Bramalea (by Nashua), Roberto did not have the best of knees, a fact which Vincent, with his expert knowledge of every aspect of breeding, noted can be a drawback with the progeny of this sire. It was to result in Roberto missing key races at the peak of his career.

After running him on heavy going at the Phoenix Park in the Vauxhall Trial Stakes (7 furlongs), a traditional trial for the 2000 Guineas, Vincent was warned not to risk him in such conditions again, as his knees could have suffered permanent damage. Vincent had no qualms then in pulling him out of the 1973 Eclipse Stakes on the morning of the race, even though he was odds-on favourite (it was run at Kempton that year because of reconstruction work at Sandown). Later Vincent took the same decision when the horse was being aimed at a second successive Benson & Hedges at York. And he took that decision, after spending nearly two hours inspecting the soft going, in the best interest of the horse, despite public fury and criticisms voiced in the media.

A Stewards' Inquiry was held before the start of racing into the circumstances of his decision to withdraw both Roberto and Roberto's half-brother, Cambrian, entered in the Acomb Stakes, at the eleventh hour. The official statement from the Stewards spoke of 'no material change in the going' and they fined the trainer £25 in addition to a fixed penalty in respect of each horse (though Sir Noel Murless said that the Stewards fined the wrong man in Vincent O'Brien!).

Vincent had hoped that Roberto could end his racing career on a high note by winning the Champion Stakes. However, he suffered a setback in training and was retired to stud duties at his owner's Darby Dan Farm in Kentucky. Compared with the valuations subsequently put on The Minstrel, Alleged, Golden Fleece and El Gran Senor, his syndication at £1.35 million seems small in retrospect, taking into account the fact that he not only sired good horses but was also a successful sire of sires.

Among his sons was Touching Wood, the 1982 English St Leger winner, and Driving Home, an outstanding champion in Canada, as well as Lear Fan, At Talaq, Bob Back, Sookera, Critique and Read Shadai.

He died at Darby Dan Farm in August 1988 shortly after the death of his owner-breeder John Galbreath. That same year had been one of his most successful, with a trio of high-class US three-year-olds, Sunshine Forever, Brian's Time and Dynaformer. His European runners included smart performers such as Al Mufti, Tralos, Zalazl, Tursanah and Mamaluna. He also figured as broodmare sire of the brilliantly fast Warning, while five of his sons sired Group or Graded winners, so his influence looks set to endure.

All the more reason to conclude that Vincent O'Brien and John Galbreath were correct in opting for Lester to ride him in the Epsom Derby.

Enter now yet another millionaire into the world of Vincent O'Brien, who unlike Charles Engelhard and John Galbreath – both American to the core – was Irish natural born, a self-made man who represented the classic example of one who made it right to the top of the ladder from the humblest beginnings.

John A. Mulcahy, 'Jack' to his friends, was born in Dungarvan, County Waterford, and took the emigrant ship to the United States at the age of 18. He returned a millionaire, having joined the Quigley (furnace-making) Corporation and worked his way up to become treasurer and then President and majority stockholder.

Vincent was introduced to John Mulcahy by the latter's

brother, Dan, an old friend of the O'Brien family and attached to the Munster and Leinster Bank (now A.I.B.) in Cork, where Vincent had maintained an account since he started training.

One day, during a fishing expedition, the talk turned to horses and racing. John Mulcahy had read that Vincent was the top trainer in the world, and wanted to know what rewards there were in it for the trainer, especially when he trained a Classic winner. He was told that all the trainer got was a percentage of the winning prize money – that is if he did not gamble.

'I couldn't believe that this man who was known around the globe was getting nothing more than a fee for the expertise he used in picking and training top-class horses,' John Mulcahy told journalist Seamus McConville in a contribution to the book *Horse Racing* (edited by Finbarr Slattery).

No one knows how many fish were caught during that long day on Lough Currane but Vincent O'Brien 'netted' a new owner in John Mulcahy. And at the same time the millionaire, with his experience of how business worked in the States, impressed upon Vincent that in future he must *always* get what he called 'a slice of the action' whenever he went to the sales and bought a yearling or when, in time, one of the horses he trained to become a Classic winner was syndicated as a stallion. In a word, he must not rely on winning percentages alone. He must become an entrepreneur in his own right.

John Mulcahy suggested that Vincent start by pressing for at least a 5 per cent slice of the action in every horse he took into Ballydoyle to train.

'Vincent said he couldn't do that but I told him there was no deal as far as I was concerned unless he did,' recalled John Mulcahy.

So a new partnership was born and with it a complete change in Vincent's modus operandi. Already Vincent and 'Bull' Hancock of the Claiborne Stud Farm in Kentucky had become close friends, and John Mulcahy, with his shrewd business brain, saw immediately how this could be utilised to translate the philosophy he had expounded to the Master of Ballydoyle into something that would make a highly significant impact on the racing scene.

The idea simply was that instead of all the Claiborne yearlings being sent to the sales, some of them would be trained by Vincent O'Brien and another percentage in the States (a number running in 'Bull' Hancock's own colours and others in his friend Bill Perry's colours). Vincent and his patrons not only got Apalachee and Lisadell in the first lot but also a slice of the action. And one of the most successful horses of all that arrived at Ballydoyle through this concept was Thatch, rated the outstanding miler in Europe in 1973.

Like all owners John Mulcahy had his ups and downs and he regarded it as a 'hell of a loss' that Cloonlara, carrying a foal by Northern Dancer, was killed by lightning at Claiborne. He never realised his great ambition to be part owner of an Epsom Derby winner. But the influence he had on Vincent O'Brien as a result of that day's fishing on Lough Currane was in a way more invaluable than if he had seen his colours carried to victory at Epsom by a horse trained at Ballydoyle.

23

'Let The Pilot Do The Flying'

Robert Sangster has always operated by one golden maxim: when you board a plane, you leave it to the pilot to do the flying. 'When the passengers decide to fly the plane themselves, then it's time for you to get off,' says Sangster.

He never deserted that maxim once he decided to team up with Vincent O'Brien – a partnership that was to develop into one of the most powerful and successful in racing history.

Robert Sangster recalled the time in 1977, the year of The Minstrel and Alleged, when he had to leave the 'flying' to his trusted 'pilot' Vincent O'Brien – 'the best trainer in the world' – and a valued friendship was nearly killed in the process.

After the Epsom Derby The Minstrel and Alleged worked together on the Ballydoyle gallops. It was not a formal trial as such, for as Robert Sangster pointed out, Vincent does not normally go in for that sort of thing. 'He knows the ability of each individual horse so well that it is not necessary for him to hold trials to ascertain what he has already concluded in his mind,' said Sangster.

Alleged came out ahead of the 1977 Derby winner on the gallops that summer morning and when Vincent rang Robert Sangster, he sounded very excited, informing him: 'We've got an exceptional horse on our hands.'

Now came the moment of decision – which colt would

the stable run at the Curragh, as it was most unlikely that the two would be pitted against each other?

Alleged, of which Robert Sangster owned a third at that stage, was running in the colours of another part-owner, the Californian multi-millionaire, the late Bob Fluor, of the Fluor Corporation. He was in the game for sport, certainly not for money. He wanted all his friends to be at the Curragh the day Alleged ran in the Irish Derby.

'Vincent didn't want to upset Bob Fluor, who was one of nature's gentlemen,' said Robert Sangster. 'I could see he was worried when we were together at the Royal Ascot meeting. "What do you think?" he asked me. "Well, Vincent you are the trainer," I replied. "As far as I am concerned, the final decision rests with you and with no one else. You can take it from there." ' And Vincent did.

In deciding on whether to run Alleged or The Minstrel at the Curragh, he was swayed in favour of running the Epsom Derby winner because he believed that if it came up firm, then these conditions would suit The Minstrel better. Secondly, his long-term target for Alleged was the Prix de l'Arc de Triomphe and he wanted nothing to stand in the way of the achievement of that goal.

The decision was conveyed to Bob Fluor that Alleged was not after all to run at the Curragh. He did not like it. He made his feelings known to Robert Sangster and Sangster admits that his Californian friend, 'wasn't at all happy' at having to go back to all the people he had told to prepare for a real old bash at the Curragh that the deal was off.

'I thought at one point we were going to fall out over it,' Sangster recalled, 'but our friendship was too firmly based to actually break on it. Happily it survived.'

Sangster was proved correct in leaving it to the pilot to do the flying. The Minstrel duly won the Irish Derby by 1½ lengths, though he had to survive an objection by the second, Lucky Sovereign, after veering outwards across the course, and the Stewards held an inquiry into possible interference. And Alleged justified Vincent's judgement in winning the Prix de l'Arc de Triomphe on the first Sunday in October.

In two races The Minstrel and Alleged netted £213,640.57 (the Irish Derby being worth £72,795 and the Prix de l'Arc de Triomphe £140,845.57).

Robert Sangster said emphatically, 'Lester had two inspired rides that season – first on The Minstrel in the Epsom Derby and then on Alleged in the Arc.

'Before the Arc we had a meeting in the George V Hotel,' he went on. 'Vincent knew that Alleged was badly drawn. I knew it also. We both knew it rested on Lester's genius to overcome the luck of the draw and produce Alleged in the straight with every chance of winning. Fortunately, as Lester predicted to us, the field didn't go the crazy pace that you often get in the Arc and that was because a number of riders felt they were in with a chance of winning, so were holding back their mounts for a late run. Lester had Alleged close to the leaders as they reached the top of the hill and soon he was second. He went for his race as they turned into the short straight and nothing was going to catch him once he took the lead. Yes, it was undoubtedly his best piece of riding that season, apart from the brilliance he showed when winning at Epsom.'

Alleged turned out to be one of the best and most profitable buys in the whole history of bloodstock transactions.

'When he was offered for sale as a yearling at the 1975 Keeneland July Sales,' recalled Robert Sangster, 'he was led out unsold at $34,000. He was very immature and scrawny looking and, indeed, one onlooker went so far as to comment that he was like a drowned rat in appearance.

'Billy McDonald (acting on Sangster's behalf) spotted something in the colt that he liked, so he helped trainer Monty Roberts to buy him privately for $34,000. Monty had the idea that he would re-submit him as a two-year-old at a sale in California.

'I didn't make it to the sale in California but Billy McDonald was there acting for me and knew where to contact me. He bought Alleged for $120,000 before he went into the ring. On my instructions the colt was then allowed to be put up for auction and I was actually prepared to let him go if he reached $200,000. Billy bought him back for $175,000.

'Hoss Inman was the underbidder. After Billy had signed the docket, Hoss, wearing a white Texan hat, came up to him and asked, "Will you take a profit?"

'Billy rang me and I told him, "Ask for $200,000 and if he agrees, the horse is his."

'Billy asked $225,000. Hoss's reaction was – "$200,000 dollars is my limit. No deal, son."

'I was so lucky that Billy decided to add on that additional $25,000 and that Hoss dug in his heels at $200,000.

'So we kept Alleged and the plan initially was that we would have him trained in California by Tom Pratt. But, fortunately, I was advised that the horse wouldn't be happy on the dirt tracks, that the spins he had already had on this surface had affected his knees somewhat. There was nothing for it but to send him to Europe and that meant, of course, putting him into training with Vincent O'Brien.' Again destiny was operating in Vincent's favour.

'I was bid $1 million for Alleged after he won the Great Voltigeur at York in 1977 by 8 lengths and trailing behind him were Hot Grove, second to The Minstrel at Epsom, and Lucky Sovereign and Classic Example, second and third respectively to the same colt in the Irish Derby. Some commentators raved about that performance by Alleged and Vincent told me afterwards that he could hardly believe the ease of it.'

Robert Sangster turned down the $1 million bid for Alleged. Instead, he actually bought out Shirley Taylor's share and now he was sitting on a gold mine – even though Alleged was to be beaten in the St Leger on his way to Longchamp.

After winning the Prix de l'Arc de Triomphe for the second year running in 1978, Alleged was syndicated for $13 million in Kentucky. Set that against the $120,000 that Sangster originally paid for him and you can really appreciate what a bargain he was when Billy McDonald picked him out.

Robert Sangster explained how the figure of $13 million was reached in assessing Alleged's value. 'Normally a stallion will cover forty mares in a season. We assumed that Alleged would be standing for a fee of not less than $80,000. On that basis he had the potential to earn $3.2 million a year and the valuation in these instances is done on a four-year calculation of overall earnings and thus the syndication figure of $13 million.'

The Minstrel, bought at Keeneland for $200,000, was syndicated for $9 million. But it did not end there.

Assert, who was purchased in France by David O'Brien for Robert Sangster and who would win the French Derby and the Irish Derby in 1982 for Vincent's son, cost only £16,000.

'I sold 50 per cent of Assert for $14 million dollars,' said Robert Sangster as matter-of-factly as a farmer telling one how he had sold ten head of cattle at a fair in Ireland.

Robert Sangster also made a 'killing' with Storm Bird, which in light of the figure he commanded – set against his failure to win anything as a three-year-old – had to be rated another of the great bargain buys.

This Northern Dancer colt (out of South Ocean), closely related to Nijinsky and The Minstrel, was picked out by Vincent O'Brien at the Keeneland Sales and bought by the BBA (Ireland) on behalf of the Sangster-O'Brien Syndicate for $1 million.

Rated the top juvenile in Europe after five successive wins as a two-year-old Storm Bird was installed winter favourite for the English 2000 Guineas and at the same time was viewed as the potential Epsom Derby winner.

At that point, according to Robert Sangster, he was valued at $20 million. He was insured by his owner for $15 million with Hughes, Gibbs & Co. in the City for a premium of £208,000. That was before his mane and tail were cut off before the season had opened in a sad, bizarre incident (Vincent O'Brien was on a winter holiday with Jacqueline; David, then his assistant, was holding the fort at Ballydoyle and had to handle the clamourings of the media).

Vincent maintained at the time that Storm Bird was unaffected by the experience and all seemingly went well with him. However, when he was taken to Naas racecourse for a public gallop he showed little of the sparkle of his two-year-old season. The bad ground could hardly be advanced as the sole reason. Then he suffered a minor setback.

That was enough to cause Storm Bird to miss the English 2000 Guineas. Vincent was confident, however, that he would have him ready for the Derby. Indeed, he came back strongly into the ante-post market but then disappointed in his final work-out and was withdrawn.

Now Robert Sangster takes up the story of how Storm Bird came to be sold for twenty-four times his original purchase price – even though he failed to win a Classic.

'I remember we were in the Hyatt Regency Hotel in Lexington during the Keeneland July Sales that summer – Vincent, John Magnier and myself. I was just leaving the breakfast table when bloodstock agent George Harris came over and asked me what value I would put on Storm Bird. I said "$15 million". I didn't think any more of it until that evening George came to me again after the sales session and told me he had a client who was willing to pay $15 million.

'I pointed out that when I had put a valuation of $15 million on Storm Bird, I did not mean that I would sell at that price. It was simply a *minimum* valuation on the colt – a figure below which there could be no negotiations. George Harris was not in the least taken aback by that. He replied – "My client is quite willing that negotiations start from a base of $15 million".

'Immediately I went into private discussion with Vincent and John, knowing now that George Harris and his client really meant business. We decided that we would not sell for less than $25 million.

'So Vincent and John accompanied me to George Harris's suite and after an hour's negotiations, it was clear that they were prepared to go to $24 million at least to acquire the colt. We gave the impression that we were playing tough by asking for time to consider, and then later went back to George Harris's suite and shook hands on $24 million. Every time I reflect on that amazing day, I just cannot believe how smoothly the whole business went. At the time $24 million became like so many chips in a big poker game in Las Vegas in the cut and thrust of negotiation. You know what I mean, you forget momentarily the astronomical sums you are dealing with, as you battle to clinch the deal.'

George Harris was acting for Robert Heffner, an oil and gas magnate from Oklahoma (and no relation to Hugh Hefner).

Storm Bird remained in training with Vincent O'Brien. The target now set for the colt was the Prix de l'Arc de Triomphe and if he were to win it, there was no doubt that it would compensate in one magnificent stroke for missing out on the English 2000 Guineas, the Epsom Derby and possibly the King George VI and Queen Elizabeth Stakes.

Vincent decided that Storm Bird should have a preliminary run in the Prix du Prince d'Orange at Longchamp on Sunday, 20 September 1981. The going was soft.

Robert Sangster lunched at the Pre Catilan restaurant near the course with Robert Heffner's lawyer and accountant. 'The thought of Storm Bird losing did not enter our minds that day,' recalled Robert Sangster. 'It was simply a question of how much he would win by. He started favourite at 7–4.' Ridden by Pat Eddery, the colt was in the lead after half a mile but was soon beaten and finished seventh behind the Aga Khan's Vayrann (Yves Saint-Martin) and Bikala.

'I never saw Vincent so shattered after any failure as he was that afternoon in Paris,' said Robert Sangster. 'I recall about twenty pressmen crowding around me, asking me what had gone wrong. All I could say was: "I do not know. I don't own the horse any more. I cannot explain it."

'I recall Tommy Stack going down to where Storm Bird came in. He said to me, "He would not blow out a candle."

'He had not seen a racecourse since the Dewhurst

Stakes. It was now mid-September. I think he lost interest in racing in the meantime as he had not been asked a serious question for a year. All right, I know he had been worked at home and that he had looked exceptional at times, and that his work had led Vincent to believe that he would come good at Longchamp. Yes, it was a great shock. Perhaps if he hadn't suffered that setback when his tail and mane were cut, things might have been different. We'll never know.'

Storm Bird did not contest the Prix de l'Arc de Triomphe. He was syndicated for $30 million to stand at the Ashford Stud in Kentucky. As a sire carrying on the valued Northern Dancer line, he did not lack patronage and soon the winners began to flow. In 1989 he finished fourth in the British and Irish sires list thanks to the exploits of the top-class four-year-old filly Indian Skimmer and the Irish 2000 Guineas winner, Prince of Birds (who was sold to Japan). The Ashford Stud sire was also represented by the Italian 1000 Guineas winner, Lonely Bird, and the US graded stakes winner, Conquering Hero.

Golden Fleece was bought for $775,000 at the Keeneland Sales in July 1980. He was unbeaten in four races, including the 1982 Epsom Derby.

In a spin on the course the morning before the Derby the colt had coughed a few times and there was a distinct possibility that he might not run.

'He didn't cough again that day, even though Vincent, with his attention to detail, had posted a man specially outside the colt's box to listen for the tell-tale sound,' said Robert Sangster, and the horse duly lined up for the Classic. But even though Golden Fleece has come to be rated one of the most brilliant Derby winners of recent times, Robert Sangster believes that 'only 70 per cent of his best' was seen that day at Epsom – which makes his performance in victory all the more incredible.

Sadly, he had sickened within a fortnight of his Derby success and all the hype about a possible Curragh clash between Assert and himself became so much pie in the sky. Initially the connections consoled themselves with the view that he had contracted a bad cold and hopes rose that he would soon be back in strong work. However, a swelling appeared in his hind leg and that had the effect of making up minds very quickly.

Golden Fleece's racing career was over. He was retired to stud at Coolmore. Eighteen months later he was dead, the victim of cancer.

'His premature death was a tragedy – a tragedy for Coolmore and for the Irish breeding industry,' said his owner.

'Life is all about timing,' Robert Sangster says, and the timing was just right when he became involved with Vincent O'Brien and John Magnier as the main partners in 'The Syndicate' – established to buy yearlings, mainly American-breds, at sales such as Keeneland – and in the creation of the world-renowned Coolmore Stud complex.

At that point in the 'seventies he had already 'been in horses' for about five years and had acquired a property near Macclesfield in Cheshire that would eventually become the Swettenham Stud.

The challenge was now there: could he go into racing and breeding on a big scale and make it pay? The fateful year was 1974 – the first year of stallion involvement.

John Magnier at that time was boss of the 300-acre Grange Stud near Fermoy, where his late father had stood the great National Hunt sire, Cottage (died 1942). John had also founded Castle Hyde Stud in 1971 and together with Robert Sangster he would be involved in Sandville Stud.

Meanwhile the original Coolmore Stud, a few miles north of Fethard in South Tipperary, was owned by Tim Vigors, renowned internationally both as a horseman and as a bloodstock agent who thought big and went in big when he wanted to acquire a horse.

John Magnier and Robert Sangster, having joined forces to purchase two horses, Green God and Deep Diver, and then a third, Sun Prince, concluded that they were having to get involved in a lot of competition with other breeders – Tim Rogers of Airlie Stud, for example, and the bloodstock agents acting for big international interests. They were even competing with studs on their own doorstep.

It did not seem to John and Robert, or to Vincent, to be the correct way to continue. Why should studs that had much in common bid against one another when they could bid together – all for one and one for all? Why not a pooling of resources?

Then the trio hit on the inspired idea. 'We decided that we would make our own stallions,' said Sangster.

A three-year plan was decided upon. But first there was the amalgamation of the studs to form a corporate entity, a type of structure that was to become a blueprint of its kind in the breeding world.

Coolmore Stud became a member of Coolmore, Castle Hyde and Associated Stud Farms, a title which confirmed the link of the Magnier family in the new venture. Grange and Sandville were also in the new company's title, and so too was Beeches Stud, owned by Robert McCarthy and situated just across the Tipperary border at Tallow, County Waterford.

Soon two more studs had been incorporated into the complex, Longfield and Thomastown Castle.

As for 'The Syndicate', Robert Sangster recalled: 'I remember the day John Magnier and myself went to see Vincent. It was the day that we virtually put "The Syndicate" together.

'The first venture was really when we bought Boone's Cabin, which was in training at the time with Vincent. He had won the Wokingham Stakes in 1975 with Lester in the saddle. He did not quite make it as a stallion and was later sent to Australia where he did moderately well. Through Tim Rogers, I acquired a share in Blood Royal, winner of the Queen's Vase at Ascot in 1975, with Lester again riding.

'I remember that the decision was taken with Tim Rogers to merge share ownerships in certain unbeaten two-year-olds we purchased in order to avoid clashing head-on for the same animals but we never did manage to get our two syndicates together.'

As time went on other people joined – and left – the

syndicate but the 'Big Three' have stayed together. They knew when they started on their three-year plan in 1975 that buying some of the best yearling colts, put up either privately or at public auction in Europe and the United States, could not of itself be guaranteed to throw up a top-class horse. However, if there was even one, the resultant syndication for stud purposes would more than justify the whole venture. In a word, if you bought a package of five, six or seven in a year and one clicked, the entire operation would be well worth while.

The year 1975 will always stand out as a red-letter one for Robert Sangster and also for Vincent O'Brien and John Magnier. From their assault on the yearling sales that year, 'The Syndicate' brought back to Ballydoyle a package of horses that included The Minstrel, Alleged, Artaius and Be My Guest. The invasion of Keeneland that same year was really the turning point. But there were a few inspired purchases at sales in Europe also. Everything they touched over a decade from 1975 to 1984 seemed to turn to gold. Godswalk, Golden Fleece, El Gran Senor, Sadler's Wells – and, of course, while Assert was not bought by Vincent, he won both the French Derby and Irish Derby for Robert Sangster. A flood of victories in Europe's top races ensued and each champion was stamping himself in the process as a valuable stud property to realise profits from syndication that became the envy of the world in the boom days.

The statue of Be My Guest (bought for a then European record price of 127,000 guineas from the Moyglare Stud crop at Goffs in 1975) occupies a proud place inside the entrance to the Coolmore Stud complex. He was the first of Coolmore's own when he was put to stud in 1978 after a racing career that saw him win three Group races, including the Waterford Crystal Mile. The same year Godswalk (bought for $61,000 as a yearling), a brilliant sprinter – his three victories included the King's Stand Stakes – also began stud duties at Coolmore. Then in 1979 came Try My Best, with a championship-winning two-year-old record behind him and, significantly, of a Northern Dancer pedigree. But all changed, changed utterly once the emphasis turned to the Northern Dancer blood.

Robert Sangster pointed out that Danzatore (Northern Dancer – Shake A Leg), after three brilliant wins as a two-year-old, including a six-lengths win in the Beresford Stakes, was installed winter favourite for the 2000 Guineas.

'But when Vincent found in the approach to the New-market Classic that Danzatore was not working as well at home as Lomond (Northern Dancer – My Charmer), he decided to run the latter. Lomond, which at one point had been at 20–1 in the ante-post lists, won at 9–1 in the hands of Pat Eddery.' Lomond won in the Sangster colours, and was retired to stud at Coolmore while Danzatore was exported to stand Down Under. Both made excellent sires.

'There is no ante-post betting in France or in the States and trainers there are not placed in the position, therefore, that people who have gone for a "killing" at ante-post odds on some colt will try to force a trainer to run a colt in a particular race,' said Robert Sangster.

'Fortunately for me and the interests of Coolmore, Vincent wasn't prepared to bow to such pressure in the case of Danzatore. He did the unpopular thing, as I have indicated, in running Lomond instead and that, I maintain, is the way it has to be – and should be.

'The 'seventies and early 'eighties were highly profitable years for us,' said Robert Sangster. 'The market crashed in 1985 and 1986.'

Sangster dominated the scene as leading owner – thanks to Vincent O'Brien – before the Maktoum brothers of Dubai arrived on the scene. In eight Flat seasons up to 1985 he was crowned Britain's leading owner. Then his apparent invincibility was broken. It coincided with the fact that, after Law Society's victory in the Irish Derby in 1985 and Leading Counsel's success in the Irish St Leger the same year, the only other Classic winner from Bally-doyle for the rest of the 'eighties was Dark Lomond's Irish St Leger win in 1988.

Sheikh Mohammed became the 'king' and in one season

alone (1987) won £1,232,000 in prize money. The same year Sangster had to be satisfied with third place and £468,000. In 1989 Sheikh Mohammed made a sweep of four Irish Classics.

With the recession in the bloodstock industry, headings telling of Sangster and 'The Syndicate' spending small fortunes at Keeneland were replaced by awe-inspiring, almost frightening spending by the Maktoum brothers.

But even though the glory days of The Minstrel and Alleged might have been past, Robert Sangster proved that he could survive in one of the toughest businesses of all. As he explained: 'When people see headings in the papers like "Sangster on Spending Spree", they think I am only a buyer. I can understand that. But in a way I am my own Chancellor of the Exchequer, seeking all the time to keep the books balanced. What many don't realise is that I sell as well as buy. In 1987 I sold over £22 million worth of bloodstock. I bought less than £1 million that same year.'

Some thought that he would never sell Vernons when it was linked for so long with the family but he showed that he was not swayed by sentiment when he remarked: 'In this life everything is for sale except the wife.'

'It was an offer I could not refuse,' he added, pointing out that it enabled him to clear off about £40 million in loans raised from the banking institutions. During the 'rationalisation' programme, he had on his own admission 'to reduce quite dramatically my borrowings from the bank'. He did not mind admitting that he had made a mistake in the case of the much-heralded decision to set Michael Dickinson up as his private trainer at Manton. The purchase and modernisation of the 2300-acre Manton estate set Sangster back £8 million and the annual running costs totalled £1.5 million. Michael Dickinson in his first year of operation at Manton – 1986 – won only four races worth £13,965.

Some would say that Sangster showed a ruthless edge in getting rid of Michael Dickinson. The outlay, however, had been so heavy that he just could not afford to wait for success. 'It was the first time I've ever sacked a trainer,' he said. 'Looking at it now, he was five years ahead of his time. But what had worked with geldings when Michael was a National Hunt trainer probably upset more highly strung young colts and fillies. I could no longer afford the time for him to perfect his theories.'

Frequently quoted as saying that 'horseflesh is an international currency' and having more than once proved at Keeneland, as in the case of Golden Fleece, his conviction that 'you must buy the best regardless of price', Robert Sangster arrived at the point as the recession hit the market that – as he put it to me – 'it is important in this business to try and spread the risk, especially in a situation where the inflated syndication fees of the 'seventies no longer operate.'

He viewed Classic Thoroughbreds as 'an ideal way' of spreading the risk among a sizeable number of people. 'No one will be that badly hurt if the company does not hit the jackpot eventually. Those who invested in it were able to afford their shares, whether they went in for some hundreds of pounds or some thousands.'

He admitted that he had invested heavily himself in Northern Dancer blood. 'That blood will not devalue,' he said, adding that at the 1988 Keeneland July Sales 42 per cent of the horses sold were of the Northern Dancer line.

In the all-conquering days when the Triumvirate he formed with Vincent and Lester proved invincible, he was happy to exclaim to the world, 'Let the pilot do the flying.' Little wonder that at the same time he should say of Vincent that he was, beyond doubt, 'the best trainer in the world'.

24

The Floating Cocktail Party

'Bloodstock agent' is how Billy McDonald would probably describe himself. One of the percentage men. But he is much more than that. He moves easily in the circles frequented by the big names of the racing world and the social roundabout. He can be found at all the big yearling sales – from Keeneland to Saratoga to Deauville.

Destiny could not have thrown together two more different people, to the benefit of Vincent O'Brien's career as a trainer, than Robert Sangster and Billy McDonald. Sangster is shrewd and calculating in his investments in business and bloodstock. Billy is unpredictable and untrammelled, the world his oyster waiting to be cracked by the sheer ebullience ingrained in that smallish, round, compact frame. He is what the Irish term 'a born character', able to live in the style of a millionaire even when fortune may not be exactly smiling on him.

Robert Sangster has never forgotten Billy McDonald for being the key figure in the inspired purchase of Alleged in California. It was one of those strokes of genius, born of a moment when the eye tells the heart something over and above cold, calculating reasoning and you must go with the eye or else regret it for the rest of your life. The tag of 'The Man who Bought Alleged' has followed Billy ever since. That tag has served him well, especially in the valley periods.

Of course, he also earned the tag of 'The Man Who Discovered Fairy Bridge'.

Billy acknowledges that his star was set right in the constellation the morning in Kentucky that he spotted the filly. He was in the Bluegrass country looking at yearlings on the stud farms in advance of the Keeneland July Sales.

'It is generally the custom to put them out at night in the paddocks because of the heat,' he told me.

'It was early morning and I saw this filly in a paddock with other yearlings. She was very small but what really caught my eye was that when the man came with the bucket of feed, she beat all the others nearly 100 yards in racing towards him. I took a mental note there and then, enquired about her breeding and said to myself that when she came into the ring eventually we would not let her go.

'I rang Vincent at Ballydoyle and I told him – 'I have seen this filly in a paddock and she's an absolute flyer.'

'He came to Keeneland Sales in due course and went to look at her. He loved the pedigree. She was by Bold Reason out of the Forli mare, Special, who in turn was a sister of Thatch and a half-sister to the top-class King Pellinore. She was small but Vincent repeated more than once that she was "a very nice filly".'

Vincent O'Brien was standing with John Magnier and Billy McDonald when the filly came into the ring.

Billy McDonald did the bidding, securing her for $40,000. 'Vincent, Robert Sangster and John Magnier took a quarter share each and I retained a quarter share myself,' recalled Billy McDonald.

'The filly went into training with Vincent and won twice in succession as a two-year old at the Phoenix Park in July of 1977, winning her second race by five lengths.

'She was the dam of Sadler's Wells.'

It's history how Sadler's Wells, after being retired to stud at Coolmore, had by the close of the 1989 Flat season attained a new pedestal in international sire ratings.

Robert Sangster is happy, then, to have Billy McDonald keeping an eye out for him for another potential Alleged or Fairy Bridge. He, likewise, had tremendous faith in P. P. Hogan's eye – P.P.'s good eye, that is!

Lightning can always strike a second time.

Now it's a morning in July 1988 and I am joined at breakfast in the Hyatt Regency Hotel in Lexington by Billy McDonald, who has been out looking at yearlings since 5 a.m. Over the grapefruit and cereal, the bacon and eggs, sunny side-up, and the hash-brown, I get talking to Billy about some of the legends, particularly those that have emerged out of his Deauville days.

He leaves me briefly to talk to 'Gordie', a tall, elegant gentleman without an ounce of spare flesh on him – one you would never imagine at first sight was 66 years old. 'Gordie' happened to be Sir Gordon White, Chairman of Hanson Industries, one of the sixty top companies in America but better known today on this side of the Atlantic as sponsors of the Ever Ready English Derby since 1984. Sir Gordon is a man in love with racing, the magic it breathes and the uncertainty it brings when you are an owner. Apart from his stake in Reference Point, the 1987 Derby winner, he also has shares in twelve Robert Sangster homebreds.

They talk almost in awe in the racing and bloodstock world of the parties Billy threw on his 'yacht', which he christened 'The African Queen' and which could not bear comparison with the yachts of some of the millionaire owners who came to the parties.

'Mind-boggling' is how one journalist described the parties Billy threw after Alleged had won the Prix de l'Arc de Triomphe in 1977 and 1978. On the only occasion Billy's yacht left port, it was christened 'The Floating Cocktail Party' by the Deauville 'set'. That was a run of twenty minutes up the coast to Honfleur – 'a booze cruise', as Billy dubbed it.

Billy had rented the yacht. The bill for the rent, plus the cost of the monumental parties on board, ran into literally thousands of pounds. Did he regret the obvious waste? 'I made back in one session at the sales the rent of the yacht and all the rest.'

Betting he admits now to be 'a stupid occupation'. But Billy wouldn't be Billy if he hadn't got bitten by the stupidity of it and paid for it. The biggest bet he ever had was on the Vincent O'Brien-trained colt, Marinsky (Northern Dancer – Thong) a half-brother to outstanding miler Thatch, in the 1977 July Cup at Newmarket.

'He was backed down to 5-4 favourite but I was on at 7-2. He beat Gentilhombre comfortably by 1½ lengths but then came the announcement of the Stewards' inquiry and objection. Marinsky was deemed to have hung left and bumped Gentilhombre coming into the last furlong and was relegated to second place, though most observers felt he was the winner on merit. Earlier at Epsom he was disqualified for biting another horse in the Diomed Stakes, after looking a winner at the distance. Can you beat that? If only they had raced him in a muzzle that day, as they did afterwards.'

'A very bad blow,' Billy confesses to me about that shattering reverse over Marinsky in the July Cup. And then with a shrug of the shoulders, he adds: 'You would only drive yourself crazy if you kept thinking back on a day like that.'

He had an interest in Alleged and in Fairy Bridge and he sold those interests to Robert Sangster to get the ready cash 'to pay a bookmaker'. I hadn't the courage to ask him if it was over the go-for-broke bet on Marinsky and Lester Piggott. He had been 'bitten' badly enough as it was without my enquiring more!

Billy McDonald was born in County Down. His family were very prominent in the show jumping world, his father being President of the Northern Ireland Show Jumping Association. From the time he was knee-high to a grasshopper, Billy had an absorbing interest in racing and bloodstock and, as he put it, he 'travelled on Vincent O'Brien's shirt tails when I started going to the Sales.'

He readily admits that anything he learned about the judgement of a yearling he learned from the Master. It is not surprising to hear him contend unequivocally that

Vincent has the greatest eye in the world when it comes to judging a yearling.

'Nobody advises Vincent O'Brien. He is the leading light and I would not speak about anyone else in the same breath as him.'

Billy maintains that there are carping critics of Vincent O'Brien who like to advance the argument that he had vast resources at his back when he picked out champions like Golden Fleece and El Gran Senor. 'But what these people invariably forget is that all through his life Vincent was able, with that uncanny eye of his, to buy *real* horses inexpensively.

'I do not know of any other man who would have bought Apalachee, and it was the same with Lomond. He can see things about a horse that I venture to say no one else can see. Many people can see the faults that it's easy to see – the things that people in the bloodstock business could crab a yearling for; there is no kudos for that.

'But Vincent can look beyond this aspect, can even forgive where his inner eye has caught something special in a colt or filly, as in the case of The Minstrel. Now there was a classic instance where he went dead against the experts crabbing this Northern Dance colt because he was so small and, even more so, because of those four white stockings. He went to $200,000 for him and while many told him he was crazy, he proved in the long run that he had acquired a real bargain at that price.

'You see, money wasn't the criterion that mattered – it was judgement, and many of those who passed up The Minstrel had reason to respect even more Vincent's uncanny eye and his judgement, especially when the colt was syndicated for $9 million.'

Turning to the vital criteria that sway Vincent O'Brien, Billy said that Vincent 'places tremendous importance on the fact that a colt must have a man's head and a good eye.

'He spends more time endeavouring to assess the character of a horse by looking at the eye and the head than at anything else. He also places a lot of emphasis on the fact that the legs must be right.

'He will, of course, have spent hours on end studying the pedigrees before he ever looks at a colt or filly. He told me once that when he was four he used to sit on his father's knee and reel off the breeding of the horses in Dan's yard, as another child would recite his sums. He is a walking encyclopaedia where pedigrees are concerned.

'Having assessed the pedigree of a yearling exhaustively, he will seek to look into its soul – through the eye. "The eyes, Billy, are the mirror of the soul and the eye can reveal bravery and courage," he advised me once. And if he doesn't see a certain look of kindness in the eye, a certain expression that rules out the tell-tale trait of a rogue, then he can pass one by – despite its pedigree. Sometimes he will discover the look of eagles as he discovered it in Nijinsky and then he knows with an exactness beyond words that he has found a champion. You can't learn that from books – Vincent started to acquire it from the first moment that he began going around with his father and he graduated, you might say, with a degree in the judgement of horseflesh that no one in the world has ever been able to match.'

'A hell of a guy,' is Billy McDonald's tribute to Robert Sangster. 'He does not forget old pals and that for me is the sign of someone you really respect. I remember when Law Society won the Irish Derby in 1985. I was standing with the owner, Stavros Niarchos and with Robert and Vincent. Robert, no doubt thinking at that moment that Law Society had been sired by Alleged, turned to Niarchos and remarked: "There would never have been a Law Society but for this man. He bought Alleged for me." Niarchos's reaction was: "Oh, really".'

Like Billy McDonald, Pat Hogan – just 'P.P.' to everyone in the racing world – is a born character, indeed a legend in his own lifetime.

He talked to me one day in April 1989 of the warm friendship between the O'Brien and Hogan families. He recalled Vincent staying in the family homestead in Greenpark, back in his school-boy days.

As Vincent O'Brien acknowledges that much of what he learned in his youth about horses evolved from going around with his father, so P.P. Hogan similarly acquired a storehouse of knowledge from his father, Joseph P., who was reputed to be one of the best judges of horseflesh in the South.

Joe Hogan, in fact, was born and bred into the world of horses and in his day was reckoned to be the most dashing man to hounds in Munster.

Vincent's father, Dan, and Joe Hogan, of course, would meet one another at the Fair of Cahirmee and other horse fairs and they would also meet at the point-to-points and no doubt at times they would be in friendly competition for a horse they had both set their eyes on to purchase.

P.P. developed into an outstanding amateur rider and in his prime he was maintaining a high average of winners against the best competition imaginable – none less than Martin Molony and Aubrey Brabazon, for example.

He carried on the family tradition of seeing the hunt as an integral part of life and in 1989, he was still riding to hounds – a 'young' 67!

P.P. came up in a hard school – a school in which you learned to do things for yourself and in which there were no silver spoons knocking about. He recalled bringing home 15 horses from the Fair of Cahirmee in Buttevant to Rathcannon – a distance of 21 miles. 'I rode one of the horses and led the other fourteen.'

Don't ask me to go into details on how he managed that. He tied a knot on the lead horse's tail and with a make-do string linked him to the others and off he went.

'You could buy any kind of horse at Cahirmee – a horse for the Cavalry Corps of some army, a hunter – you name it, you could have it, if you had the ready cash to do a deal.'

You trusted your own judgement and if you had an eye for a bargain, you could get a real one.

P. P. Hogan brought the knowledge he acquired in hard schools in the South to the yearling sales. The judgement was the same, only now you were picking out yearlings that would become potential stallions.

'I suppose you could say it's a little bit of a gift from God himself,' was how he summed up the 'eye' for picking out a potential champion.

That may have seemed, in a way, to over-simplify it – but the P. P. Hogans and the Vincent O'Briens belong to a rare species.

'He has done everything,' was his tribute to Vincent O'Brien as a trainer.

'He started small in Churchtown and he went on to develop Ballydoyle into one of the best stables in the world.'

Would you say he was the greatest, I asked?

'He has to be, he must be because no other trainer has come any way near his record, both over the jumps and on the Flat. And no trainer can ever equal that record because no one will ever mix it with such success. Yes, Vincent must stand as a man apart.'

P.P. could aptly be described as the uncrowned 'King' of the point-to-point circuit.

It has been nothing for him to turn out 40 winners in a season and one year he had a total of 48 winners. No trainer has managed to break his dominance of the hunter chases.

On Sunday, 15 February 1987, he had his greatest day as a trainer. Incredibly, he trained eight winners spread between Kilworth in County Cork and Scariff in County Clare. At Kilworth alone he scored six.

P. P. Hogan trains about 40 horses on his 400-acre spread at Rathcannon, which is roughly nineteen miles from Limerick and an easy drive from Vincent O'Brien's birthplace in Churchtown.

No story matches the one as to how he came by the eye grafted on to balance his good eye ('I have only one little eye now,' is how he puts it himself).

The squeamish, reading this book before dinner in the evening, wouldn't be too happy with me if I related it here. Perhaps if you get P.P. in the right mood he will tell you – if you are passing by Rathcannon some time.

Suffice it to say that as he looked at a filly one day at a yearling sales in the company of Robert Sangster, he was heard to remark: 'The fellow that had this eye before me must have had a great eye for the women but certainly not for horses!'

Robert Sangster, who has a great affection for P. P. Hogan as he has for Billy McDonald, is tickled pink every time he thinks of P.P. sending cards home from Paris and placing himself firmly in the 'Sang George' Hotel.

Out of a trip to Paris, in fact, emerged one of the stories about P. P. Hogan that has passed into racing lore – the story of how he 'cashed in' to make a nice killing for himself.

David O'Brien, before he commenced training in 1980 and when he was looking for yearlings, went to Moyglare Stud with Philip Myerscough to view the yearlings there. He saw a Be My Guest colt out of Irish Bird and liked the horse so much that he decided to go to the Goffs Sales in Paris to buy him. P. P. Hogan, who was Robert Sangster's manager at the time, had seen the horse also and with Robert Sangster's support, they went to the Sales and David bought the horse which was knocked down to him for the French equivalent in francs of £16,000. Be My Guest was a first season sire and Assert's dam had, at that time, produced nothing much, so there was no reason to expect that he would make a very high price. It was an inspired purchase by David O'Brien, who, as he paid for Assert, could never have imagined that such a cheap colt would win the French Derby and the Irish Derby in 1982.

Robert Sangster was reputed to have given P. P. Hogan a share in Assert and when the colt was syndicated for $25 million, Sangster told P.P. that he could, if he wished, convert his stake into stallion shares.

But Pat decided to convert the major portion of his stake into hard cash as land had come on the market near him and he wanted to buy it.

I put it to him that the accepted story in racing circles was that he got £1 million to £1.25 million. 'Is that what they say?' he countered with that hearty laugh of his and then added with a whimsical smile: 'You know, I still have some bit of the action.'

25

Eddery On El Gran Senor's Epsom Defeat

'If you don't stay, you don't win.' In that cryptic seven-word sentence ace big-race rider Pat Eddery summed up the reason why El Gran Senor was short-headed in a photo finish in the 1984 Epsom Derby.

The fierce debates will go on down the decades about the so-near-and-yet-so-far sole reverse for the Vincent O'Brien-trained 'wonder colt' at the hands of Secreto, trained by Vincent's son, David. A framed cheque in John Magnier's office at the Coolmore Stud in County Tipperary brings home even more forcibly what that single defeat meant to the connections of El Gran Senor. It was a cheque from Ladbrokes for £170,800. It represented John Magnier's winnings from the £10,000 each-way bet he had on Secreto at ante-post odds of 16–1.

'I put on that bet as a saver. I saw Secreto as the only danger. There was no need for me to have a bet on El Gran Senor. You see, I owned a bit of him.' Owning 'a bit' of this colt, if he had retired with the Epsom Derby under his belt and with no blemish on his racing record, would have meant far, far more in his greatly-enhanced value as a stud property than the £170,800 – a mere drop in the sea, you might say – that John received from Ladbrokes.

'Ladbrokes closed my account after paying me my cheque,' he added with a smile.

'My reaction all the way through at Epsom that day was

to wait as long as possible,' said Pat Eddery. 'El Gran Senor could "take" any of those in front of him, I knew, with his acceleration. It was merely a question of keeping him covered up until inside the final furlong.

'I was fourth into the straight behind Al Talaq, Telios and Claude Monet. I was travelling so easily that I wasn't in the least worried about any of these. I felt I had a stone in hand.

'El Gran Senor had so much talent, so much class, so much speed – was so vastly superior, in fact, that he was running all over them despite my efforts to keep him covered up to the last possible second.

'Look, they simply died ahead of me. And when I saw Claude Monet go like the rest, I found myself in front, even before we hit the hill. El Gran Senor didn't stay in that final furlong when Secreto came at him. If you don't stay, you don't win. It's as simple as that. Never was that maxim borne out as clearly as it was that day at Epsom.'

Certain critics had suggested in the aftermath of Epsom that El Gran Senor proved at the Curragh that he could get 12 furlongs and that even *Racehorses of 1984* had concluded that 'a short-head defeat in the Epsom Derby and a victory in the Irish Sweeps Derby are testimony to El Gran Senor's effectiveness at a mile and half.'

'I see it differently,' replied Pat emphatically. He stressed that he was talking from the first-hand knowledge gained from having ridden the colt on *both* occasions.

'As far as I am concerned, the Curragh proved quite conclusively that El Gran Senor did *not* get a mile and a half in a truly-run 12-furlong Classic race,' he explained. 'That particular Irish Derby suited him to perfection. There was a small field of only eight runners, the smallest in twenty-five years. There was no pace early on; in fact, they went so moderately that I was able to sit there knowing that I could wait and utilise El Gran Senor's speed to the fullest possible advantage in what was going to develop into a sprint finish, which it actually became. It was *no* test of stamina.

'To revert to Epsom, I rode the race I planned to ride and that my experience told me would lift the Derby – if

El Gran Senor had shown the stamina to get the distance. People, I know, will go on talking about it for years but, let me repeat, a colt either stays the distance of the Epsom Derby or he doesn't, as was proved so conclusively when Blushing Groom failed behind The Minstrel in 1977. There are no two ways about it. El Gran Senor didn't get the 12 furlongs that day. The hill at Epsom found him out.'

Tipperary-born Christy Roche, who that day had the greatest triumph of a career that saw him ride for both Paddy ('Darkie') Prendergast and Vincent O'Brien, advanced the theory that Pat Eddery got too good a run on El Gran Senor on the inside and when Claude Monet 'died' he was suddenly left with nothing in front of him. Roche doubted beforehand whether El Gran Senor might really get the mile and a half, especially up the last testing hill at Epsom and that was what inspired him to keep 'working like hell' on Secreto.

In retrospect, however, Roche admits that if Claude Monet had stayed ahead of El Gran Senor for just a little longer, then 'Pat might have been able to come at me with a short, sharp run and in that case I believe he would have won it. It was being left in front too soon that killed any hope he had of victory.'

'El Gran Senor was unbeatable up to 10 furlongs,' said Vincent O'Brien. Unconsciously, he touched the heart of the matter – for El Gran Senor was, surely a 'wonder colt' at a mile and quite brilliant up to 10 furlongs, but a question mark remained once the distance was pushed to a testing – and that is the operative word – 12 furlongs.

The final word comes from Capt Michael Byrne, who at the end of 1989 retired as Senior Irish Turf Club Handicapper. 'El Gran Senor was the best miler we have rated in the International Classifications since they were first published in 1977 – the best I have seen in twenty years as an official handicapper. The quality of his closest rivals in the 1984 English 2000 Guineas attests to his brilliance. Runner-up that day was Chief Singer, rated higher at the distance than all the remainder at any age at the end of 1984. This he achieved by winning the St James's Palace Stakes by 8 lengths in record time. We also rated Chief

Singer the leading all-aged sprinter in Europe after he beat a very good field for the Norcross July Cup.'

Capt Byrne added very significantly: 'I do not subscribe to the school that criticised Pat Eddery after El Gran Senor had been beaten by Secreto at Epsom. The colt went from pulling the proverbial roller 2 furlongs down to struggling close home. I consider that Pat's skill and judgement got the colt as close as he did that day. Winning the Irish Sweeps Derby subsequently proved nothing. It was run exactly to suit him and even the fourth finisher that day, March Song, went on to take advantage of a favourable handicap mark at Dundalk two weeks later.

'To sum up – El Gran Senor was a superb miler; most probably a high-class Group 1 horse at 10 furlongs, but very average in the context of Group 1 at a mile and a half.'

El Gran Senor was unbeaten in four outings as a two-year-old, his victories including the Railway Stakes, the National Stakes and the Dewhurst Stakes. Pat Eddery has a vivid memory of his first outing as a three-year-old in the Gladness Stakes (7 furlongs) at the Curragh on 14 April 1984.

'I got him as relaxed as I could as I knew from riding him in the four victories he scored as a two-year-old what tremendous speed he had. But even I wasn't prepared for the sheer class and speed he displayed that day. We literally left the field standing. I knew then that he was an exceptional colt and that he would never get beaten at a mile certainly.'

Already, without knowing it, Pat was presaging the worst, for in assessing that El Gran Senor was arguably one of the greatest milers of modern times, he was pin-pointing his Achilles heel – the nagging doubt about his ability to get an extra 4 furlongs when the tap was really turned on in a truly-run Classic event.

While he was under contract to Vincent O'Brien and Robert Sangster, it was Pat Eddery's practice to go over to Ballydoyle a week before the start of each Flat season when he might ride 10 horses a day.Thus he got the 'feel' of the horses that were new to him, before they saw a racecourse for the first time.

'Vincent never gave me instructions,' he said. 'Yes, he would discuss the other horses in a race and their comparative merits. In the parade ring before I went out – while we were chatting – he might see one being led past and remark: "That's a nice horse." But once Vincent was happy that you were acquainted with the horse you were riding for him, especially if it was a Classic or some other big race, then he did not feel it necessary to burden you with a detailed list of instructions.

'I rode great horses out of his yard: Golden Fleece, El Gran Senor, Sadler's Wells, King's Lake, Law Society; I could go on – they were marvellous years.'

In 1986 Greville Starkey's tactics were widely criticised when his thrilling late run on Dancing Brave from a seemingly impossible position failed by just half a length to catch Shahrastani and Walter Swinburn in the Epsom Derby. Starkey was unable to take the mount in the King George VI and Queen Elizabeth Stakes at Ascot because of injury. As Vincent O'Brien's horses were under a cloud because of the virus that had hit the Ballydoyle stable, Pat Eddery was available and quickly snapped up to ride Dancing Brave. He made the most of the opportunity by producing Dancing Brave with an irresistible run in the straight to cut down Shahrastani, who in finishing fourth had clearly run below his best. It had been noticeable that he sweated up during the preliminaries.

Meanwhile, Khalid Abdullah had been endeavouring to woo Pat Eddery away from his Ballydoyle contract. The quest for Eddery's signature had been long and sustained and pre-dated the 1986 Epsom Derby. When the contract was eventually signed it was widely reported to be worth £2 million to Eddery, who in the words of Brough Scott became 'the world's priciest rider'.

It was a near fairy-tale story, the rise of Pat Eddery. From carefree days in his native Blackrock in County Dublin to being, overnight, the most sought-after big-race jockey in the world, with an Arab Prince prepared to make him an offer he could not refuse. It was to see him end a happy five-year association with Robert Sangster and Vincent O'Brien.

It had all started for him at Seamus McGrath's stable at Glencairn, County Dublin where his father, Jimmy, had been first jockey. Riding was in his blood. He recalls that he rode his first racehorse when he was seven. Not surprisingly, he was apprenticed to Seamus McGrath 'There were a lot of boys there, and I was well down the list, so I felt I would have to move,' he told Tom Mac-Ginty, Racing Correspondent of the *Irish Independent*. 'Seamus McGrath could not have been more helpful. He drew up a list of trainers in England and my father decided Frenchie Nicholson was the one to whom I should go.'

It was an inspired move. Pat Eddery never looked back, for Frenchie Nicholson had already established a well-deserved reputation for training jockeys. Young Eddery was to prove his star pupil.

He progressed quickly to succeeding Duncan Keith as first jockey to Peter Walwyn (his apprenticeship ended in September, 1972). He was champion jockey at the age of 22 for the first of four successive occasions in 1974 with 148 winners and that season also saw him ride his first Classic winner – on Polygamy for Peter Walwyn in the English Oaks.

In 1975 he won the Epsom Derby for Walwyn on Grundy and this colt, having been runner-up in the English 2000 Guineas and victor in the Irish equivalent, went on to win the Irish Sweeps Derby and the King George VI and Queen Elizabeth Stakes.

For seven seasons Peter Walwyn and Pat Eddery were to prove a powerful partnership, and it was a difficult decision, a very difficult one for him, to leave Peter's stable to team up with Vincent O'Brien and Robert Sangster towards the end of the 1980 flat season.

'O'Brien Makes Eddery an Irresistible Offer', read the headline in *The Times*, and Michael Phillips reported that 'try hard as Peter Walwyn did to match the offer from

Ballydoyle, which is believed to run into six figures annually besides any perks, it became clear that Eddery was bent on accepting O'Brien's offer.'

Michael Phillips summed up: 'As I see it, Eddery's switch of allegiance to Ballydoyle can be likened to Kevin Keegan's move from Liverpool to Hamburg. Personalities do not come into it. It is purely financial.' Ironically enough, when later Pat Eddery switched his allegiance from Ballydoyle to Prince Khalid Abdullah, he was unstinting in his praise for the genius of Vincent O'Brien. Again personalities did not enter it. The move was purely financial.

The critics who were so vociferous when Eddery was beaten a whisker by Secreto in the 1984 Epsom Derby were silenced finally as he won the Prix de l'Arc de Triomphe at a packed Longchamp on 5 October 1986, the crowd being swelled by an estimated 10,000 British and Irish racing enthusiasts.

With an electrifying last furlong run, Eddery beat the French Derby winner of that season, Bering, with Bakharoff third. And when he won on Trempolino the following season from Tony Bin and Triptych, he was completing three-in-a-row, making it four wins in all in this race (he had won on Detroit in 1980) – the same total as Yves Saint-Martin (1970, 1974, 1982 and 1984).

After the Longchamp race, Pat Eddery was quoted as saying: 'Dancing Brave is undoubtedly the best horse I have ever ridden.'

However, when I met him during a quiet moment at Newmarket on the eve of the 1989 2000 Guineas and asked him in cold retrospect to give his view on the comparative merits of Golden Fleece and Dancing Brave, he said: 'Golden Fleece of his year was the best I had ever ridden up to that point in my career. I rode Dancing Brave in the King George VI and Queen Elizabeth Stakes and in the Arc. He gave me the feeling that he was an exceptional horse. Therefore, I will not put one ahead of the other'.

Cash Asmussen went to Ballydoyle at the start of the 1987

flat season on a two-year contract with Robert Sangster and Vincent O'Brien – and it goes without saying that he arrived to a fanfare of trumpets.

Taking over the mantle worn with such distinction by Lester Piggott and then by Pat Eddery imposed its own special challenges, its own strains from the outset. Cash, then 24, had achieved everything he wanted to achieve in France, where he had been champion twice at that stage. The lure of being number-one jockey to Vincent O'Brien was too good a chance to miss. Then, too, as 'a student of this game', he knew he would be joining a great 'university' of racing as it were – and he did not hide the fact that he wanted to learn from the Master.

Before he left Paris, he told racing writer Desmond Stoneham: 'I just wanted to join one of the most powerful stables in the world. Vincent O'Brien has done phenomenal things. I hope to benefit from his knowledge. An amazing number of champion racehorses have been through his hands and I hope to be involved with future ones. My ambition also is to ride as many Classic winners as possible.'

Ireland had its own appeal for him, too, in another sense. His great-grandmother was born in Ireland and the talented Texan is a devout Roman Catholic.

He could not have foreseen that things would go so badly wrong in Ireland in the final analysis and that he would be terminating his contract a year earlier than it should have ended. He had become accustomed to hearing the cry 'Bravo Cash' or 'Allez Cash' as he booted home the winners on French tracks. He had captured the hearts of the French racing public, not only by his success in the saddle but also by his jovial character.

The contract with Ballydoyle and Robert Sangster was terminated 'by mutual agreement'. Cash had an attractive offer to go back to France and he realised that the establishment of Classic Thoroughbreds had created an entirely new situation for Vincent O'Brien. If 'aggro' was arising with a section of the Irish racing public over the way he was riding, then he did not think it was right that this should spill over into affecting a new operation at Ballydoyle.

'I do not feel bitter at what happened,' he said. 'I have nothing to hide. I can hold my head high. During my stay in Ireland I made a lot of friends and I still cherish those friendships very much.'

The summer of 1987 became the summer of Cash Asmussen's discontent – not with Ireland and its people as a whole but at the 'stick' he had to endure at the hands of a vociferous section of the race-going public. He also came to be concerned at what he described at the time as 'a lot of negative press'.

'It got to the stage where I believed these people were playing a sort of game with me. Sure, they could be mad, but they were never vicious mad, as you can find it in other countries where racegoers can be far more vocal and objects can even be thrown at jockeys by disgruntled punters. I got the feeling at times that these Irish racegoers were doing it more in a joking manner and, therefore, I was never troubled by any sense of viciousness.

'No, it never did get to the point where I held anything against Irish racegoers as a body or against the Irish generally.

'I love the Irish people as they live for racing. Go into any pub, into any church or any bank and 98 per cent of the people you meet know racing and you're amazed how many know the form book. When people live for racing, it makes a professional feel really good.'

When Golden Temple, a Golden Fleece filly owned by Stavros Niarchos, failed to land the odds of 4–9 laid on her in a field of seven at the Phoenix Park on Saturday, 22 August 1987 it resulted – as Con Power reported in the *Sunday Press* – in 'the kind of railing never before handed out to any jockey in this country'.

Cash Asmussen dismounted to the strains of 'California Here I Come' being sung by one disenchanted punter. No doubt the idea was to get under the American's skin. At all times, however, Cash kept his cool. In his dealings with the racing press he was courtesy personified and even those who were among the harshest critics of some of his performances could not but admire him for the way he took it on the chin.

The final irony of his riding in Ireland was that no one ever questioned his integrity. It came down, as in the case of Golden Temple, to whether or not you agreed with the tactics he adopted in races he lost and whether you were satisfied with his record in tight finishes.

Those who love to delve into statistics were quick to point out that a glance at 22 short-head, head and neck finishes that Cash was involved in revealed that he came out best in only six as against being on the losing end in sixteen. And in the case of twelve photo finishes in this overall total of 22 races, he was first in three (one subsequently meriting a disqualification) and failed in nine.

They would contrast his record with the fantastic strike rate of Australian Garnie Bougoure in photo finishes when riding for Vincent O'Brien and Phonsie (when Vincent was under suspension as a result of the 'Chamour Affair').

There is little doubt that the failure of Golden Temple at the Phoenix Park on 22 August 1987 really brought matters to a head. Golden Temple was something of a 'talking horse' from the outset but she was never going to be a world beater and in the end punters, who had installed her favourite again and again, had to accept the inevitable and question her willingness really to battle in a finish.

Beaten into fourth place on her debut at the Curragh, she won her next two races, one of them the McGrath Stakes (Listed) on Budweiser Irish Derby Day.

Starting at 4–5 for the Brownstown Stud Stakes at Leopardstown on Monday, 3 August she was at the rear of the field early in the race and had only improved into seventh place entering the straight. She ran on to take second place behind the English-trained Just Class in a field of seven.

Then came the controversial Phoenix Park race. Golden Temple was last 2 furlongs out in a field of seven but ran on between horses inside the last furlong, only to be beaten a head by the Dermot Weld-trained Claxton's Slew,

The Coolmore empire . . . Law Society (Pat Eddery up), winning the 1985 Irish Derby (*below*) from Theatrical, is now at stud at Coolmore with Caerleon (*above right, with Bob Lanigan*), the 1983 French Derby winner and Champion Flat sire in 1988. *Above left*: John Magnier, the Coolmore boss, and (*inset*) Be My Guest, whose statue occupies a proud place inside the entrance to the Coolmore complex.

The eye of the Master . . . in the steamy Kentucky July heat, Vincent O'Brien and his son Charles look at a yearling in the barn area at Keeneland and (*below*) Vincent displays his total attention to detail.

David O'Brien and his Australian-born wife, Catherine, pictured on their wedding day, and (*below*) one of David's outstanding triumphs as a trainer, the victory of the filly Triptych (C. Roche up) over the colts in the 1985 Irish 2,000 Guineas.

Left: Vincent O'Brien and his brother Phonsie chatting with President Hillery at Punchestown in April 1986 on the occasion of the famous match between ill-fated Dawn Run and Buck House.

Right: Vincent with Bob Hawke when the Australian Prime Minister made a special visit to Ballydoyle and Coolmore during his official visit to Ireland in October 1987.

Left: Vincent with Irish Racing Board Chairman, Dr Michael Smurfit, whose father, Jefferson Smurfit Sr, was one of Vincent's first owners.

Right: Vincent with actor John Forsythe at the Curragh on Budweiser Irish Derby Day 1989, after Jacqueline O'Brien's Wedding Bouquet had won the opening race!

Left: The Heir Apparent . . . Charles O'Brien in happy mood after receiving the Bollinger 'Irish Trainer of the Year' Award on behalf of his father in December 1988.

Right: Father and son in a tactical discussion with stable jockey John Reid at the Phoenix Park.

Left: Vincent with his daughter, Susan Magnier, chatting with Tipperary-born Jimmy Fitzgerald, who trained Forgive 'n' Forget to win the inaugural Vincent O'Brien Gold Cup at Leopardstown in 1987.

Right: Vincent with the American Cash Asmussen, who had a controversial season in Ireland but contends that his career record of winners stands up to any scrutiny.

Left: Margaret O'Brien with Pauline (on Raffles) and Mark (on Taffy) in the yard of Clashganniff House where, in Vincent's day, Cottage Rake and Hatton's Grace were stabled.

Right: Vincent has found relaxation from the public gaze by fishing, shooting, golfing and hunting. Here he is seen hunting with Lord Waterford and his daughter Liz in her childhood days.

Left: Vincent on the day he received the Kaliber Award in Dublin, with Bryan Marshall (left), who rode Early Mist (1953) and Royal Tan (1954) to victory in the Aintree Grand National, and Pat Taaffe (right), who completed a fabulous O'Brien three-timer with different horses by taking the 1955 National on Quare Times.

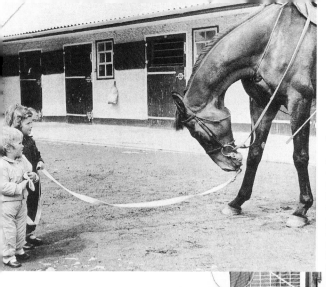

Jacqueline O'Brien's brilliance with the camera can be seen (*left*) in her classic picture of 1955 Aintree Grand National winner, Quare Times, in the yard at Ballydoyle with Liz and Sue, and again (*below*) with grandson Sean McClory with Storm Bird.

Below: The pride of Vincent and Jacqueline, their thirteen grandchildren, photographed at Ballydoyle House at Christmas 1988. Back row (left to right): Robert (O'Brien), John Paul (Magnier), James (Myerscough), Sean (McClory). Front row (left to right): David (Myerscough) holding Tara (Myerscough), Thomas (Magnier), Michael Vincent (Magnier), Samantha (Magnier), Kate (Magnier) holding Charles (O'Brien), Andrew (O'Brien) and Sophie (Myerscough).

Left: Vincent O'Brien with his first grandchild, Andrew, son of David. *Below*: Jacqueline, caught by the camera of another professional photographer, as Alleged seems to be saying to her: 'No photographs today, please!'

a 6–1 chance ridden by Irish Champion jockey Michael Kinane.

Experienced race readers were critical of Cash Asmussen for lying too much out of his ground at Leopardstown, leaving Golden Temple with too much to make up in the straight and they were sharply critical of him at the Park for getting boxed in in such a small field and being forced to come between horses at the crucial moment. Earlier in the season they had been critical of his riding of Seattle Dancer in the Nijinsky colt's opening race of the season at the Park when the Vincent O'Brien-trained Classic hope did not see daylight until too late and failed to beat the 14–1 outsider, Reet Petite, and On The Turf. Seattle Dancer was at 4–6 that day.

But in the final analysis the Golden Temple failure in mid-August brought matters to a head and his critics would assert that it meant that Asmussen's days at Bally-doyle were numbered.

It was common knowledge among the racing writers that Christy Roche could have succeeded him at the season's end but Christy decided to remain with David O'Brien out of the loyalty built up between them during the Assert-Secreto days.

Cash Asmussen was not prepared to get bogged down in detailed excuses for Golden Temple's failure at Leopardstown and the Park. He acknowledged that 'she had a lot to do at Leopardstown' but stressed that 'she didn't finish in that race as she did at the Park'.

'The opening never came for me in that Park race when it would have made all the difference between defeat and victory. When the openings come, you're a hero – when they don't, you're a villain. That just goes with the terri-tory,' he said.

Then he posed the pertinent question: 'What did Golden Temple do afterwards?'

A quick glance through the Form Book showed that in her only other outing in 1987, with Cash in the saddle and starting 2–1 favourite in a field of nine for the Group 3 Mount Coote Stud Stakes (1 mile) at the Curragh in

269

September, she held a prominent position early on but weakened in the last 1½ furlongs to finish fifth.

She had two outings the following season, when John Reid had taken over. The punters still had faith in her and installed her 6–4 favourite for the Ballycorus Stakes (Listed) at Leopardstown in July. Having led until inside the last furlong, she was run out of it and beaten a length by Cipriani (Michael Kinane). In her only other outing, over the same course, she again weakened in the final furlong to finish seventh behind the favourite, Llyn Gwynant (Willie Carson), trained by John Dunlop. Golden Temple started 9–4 second favourite that day.

Yes, Cash had a right to ask: what did she do after the Phoenix Park race that had caused such a furore and brought such a storm about his head?

'I probably arrived at Ballydoyle with too high a profile. Unless I was going to perform miracles, I suppose I could only end up putting spots on it,' he said with emphasis and a touch of irony at the memories of things past.

He came to realise that any horse out of the Ballydoyle stable that was reported to be catching the proverbial swallows on the gallops was going to start at 4–7 or even shorter on its debut. 'All the O'Brien fancied horses are at short odds – you have to learn to live with that. If one of them gets beat when the public expect it to win, then you have to be prepared to take the stick, even if the fault isn't yours.

'I can tell you this,' Cash went on, 'when you look at my record in the overall in Ireland over one season, it stood up against anyone. When they were making all this fuss about my riding of Golden Temple at the Park, I had ridden 51 winners from 129 mounts – an average of virtually 40 per cent and no Irish jockey could match that ratio.'

By the time the season ended, he had ridden 62 winners, coming second to Michael Kinane (86) in the Irish Flat Jockey's Championship.

He smiles when he reflects on the fact that his Irish percentage of winners to rides outstripped his career per-

270

centage and he contends that his career record overall again would bear comparison with that of any jockey on a global scale. He has long since passed the landmark of 2000 winners and is heading inexorably towards stake winnings on the horses he has ridden to victory of $50 million (the total was around $35 million the day Golden Temple failed to catch Claxton's Slew at the Park).

Cash Asmussen's ambition of 'riding as many Classic winners as possible' when he left Paris to take up duty at Ballydoyle was not to be realised, though he did win the Irish St Leger on the John Oxx-trained Eurobird. There was no Sir Ivor, no Nijinsky, no Alleged, nothing of the calibre of The Minstrel in the stable – the kind of champions that Lester had ridden. And neither was there anything to compare with Sadler's Wells, Golden Fleece or El Gran Senor – the kind of class colts that Pat Eddery had the privilege of riding.

Seattle Dancer was the pride of Ballydoyle when Cash arrived – the great hope for Classic glory in 1987. But though Cash won the Derrinstown Stud Derby Trial Stakes and the Windfields Farm Gallinule Stakes on him, he could only finish sixth in the Prix du Jockey Club (French Derby) and later finished second in the Grand Prix de Paris at Longchamp.

Supposing there had been a Nijinsky or a Sir Ivor, a Golden Fleece or an El Gran Senor, would there have been such an intense spotlight put on the defeats the Texan suffered on a few odds-on chances of questionable ability in the final analysis? As great horses make trainers, so jockeys gain from the super champions and ride the crest of the wave with them.

26

David Walks Away From It All

'I had always felt that some day David would walk away from it all.' Thus did Christy Roche, stable jockey to David O'Brien, sum up his feelings in the immediate aftermath of the announcement in early October 1988 that Vincent O'Brien's eldest son had decided to give up training in his early thirties. In 1984, at the age of 28, David became the youngest man ever to train an Epsom Derby winner when Secreto beat El Gran Senor, while in 1982 he won the French Derby and the Irish Derby with Assert, and in 1985 the Irish 2000 Guineas with Triptych. Never in the history of racing globally had a trainer achieved so much before his 30th birthday.

It had been on the cards for some time that David O'Brien would quit training. A few people very close to him in the stable and in the racing world had been taken into his confidence and were aware that he would be calling it a day in the autumn of 1988. Yet when the announcement came there was a deep sense of shock and people naturally speculated on the reasons why.

Christy Roche, whose relationship with David O'Brien was not just one of Master and stable jockey, but one of deep mutual respect and friendship, said, 'An out-and-out gentleman, David was too nice a guy for this game. It was not in him to give owners false hopes. He wasn't prepared to run a horse unless it could do itself justice on the racecourse.'

Roche said that David O'Brien 'was under pressure right from the very first day as a son of Vincent. He achieved in three short years (1982–84) what most trainers would spend a lifetime trying to achieve.

'He wasn't interested in making his name solely by the number of winners he turned out. He had the same attention to detail as his father. And like his father he thought big and aimed big – always. If he could not maintain things at that level, he would judge himself a failure.

'After you have won the English, French and Irish Derbys before your 30th birthday it is difficult to stay with bad horses or horses that do not come up to the mark for various reasons.'

The sad thing about David's decision to call it a day, he contended, was that the training profession had lost a genius. 'And I do not say that lightly,' he added.

'I maintain that if David had not given up training, he could have set records that in time would have had people making comparisons. To those who would knock him, I would point out that he took a £16,000 colt in Assert and turned him into a dual Derby winner. And he had the courage with Secreto to take on El Gran Senor, which many thought was unbeatable. His record in a very short spell as a trainer says it all.'

On a Sunday evening late in February 1989 at his home south of Cashel, in County Tipperary, David O'Brien talked about pressure – the pressure that can stem from working fifteen to sixteen-hour days and how that can take its toll and lead to frustration, particularly if success does not attend your efforts at the pace at which it started.

He admits that he would wake at night thinking about the horses, about his plans for them, about setbacks they might suffer, about the failure of colts and fillies to realise the potential that seemed to be there – on looks and breeding – when they were bought originally at the yearling sales.

Once he had made up his mind, that was it. He was not prepared to go into details, to elaborate, to give long interviews to the media explaining the reasons why. He was not going to get caught up refuting publicly the various theories that sprang from idle racecourse gossip. He decided to say nothing beyond the bare statement announcing that he was calling it a day and which read: 'I have taken the decision for personal reasons, and while it will mean the end of my direct involvement in training, it will in no way diminish my interest in the bloodstock industry, which is so much part of my life.'

Stallion shares would ensure a comfortable existence, even if he decided not to work again. But he was going to keep his hand in in other aspects of the bloodstock industry. The knowledge he had gained, much of it from his father before he went out on his own, would certainly stand him in good stead.

'Father thrives on pressure,' he said. 'The higher the stakes, the bigger the targets, the more he relishes it. He is phenomenal the way he has stood up to it for almost half a century, even when things may have been going badly, as when the stable was hit by a virus some years back.'

The decision to give up training was taken for family reasons, he explains. In the years he had been training he had devoted himself most of the waking day totally to the horses (to the exclusion of golf, which he loved as a form of relaxation). David felt that he had to think of his wife, Catherine, and their three young children. He was extremely anxious to give time to them.

He had always been one of those people for whom there were no half measures. You were either in something completely or not at all. It was not in him to sit back after the Classic successes he had enjoyed and bask in reflected glory, rest on his laurels and let things run for themselves. He had to maintain the pace, to aim higher, to go after new peaks. Something had to give.

When he began training on his own it was an advantage, he said, to be known, to be introduced to people you had never met before as 'the son of Vincent O'Brien'. It opened doors, it helped make a lot of contacts, it smoothed the way in a manner that he could not deny.

'But there was pressure created, too, by being Vincent O'Brien's son, through people's expectations being pitched very high and immediately they wondered aloud almost whether I could achieve all that Father had achieved. On balance, though, I could not complain. I got every chance and the breaks came my way very quickly, much more quickly than anyone of my age could ever expect.'

Approaching the end of his very first season as a public trainer – 1981 – when he was still only 25, David O'Brien had saddled more than twenty winners, including winners of Pattern races in Pas de Seul, his first runner in France, Anfield in the Railway Stakes and Ashford Castle Stakes, and Assert in the Beresford Stakes. Significantly, looking ahead to Secreto's defeat of El Gran Senor in the Epsom Derby, the Ashford Castle Stakes and Beresford Stakes were both won at the expense of better-backed colts trained by Vincent O'Brien.

David showed that he had acquired his father's eye to pick out 'a good one' when he saw Anfield in a field 'and I went to the sales determined to have him, no matter what he cost'. In fact, the son of Be My Guest made 53,000 guineas at Goffs and, having won all his three races in Ireland, only lost his unbeaten record in the mud of the Grand Criterium the Sunday after the Prix de l'Arc at Longchamp.

Then there was his outstanding training feat with Pas de Seul, rated champion three-year-old miler in England and Ireland (with a rating of 133 from *Timeform*) in 1982. In the hands of Christy Roche, Robert Sangster's Mill Reef colt had taken the Prix Eclipse (Group 3) at Saint Cloud in late September 1981, the second victory of his two-year-old career. He was then off the course for eleven months with a hairline fracture of the off-fore cannon bone, which required pinning.

He reappeared amazingly fit enough to win the Hungerford Stakes (Group 3) in mid-August 1982 at Newbury with Pat Eddery in the saddle, starting at 13–2 in a field of ten. And then, having finished fifth in the Waterford Crystal Mile Stakes (Group 2) at Goodwood on firm going, he went to Longchamp in October and on heavy going took the Prix de La Forêt (Group 1) by an impressive three lengths with Christy Roche up.

David had proved that he could evaluate with uncanny accuracy the material in his yard. Before Assert had his very first outing in a Maiden at Leopardstown and before he won the Group Two Beresford Stakes at the Curragh, David, when asked to name the best colt in his care, immediately named Assert. He was beaten by Golden Fleece in that Maiden at Leopardstown but in the Beresford trounced the previously undefeated Longleat.

The third generation of his family to embark on what many believe is the most demanding living in the world of professional sport, David O'Brien did not automatically follow in his father's footsteps when eventually deciding to train horses. As Tom MacGinty wrote in a feature in the 1981–82 edition of the *Irish Racing Annual*, this shy young man with the ever-ready smile, 'had seen too much of the problems and traumas, which grow rather than diminish with the sort of international recognition his father achieved, to think it was a sinecure.'

David admitted, himself, that he wanted to keep his options open, so he decided to study accountancy – 'Something, I knew, would be useful no matter what I did in the end. But during my years in Dublin I found I was more and more often returning home to be with the horses, and eventually decided this was what I wanted to do.'

Vincent took him under his wing as an apprentice trainer. It became a four-year course interspersed with winters in America and in Australia, where David joined Bart Cummins, an almost legendary figure down under. It was in Australia that he would meet Catherine, who hails from the same area near Perth as Jacqueline. Later Catherine came over to Ireland to stay with a cousin. She never went back, but married David.

'My father never pushed me into horses at all but I think he is very pleased that I have chosen to make it my career,' said David in November 1980 in a *Sunday Independent* interview with Frank Byrne, when the story broke that he had applied for a licence and that 1981 would see him competing for the first time in his own right as a racehorse trainer.

'Obviously,' said David very sincerely, 'it's going to be impossible to achieve all that my father has achieved in racing – but it doesn't really worry me; in fact, it's a big help to have that kind of inspiration.

'The one thing he has impressed upon me is to pay attention to detail. But I don't think I'll ever know as much about horses as he does – or even half as much.'

The 40 horses that he had in his yard adjacent to Ballydoyle were mostly two-year-olds, while the older brigade included a few cast-offs from his father's string. Among these was Adams, who became David's first runner, in the Burmah Lincolnshire Trial on the first day of the 1981 season at the Phoenix Park. Ridden by Christy Roche, who had been signed as the stable jockey, Adams started favourite. He ran a respectable race to finish seventh, giving every indication that he would be better for the run. And so it proved six weeks later at the Curragh on 27 April.

Top weight for the Athgarvan Handicap and again ridden by Christy Roche, Adams was in contention almost from the start and, taking the lead 2 furlongs out, ran on tenaciously to beat the three-year-old Forelock by a length and a half. David was on his way.

Before the end of the season, he was asked if he could foresee the possibility of training a Classic winner in his second season and his response was: 'Some of the two-year-olds have the potential. I just hope they come up to that class.' He was thinking especially of Assert.

Assert was having his first outing of the season and started at 6–1 when he ran in the Nijinsky Stakes at Leopardstown on 8 May 1982 against the Vincent O'Brien-trained Golden Fleece, who had already taken the Sean Graham Ballymoss Stakes at the Curragh on 17 April. Assert was beaten by 2½ lengths but *Raceform Note-Book* reported that 'making his run on the home turn, he closed the gap with the winner very impressively from the distance and when there was no chance of victory, was gently eased close home. He will be a force in the very top class.'

I put it to David that suggestions were made at the time that Assert was given an 'easy' race so that no blemish would be put on the record of Golden Fleece. David said quite emphatically that there was no question of Assert not being allowed to run on his merits that afternoon at Leopardstown.

'Golden Fleece already had a race under his belt that season as a three-year-old, whereas my one was only starting off his three-year-old career. It would have been madness to have given him a hard race on his very first outing. That was the last thing I wanted to do. I instructed Christy Roche to win if he could but under no circumstances was he to knock the colt about.

'Assert ran on his merits that day and Golden Fleece, the fitter of the two, had a fair bit in hand. There is absolutely no doubt about it that if Assert had been given a punishing race to try and win an event worth £8856, he might never have won the French Derby or the Irish Derby.'

As a result of his victory in the Nijinsky Stakes, Golden Fleece was installed a 3–1 favourite for the Epsom Derby, his next outing. There was speculation that David was prevented from running Assert against Golden Fleece at Epsom by Robert Sangster, who owned both colts, but David flatly rejected any such suggestion. 'It was never my intention to run Assert at Epsom. Assert was a big, long-striding horse. I decided that he would not be able to handle the gradients, would have difficulty coming down the Hill and might get unbalanced rounding Tattenham Corner.'

Assert, having won the Prix du Jockey Club (French Derby) like a really top-class colt by 3 lengths from Real Shadai (M. Philipperon), swept to an 8 length win in the Irish Derby from Silver Hawk (A. Murray). Christy Roche rode him in both victories. After being beaten by a neck by Kalaglow in the King George VI and Queen Elizabeth Stakes over 1½ at Ascot, Assert came back to 1¼ miles in the Benson & Hedges Gold Cup at York and became the widest-margin winner of this prestigious event when drawing relentlessly clear of his rivals in the last 2 furlongs to beat Norwick by 7 lengths, with Amyndas a neck away third.

As Christy Roche was injured, Pat Eddery took the ride at York and actually won that Benson & Hedges race 35 minutes after breaking a bone in his right hand – he had been tossed on to a concrete support post when his mount Kenninghall collapsed in the previous race ('I could only use two fingers in my right hand,' said Pat).

Then, with a $25 million syndication deal safely completed, Assert made his farewell Irish appearance in the Joe McGrath Memorial Stakes over 1¼ miles at Leopardstown on Saturday, 18 September and got a wonderful reception from a large crowd as he toyed with the opposition to win by 3 lengths from King of Hush (Steve Cauthen), with Punctilio (Pat Eddery) a further 1½ lengths away third.

'Ten furlongs is his best distance, but he won the two Derbys over a mile and a half and was only just beaten in the King George VI and Queen Elizabeth Stakes,' said David O'Brien afterwards, adding that soft ground would not deter the horse at Longchamp in the Prix de l'Arc de Triomphe. 'He has a light action and he won on the soft as a two-year-old.' So the die was cast and it was decided to bypass the Champion Stakes in favour of the richer and more prestigious Prix de l'Arc de Triomphe.

It would, of course, have been the crowning achievement of a truly memorable season for David O'Brien if Assert had gone on to win in Paris. Some big punters in Ireland and Britain had gone for a real 'touch' and the colt started 5–2 favourite in a field of 17. Assert, in the hands of Pat Eddery, was close up on the outside until 2 furlongs out and then dropped out of it quickly to finish eleventh, to the disappointment of the big Anglo-Irish following present.

Desmond Stoneham reported from Paris in the *Irish Field*: 'Assert's fate was probably sealed when at 10.30 on Saturday night the heavens opened and the already very soft going was quickly transformed to heavy. Pat Eddery reported that Assert could never show his true action on that soggy ground.'

Would Assert have beaten Golden Fleece if the two had met in the Irish Derby? David O'Brien said that the go-ahead had been given for the two to meet in the race, though since Golden Fleece never ran again after his Epsom Derby triumph, it must remain a matter of speculation whether the two Robert Sangster-owned colts would have actually got to the starting-gate together. The cynics will continue to exclaim that it was never on, just as they would never have seen a repeat of the Secreto-El Gran Senor 1984 Epsom Derby clash evolving at the Curragh.

'It would have taken an exceptional horse to have beaten Assert that day. We put in a pacemaker for him. It would have been a real test – a tougher test for Golden Fleece than Epsom was. The question is – would Golden Fleece's electrifying burst of finishing speed have been blunted by the time they got to the final 2 furlongs? They would have been going a really hot gallop the whole way. Assert liked it that way and would have been very much at home forcing the pace from a half a mile out, as Christy Roche did in the actual Curragh race, in which he had built up an unbeatable lead at the distance,' said David O'Brien.

Even though Secreto gave Christy Roche the greatest day of his career as a jockey when he won the Epsom Derby by beating El Gran Senor, Christy unhesitatingly put Assert ahead of him, describing him as 'a true mile-and-a-half horse'.

In one short season, David O'Brien had scaled peaks that many trainers have not even dreamt of reaching in a lifetime in the profession. Robert Sangster had so much faith in him that he had an interest in over half of the 50 horses in his stable.

David's dedication was such at this early stage of his career that he thought nothing of rising at 5.30 a.m. and not finishing his working day until 8 p.m. This routine never changed, even on his wedding day.

Jacqueline O'Brien says of David: 'He treated the horses in his care as individuals – feeding each one differently and planning individual training schedules suited to the personality, temperament and ability of each horse. I have never seen anyone who went to so much trouble to personally bring out the potential in each separate horse.

'I don't believe anyone else ever put on a bandage in his yard; he made up the feed for the horses and always did the early morning feed himself. He used to say that he could tell how the horses were by the way they behaved in their boxes after the night.

'Whenever we came up against a problem in either stable management or in the veterinary field,' Jacqueline added, 'I would go to David and expect to get a first-class answer. I would agree with Christy Roche – but obviously my view is a bit biased – that David is a great horseman.'

Those who saw 'the season of Assert' as a flash in the pan, were to under-estimate completely the quality of genius in David O'Brien's make-up. Nothing demonstrated this quality better than the way he prepared Secreto for the 1984 Epsom Derby and assessed that El Gran Senor could be beaten.

Ever cautious in his pronouncements and never known to make rash forecasts, Vincent O'Brien admitted on the eve of Epsom Derby that he was 'confident'. El Gran Senor was going to Epsom unbeaten.

Like his father, David O'Brien was not given to extravagant expressions of opinion. He repeatedly said, 'By the time he is finished with Secreto, El Gran Senor will know he has had a race.'

Secreto was at least as well bred as El Gran Senor; indeed, in the opinion of breeding authority Tony Morris, Secreto was better equipped in this department for the Derby, being by the same great Northern Dancer, out of a half-brother to a French Derby winner and, therefore, more likely to stay. Isobel Cunningham in *The Scotsman* tipped Secreto to win on the score of breeding.

Nonetheless, the public evidence in support of Secreto's claims was limited. He had won his only race in the autumn of 1983 with ease, but it was a minor event which merited a rating of 7 stone 7 pounds in the Irish Two-Year-Old Classification, 28 pounds below El Gran Senor. And while the Tetrarch Stakes, in which he ran away from Without Reserve and Deasy's Delight, over 7 furlongs at the Curragh in April, showed that Secreto had a real touch of class, the Irish 2000 Guineas, for which he started favourite, left doubts in the minds of many observers.

They were not shared by either David O'Brien or Christy Roche, despite the fact that both admitted subsequently that they had considered Secreto unbeatable that day. A modest early gallop and the fact that Secreto ran too freely in Roche's opinion, combined to bring about the defeat.

There was no weakening in the resolve to take on El Gran Senor. Thus it was that on a virtually perfect summer's day the two sons of Northern Dancer, trained in neighbouring parishes in County Tipperary, were among the 17 runners that went to the start and created one of the most debated race climaxes in racing history.

'My attitude,' said David, 'was that I had a horse in my charge that was good enough to go for the race and, therefore, I must go for the race. I could not be influenced in that decision by El Gran Senor's unbeaten record and neither could I be influenced by sentiment, though I know some people would have found it difficult to understand why I should be taking on my father.

'I didn't feel overawed by the reputation El Gran Senor had built up. Anyway, a close study of his pedigree showed that there *had* to be a doubt about his getting the distance and, furthermore, I concluded that he had shown such speed in his previous races that you had to wonder whether he could last it out up the hill.

'On breeding, I felt my horse had the better chance. So, despite the reverse Secreto had suffered in the Irish 2000 Guineas, I was not going to be deterred.

'As to the race itself, I accept that it looked all over bar the shouting 2 furlongs out. It was not until I saw El Gran

Senor beginning to wobble under Secreto's challenge that I knew we could beat him and the hill found him out in the end.

'I suppose I was sorry in a way to beat my father when there was so much at stake for El Gran Senor but, at the same time, it was a tremendous thrill for me to win the Epsom Derby and add it to the two other Derbys I had already won. There is nothing in racing for a Flat trainer to compare with winning the Epsom Derby.

'There is too much emphasis placed on keeping Classic horses unbeaten. The way I look upon it is, you win some, you lose some. A horse, I contend, must be judged on the *overall* record. If you try to protect a record, say after a colt has won the 2000 Guineas and Derby, then you may never find out his true worth – what he is capable of achieving if allowed to go for the King George VI and Queen Elizabeth Stakes and the Prix de l'Arc de Triomphe, for example.

'I don't believe for one moment that it took all that much from El Gran Senor that he was beaten a short head in the Epsom Derby. To my mind, the very fact that he ran in the race after winning the 2000 Guineas showed that he was tough enough to take plenty of racing, especially as he came out subsequently and won the Irish Derby.

'I don't think either that breeders were put off in the least by that short-head defeat. His record in the overall was outstanding – only one defeat and that by the narrowest of margins in a photo finish.'

The final word on Secreto and El Gran Senor at Epsom and what might have happened if they had met again remains with Christy Roche, who remarked: 'If the repeat of the Epsom Derby between Secreto and El Gran Senor that everyone wanted had taken place at the Curragh, it would undoubtedly have been a wonderful race. I would still have favoured my one in a true test of stamina.'

Secreto's triumph at Epsom overshadowed another outstanding achievement by David O'Brien in 1984 when the filly Alydar's Best, who had been purchased at Keeneland for $625,000, won the Grand Criterium at Longchamp. Most of the 1984 Classics had been run before Alydar's Best – who late the previous season had even been spoken of as a Derby prospect – struck winning form by taking the Pretty Polly Stakes at the Curragh and then went on to finish second in the Irish Oaks. At the end of her three-year-old career she went to America where she broke down badly.

David O'Brien won the Irish 2000 Guineas in 1985 with Triptych, wearing the colours of Alan Clore, but this brilliant mare was being trained in France by Patrick Biancone when she won the Phoenix Champion Stakes in 1987 and when she finished third to Dancing Brave in the Prix de l'Arc de Triomphe in 1986 and to Trempolino in 1987. The last of David's Classic triumphs came in 1986 when he won the Jefferson Smurfit Memorial Irish St Leger with Authaal (Christy Roche) at 8–1 for Sheikh Mohammed.

When he made the announcement that he was quitting training, he had 29 horses registered in training, 23 of them being owned by Sheikh Mohammed. In that 1988 season – up to October – he had won 14 races with seven horses for £87,634. He had experienced a lot of problems with his two-year-olds and none of the 16 had made a racecourse appearance. That was very frustrating, because the two-year-olds provide the potential Classic challengers for the following season.

Robert Sangster was quoted as saying, after David's announcement that he was quitting: 'His entire life revolved around horses. David is a very shy man and I think that perhaps he was unsuited to the hurly burly of the racing world. I also think he was probably frustrated by the lack of success with his two-year-olds.'

But when you have scaled the heights that David O'Brien did at 25 when winning two Derbys with Assert and then at 27 sealing that achievement by winning a third Derby with Secreto and when you have handled a horse of Triptych's calibre, it is extremely difficult to continue to work sixteen-hour days with horses of moderate calibre or no potential to make the top. As Christy Roche so aptly put it, David was interested more in quality than in the number of winners he turned out.

The home-loving David O'Brien came to realise that there were other things in life besides the continued quest for excellence and more Classic glory – and the constant grind that went with it.

27

A Wonderful Father

The all-pervading sense of family, and a very close-knit family at that, is what strikes you most forcibly as you converse with his children about Vincent O'Brien.

What emerges is that he has not only been a wonderful father in their eyes but also remains the father figure they look up to with total respect and pride. The imprint left in their minds from childhood days reveals a father who was great at telling bedtime stories, outstanding too at bringing to life for them the characters and the customs of his own childhood in Churchtown, taking them for fishing expeditions along the Blackwater, following the hunt with them from the time they were able to ride to hounds, going with them along with Jacqueline on family holidays to the Alpine ski slopes or to Palm Springs and entering fully into the spirit of birthday parties and of the festive occasions, Christmas most of all.

Four of his five children are married – Charles is still single at the time of writing in 1989 – and they agree that he is 'superb' as a grandfather. They emphasise how Vincent 'adores being with his grandchildren'.

'And they simply adore him also,' says Susan, wife of Coolmore boss, John Magnier.

'They can climb all over him and he doesn't mind,' says David. 'And he is so patient with them.'

Vincent has always had a great feeling for nature. The hedgehog straying on to the avenue at Ballydoyle, baby birds in their nests, the hare with young finding its way on to one of the gallops in the early morning – these capture his attention in a very special way and the world seems to stop momentarily while he tends to their needs. He will treat them with the respect he would accord a human being.

The sensitivity that is at the heart of his communion with nature impressed itself deeply on his children. 'Yes, he loves everything about nature: the animals, the birds and the trees, the flowers, the changing seasons – it has always been an essential part of his life,' said David. 'He taught me so much to appreciate.'

Combined with his love of nature is a deep belief in God. One is intertwined with the other. He cannot contemplate nature in all its beauty without seeing the Maker's hand in every facet of it.

'A very good Catholic,' is how Liz describes her father. 'I don't think I have seen him miss Mass ever, either on a Sunday or Holyday.'

Each new Flat season starts with the celebration of a Mass of blessing at Ballydoyle, attended by all the stable staff and the members of the O'Brien family and household staff. It is as important to Vincent O'Brien in his scale of priorities as the security arrangements imposed around colts like Sir Ivor, Nijinsky and El Gran Senor in the count-down to an Epsom Derby. It is a throw-back to the days in Churchtown when the local Parish Priest or Curate blessed the O'Brien challengers as they departed for the Cheltenham Festival meeting or the Aintree Grand National meeting.

The children remember kneeling down after the evening meal for the Family Rosary, a daily practice that had been inculcated in Vincent by his own parents in Churchtown. The rich Irish traditions die hard.

Susan recalls when she was a child Dad coming up to read bedtime stories to her, *Winnie the Pooh*, and other timeless favourites such as *The Wind in the Willows*.

'What I liked even more than these was when he talked to us about his own childhood days, when he talked, too, about the War years, the rationing of tea and cigarettes, the clothes coupons and his days in the LDF. He brought back the veil on a lost world to us – something it is not easy to imagine today. It all seemed so wonderful because he had made it so real and in many ways so simple and different.

'I remember how the characters he knew in Church-town and Buttevant became for me, in the telling, people I felt I knew all my life, he painted such a picture of them. And I remember laughing at funny happenings and funny sayings and being sad, too, when he related tragedies that befell friends of his in the community. He had such an exact feeling for that area of County Cork.

'I remember Christmas times past and Mother playing the organ in the little Church in Rosegreen. We joined in the hymns, 'Silent Night' and 'Adeste Fidelis', and then being brought to the Crib. Dermot and his wife, Jean, and Phonsie and his wife, Ann, joined us for the Christmas dinner and I can still recall the laughter around the table as the turkey was brought in. Later the Christmas pudding and then slices of Christmas cake and all the minerals that we kids could consume.

'We would put on our own little theatrical production during the Christmas period. I played the piano, David was on the trumpet, Liz played the viola and Jane the violin. We took it very seriously. We made the stable lads pay going in! It was all good fun and there was even a ballet performance as part of the production.

'Father taught us how to play cards but, strangely enough, he never played children's card games. If he played with us, he played poker – and he played it seriously. He had learned how to play cards, he told us, from his own father.

'As a family man, I don't think there was anyone like him. And, now as a grandfather, he has been simply wonderful to our children, Katie, Thomas, John Paul, Michael Vincent and Samantha.'

Did she really call one of the boys Michael Vincent?

'Yes, and he so quickly became "M.V.",' she laughed. There could be no finer tribute by John and Sue to Vincent

than one of the Magnier boys already being known as
'M.V.'

Christmas figures strongly in the childhood memories of
Susan's sister, Jane, as it does with all the O'Brien children. She recalls writing to Santa and the thrill it gave on
Christmas morning examining the presents. 'They came
for each of us in a pillow case.' Birthday parties, too, have
a special place in her storehouse of memories. One party
that will always remain special for her was one of the
most recent, when her father celebrated his 70th birthday
in April 1987. 'It was a wonderful party, a purely family
occasion. I think Father really enjoyed it,' she said.

Vincent could be strict in certain things, like insisting
that everyone change for dinner. 'It meant that we girls
could not arrive at table in jeans,' said Jane. And when
he gave them pocket money, he expected that they would
not toss it away foolishly. It was almost as if he was telling
them silently that the way they used their pocket money
was an indication of how they would learn to look after
their own things.

Vincent and Jacqueline believed in protecting the children when they were too young to appreciate, or cope
with, certain happenings. Liz recalled the time that Vincent lost his licence over the 'Chamour Affair'. 'Nanny had
been told not to breathe a word about it to any of us
children. I can remember an awful lot of secret whispering
and wondering what it was all about. Then we were
having tea in the kitchen with Nanny – that is us children
– and suddenly over the radio came the news that Father
had lost his licence and I think it was mentioned that he
would be moving out of Ballydoyle.

'I remember Nanny literally flying to the radio and
trying desperately to switch it off before we could hear
any more. I can still see the exact spot in the kitchen
where the radio was that evening. You never forget things
like that.'

Yet, as they got older they were included in every family
conversation over meals. 'Nothing was held back from

us,' said Liz, 'and I think this cemented the closeness of the family as a unit.'

Jane recalled the pressures created on her father whenever he had a horse that emerged good enough to win a Classic and that pressure became all the more intense the better the horse was, especially if it was in the Sir Ivor, Nijinsky or Golden Fleece class.

'I always noticed that he grew tense when one of the outstanding two-year-olds of the previous season came out and won as a three-year-old and then the spotlight came on it as a possible 2000 Guineas and Derby winner. Strangely enough, he took defeat in his stride. He was more relaxed after a bad day than he was when victory meant that he had a horse in the yard that created all the security problems surrounding a well-fancied candidate, maybe even a warm favourite for one of the Classics. He became pre-occupied with the planning ahead, with concentrating on every detail, ensuring that nothing would go wrong if he could possibly help it.'

Liz remembers that there were always people coming and going. 'We would give a hand out, if there were quite a number of guests, and particularly if Mother was away on business.' It could lead to amusing situations. Once Jane Engelhard, wife of Charles Engelhard, the owner of Nijinsky, arrived with a present of two tins of caviare. 'I think they were worth about £500 each – and we put them in the freezer. I don't think we were supposed to do that,' said Liz with a smile.

On another occasion Jane donned an apron to assist in the serving at dinner and none of the guests knew her. As she served her father, he remarked aloud to the surprise of all – and, indeed, the horror of some – of the guests, 'Thanks Darling.'

The children tell other amusing stories about their father but tell them with an affection that indicates that they love to think that the Master of Ballydoyle, so meticulous in the world's eyes when preparing a Sir Ivor or Nijinsky to win a Derby, could actually be human like any other Dad. Like the time he twisted ligaments in his leg doing a Russian dance at the Tipperary Hunt Ball. The family holiday had been booked and he bravely accompanied the rest of them on the flight to the Alpine resort – sitting it out as they went skiing day after day.

And Liz recalled going with her Father to the Prix de l'Arc de Triomphe and tearing up and down the Champs Elysées looking for a Catholic Church in which to get Mass. 'We ended up in a Jewish Synagogue by mistake!'

David remembered living at home at first when he set up on his own as a trainer in 1981. 'There I was, eating across the table from my father at meals. We talked as father and son and yet we were in opposition! It was funny in a way when races were coming up in which we both had runners. A bit of a cat-and-mouse game – and neither of us giving anything away . . .'

Being a son or daughter of Vincent O'Brien created its own special problems. But then there are those who contend that in this day and age the children of the famous or the very rich may have to pay a price in personal terms for living in the constant shadow of a parent or parents rarely out of the headlines or social columns. In fact, a treadmill can be created that can inevitably catch those who did not bargain for it on the revolving cylinder of an unremitting spotlight. It can plunge one into the whirlpool of party-going and popping champagne corks, of invitations stemming from the aura surrounding the name, into a life that, at times, can take on an unreality that weaves the spell which demands later that one must learn to cope with the legacy stemming from it.

Or you may be asked to pitch things too high in order to emulate and, in the very seeking to emulate and even go one better, you may graft beyond the danger point.

'You couldn't really do very much in public but it would be talked about,' said Liz. 'You knew you were open to public scrutiny – all the time.' Did she sometimes long to be just the daughter of an ordinary person?

'We knew it couldn't be that way. In a way it was contradictory. We had our own circle of friends and when you are in the middle of something, you cannot see it from the outside. You cannot see yourself in the terms in which others are viewing you.'

In this she touched the heart of the matter. The children of Vincent O'Brien may have been acting totally as themselves, being quite ordinary within the family circle, but others outside that circle could not accept them as anything less than the offspring of Ireland's most famous racehorse trainer, an international figure known from London to Keeneland, from Paris to Australia, and all the way back to Ballydoyle. Known, in fact, wherever people followed racing.

Charles, who was born fifteen years after Liz, is seen today as the Heir Apparent, the son who is being groomed to take over at Ballydoyle when Vincent steps down. He is an extrovert like his mother, the complete opposite to the shy, retiring David.

Shortly before his father celebrated his 70th birthday in 1987, Charles, just twenty, had recently returned from a six-month sojourn at Brian Mayfield Smith's training establishment in Australia. He was preparing to leave for the States, where he planned to join the Californian stable of the very successful John Gosden, who had been an assistant for a time at Ballydoyle (John has since returned to train in England).

'My father never "pushed" me towards a career in racing,' Charles confided. He had gone into accountancy first, like David. 'I suppose the reason I went into accountancy initially was that my parents wanted me to make up my own mind, to see if I would prefer another life rather than racing. I am thankful to them for that. But I realised from the start that I loved being with horses. I suppose you could say it was in my blood.'

Charles will be taking over his father's establishment and the runners will be from Ballydoyle – and Ballydoyle has an image that extends far beyond the shores of Ireland, and a reputation to uphold that goes right back to the early 'fifties and will have extended over a span of forty years.

It is like the Abbey Theatre in Dublin or the National

Theatre in London, La Scala in Milan or the Metropolitan in New York. The very rafters ring with tradition – great moments, great performances, great individual performers soaring to undreamt-of heights.

Today Charles accompanies his father on the round of the barns at Keeneland looking over the yearlings in the sun-drenched Kentucky heat – just as Vincent before him accompanied his father, Dan, when he was going to fairs or to farms looking at horses he had an eye to buying. It is Charles who is seen at his father's elbow at race meetings and, in fact, the media have come to accept the two of them together – just as Vincent and his father were inseparable in the years directly before the Second World War and in the early War years before Vincent set up on his own after his father's death.

No one will envy Charles the mantle that he will assume when he becomes the Master of Ballydoyle. The challenge he faces will be an awesome one.

Epilogue

The trainer, like the great actor, must be judged in the final analysis on his days on the high plains of achievement.

As with the late Laurence Olivier: his first spell-binding Richard III during the Old Vic season of 1944, and later his great performances as Othello and Macbeth, performances which outlive some of the film roles he took that were beneath his talents.

There are those who would seek to make lasting judgements on Vincent O'Brien solely on the record of the Ballydoyle stable in the Classics and other major races run in the last six years of the 'eighties and, more particularly, since Classic Thoroughbreds was established.

In the period since El Gran Senor was short-headed in a photo finish to the 1984 Epsom Derby to the end of the 1989 Flat season, the only Classics that came the way of the Ballydoyle stable were Law Society's triumph in the 1985 Irish Derby, Leading Counsel's success in the Irish St Leger the same season and Dark Lomond's win in the same race in 1988.

The high hopes entertained for Saratogan in the 1989 English 2000 Guineas were not realised. In fact, none of the two-year-olds in which Classic Thoroughbreds had an interest, including the unbeaten Classic Fame and Classic Secret, trained on to hit the headlines like Nashwan or Old Vic. The shares that reached a high of 41p at one point prior to the 1989 English 2000 Guineas fell back dramatically to a figure below 20p following Saratogan's failure and other setbacks.

But to judge Vincent O'Brien's place in racing history on his record in the latter half of the 'eighties is to miss out completely on all the peaks he conquered over five decades and more, including being six times in the top three on the Flat in Britain, winning the championship twice and also being twice champion trainer under National Hunt Rules.

The immortals in sport are judged by the standards they set themselves. And such were the standards that Vincent O'Brien set that it would be well-nigh impossible to maintain them season after season.

Ballydoyle came to represent Classic success indelibly in the public mind – and nothing less. It came to represent horses of the calibre of Sir Ivor, Nijinsky, Alleged, The Minstrel, Golden Fleece and El Gran Senor. It was not for nothing then that the name 'Classic Thoroughbreds' was chosen for the new public company. Vincent O'Brien had the right to fly that flag over his flagship.

Four days before he celebrated his 70th birthday I recalled while chatting to him that Ernest Hemingway had once said that the writer never retires. And Hemingway, after a lean period, bounced back to win the Nobel Prize for Literature with *The Old Man and the Sea*. Dr O'Brien smiled at that.

Many a trainer half his age would have been defeated by the virus infection that hit Ballydoyle in 1985 and caused even more havoc to the stable's prospects the following season. But the Master of Ballydoyle has always shown himself to be a man of resilience and courage. Indeed, durability could be said to be his middle name.

He was 72 when he was supervising the preparation of Saratogan for the 1989 English 2000 Guineas. It was 45 years back to the 1944 season when he sent out Drybob to dead-heat for the Irish Cambridgeshire and Good Days won the Irish Cesarewitch. It was 51 years since the 1938 Cambridgeshire, which he helped his father win with

Solford, while the Irish Cesarewitch was won in 1941 by Dan O'Brien, again with his son's assistance.

No one was more deserving of the Doctorate conferred on him by the National University of Ireland in 1983 (he actually received an honorary LL.D.).

The impact that Vincent O'Brien made in his long career as a trainer on those involved in racing and breeding world-wide was borne home to me quite forcibly on a Sunday morning in March 1990 as I sat talking to Charles Taylor, President of Windfields Stud Farm and Chairman and Chief Steward of the Jockey Club of Canada, in his home in Toronto.

Charles, who is son of the legendary F. P. Taylor (whose name will always be linked with the peerless sire, Northern Dancer, and with colts like Nijinsky and The Minstrel that helped put Vincent O'Brien on a pedestal apart as a Flat trainer) and a former foreign correspondent for *The Globe and Mail* in his own right, said in tribute to the Master of Ballydoyle: 'I like to quote my late father, who always said, "there is no greater trainer in the world than Vincent O'Brien". And then he would add with a knowing twinkle in his eye, "The only reason I do not say he is the greatest is that I do have many other trainer friends!"

'I share the total respect my father had for Vincent. What always struck me during my visits to Ballydoyle was the meticulousness and thoroughness of the entire training operation and the total attention to detail. I have never seen anything like it anywhere else in my lifetime.'

Charles recalled being at Epsom the day El Gran Senor and Secreto, both bred at Windfields Farm, fought out their memorable finish to the 1984 Derby. If El Gran Senor had won, it would have been Vincent's seventh triumph in the race but ironically he was denied the moment by his own son, David. 'I remember David saying to his parents, "I'm sorry", but of course they were both thrilled for their son.'

Peter O'Sullevan, who has known him for over 40 years, said, 'As a visitor to Ballydoyle from the early 'fifties, one of the features which, to me, reflected the prosperity generated by M. V.'s talent was the speed with which the personnel's bicycle shed gave way to a carport.

'It should always be remembered that Vincent and his long-time contemporary, Paddy ("Darkie") Prendergast, did more than any other two personalities to put Ireland on the international racing map.'

Brough Scott said, 'There have been, and will be, many great trainers through the ages but there will be only one Vincent O'Brien. For he has been unique, in both the range and manner of his achievement. He was the pioneer.

'No one else had so completely conquered the high ground of the jumping game and then moved to similar eminence on the Flat. And he was the first to develop the high-tech, high-finance blending that has become the modern training norm.

'But for all his energy and ambition, the real key to Vincent's success lay in something you will never find in books or ledgers, something he was born with, something as Irish as Tipperary: a genius with a horse.

'When it's all over, that will be the part of O'Brien's legacy which many will seek but none can find. It's that which sets a standard against which all greatness will have to be judged.'

He has to be classed The Incomparable.

Writing of Lord Olivier in the *Sunday Times* after his death in July 1989, Garry O'Connor said that he had no rival on the stage – and Olivier knew it. 'Some thirty-five years after being presented by Sir John Gielgud with the sword Edmund Kean had used when playing Richard III, Olivier was asked if he would, in his turn, pass on the sword, and if so, to whom. He answered: "No one. It's mine." '

If there is a similar mythical sword in the racing world, it rests with Vincent O'Brien.

He will not need to pass it on.

THE FABULOUS VINCENT O'BRIEN RECORD

(Compiled by Annie and Tony Sweeney)

Appendix 1
Big Race Successes At Home

ON THE FLAT

IRISH 2000 GUINEAS
1959 El Toro (T. P. Burns)
1978 Jaazeiro (L. Piggott)
1981 King's Lake (P. Eddery)
1984 Sadler's Wells (G. McGrath)
1988 Prince of Birds (D. Gillespie)

IRISH 1000 GUINEAS
1966 Valoris (J. Power)
1977 Lady Capulet (T. Murphy)
1979 Godetia (L. Piggott)

IRISH DERBY
1953 Chamier (W. Rickaby)
1957 Ballymoss (T. P. Burns)
1970 Nijinsky (L. Ward)
1977 The Minstrel (L. Piggott)
1984 El Gran Senor (P. Eddery)
1985 Law Society (P. Eddery)

IRISH OAKS
1964 Ancasta (J. Purtell)
1965 Aurabella (L. Ward)
1969 Gaia (L. Ward)
1979 Godetia (L. Piggott)

IRISH ST LEGER
1959 Barclay (G. Bougoure)
1966 White Gloves (L. Ward)
1969 Reindeer (L. Ward)
1975 Caucasus (L. Piggott)
1976 Meneval (L. Piggott)
1977 Transworld (T. Murphy)
1980 Gonzales (R. Carroll)
1985 Leading Counsel (P. Eddery)
1988 Dark Lomond (D. Gillespie)

TETRARCH STAKES
1968 Harry (L. Ward)
1969 Sahib (L. Ward)
1971 Minsky (L. Piggott)

1972 Homeguard (J. Roe)
1973 Dapper (L. Piggott)
1974 Cellini (L. Piggott)
1982 Achieved (P. Eddery)
1983 Salmon Leap (P. Eddery)
1985 Northern Plain (P. Eddery)
1988 Prince of Birds (J. Reid)
1989 Saratogan (J. Reid)

ATHASI STAKES
1962 Lovely Gale (T. P. Glennon)
1968 Rimark (L. Ward)
1972 Arkadina (J. Roe)
1974 Lisadell (L. Piggott)
1979 Godetia (L. Piggott)

TRIGO STAKES
1957 Ballymoss (J. Power)
1960 Die Hard (G. Bougoure)
1962 Larkspur (T. P. Glennon)
1965 Donato (J. Purtell)
1966 Beau Chapeau (L. Ward)

DERRINSTOWN STUD DERBY TRIAL STAKES
(Formerly Nijinsky Stakes)
1972 Boucher (J. Roe)
1974 Hail The Pirates (L. Piggott)
1976 Meneval (L. Piggott)
1982 Golden Fleece (P. Eddery)
1983 Salmon Leap (P. Eddery)
1984 Sadler's Wells (G. McGrath)

GALLINULE STAKES
1953 Chamier (W. Rickaby)
1965 Baljour (J. Purtell)
1969 Onandaga (L. Ward)
1970 Saracen Sword (N. Brennan)
1971 Grenfall (J. Roe)
1973 Hail The Pirates (L. Piggott)
1974 Sir Penfro (T. Murphy)
1975 King Pellinore (T. Murphy)
1976 Meneval (L. Piggott)
1977 Alleged (L. Piggott)
1978 Inkerman (L. Piggott)
1980 Gonzales (L. Piggott)
1984 Montelimar (P. Eddery)
1987 Seattle Dancer (C. Asmussen)

PRETTY POLLY STAKES
1959 Little Mo (G. Bougoure)
1964 Ancasta (J. Purtell)
1967 Iskereen (L. Ward)
1969 Rimark (L. Ward)
1979 Godetia (L. Piggott)
1980 Calandra (L. Piggott)
1988 Dark Lomond (J. Reid)

DESMOND STAKES
1964 Restless Knight (J. Purtell)
1966 White Gloves (L. Ward)
1967 White Gloves (L. Ward)

1987 Seattle Dancer (C. Asmussen)
1988 Kris Kringle (J. Reid)

1969 Reindeer (L. Ward)
1972 Boucher (J. Roe)
1973 Hail The Pirates (L. Piggott)
1974 Sir Penfro (T. P. Burns)
1976 Niebo (L. Piggott)
1977 Be My Guest (T. Murphy)
1981 Belted Earl (P. Eddery)
1985 Sunstart (P. Eddery)
1986 Wise Counsellor (P. Eddery)
1987 Entitled (C. Asmussen)

BLANDFORD STAKES
1959 Little Mo (G. Bougoure)
1961 Silver Moon (G. Bougoure)
1965 Donato (J. Purtell)
1968 Wenona (L. Ward)
1970 Riboprince (L. Ward)
1971 Wenceslas (J. Roe)
1972 Manitoulon (J. Roe)
1974 Richard Grenville (L. Piggott)
1975 King Pellinore (L. Piggott)
1980 Gonzales (T. Murphy)
1981 Magesterial (P. Eddery)
1982 Lords (P. Eddery)
1983 South Atlantic (P. Eddery)
1988 Kris Kringle (J. Reid)

BALLYMOSS STAKES
1967 White Gloves (L. Ward)
1969 Selko (L. Ward)
1973 Cavo Doro (L. Piggott)
1982 Golden Fleece (P. Eddery)

JOE McGRATH MEMORIAL STAKES
1978 Inkerman (L. Piggott)
1979 Fordham (T. Carberry)
1980 Gregorian (G. McGrath)
1981 King's Lake (P. Eddery)

PHOENIX CHAMPION STAKES
1984 Sadler's Wells (P. Eddery)

PHOENIX STAKES
1976 Cloonlara (T. Murphy)
1981 Achieved (P. Eddery)

RAILWAY STAKES
1962 Turbo Jet (T. P. Glennon)
1965 Glad Rags (J. Purtell)
1968 Sahib (L. Ward)
1969 Nijinsky (L. Ward)
1970 Minsky (L. Ward)
1971 Open Season (J. Roe)
1975 Niebo (L. Piggott)
1976 Brahms (L. Piggott)
1978 Solar (T. Murphy)
1980 Lawmaker (T. Murphy)
1982 Ancestral (P. Eddery)
1983 El Gran Senor (P. Eddery)
1984 Moscow Ballet (P. Eddery)

ANGLESEY STAKES
1959 Arctic Sea (G. Bougoure)
1962 Philemon (T. P. Glennon)
1965 Bravery (J. Purtell)

1969 Nijinsky (L. Ward)
1970 Headlamp (L. Ward)
1971 Roberto (J. Roe)
1973 Saritamer (L. Piggott)
1975 Niebo (L. Piggott)
1977 Solinus (T. Murphy)
1980 Storm Bird (T. Murphy)
1982 Caerleon (P. Eddery)
1984 Law Society (P. Eddery)
1985 Woodman (P. Eddery)
1987 Lake Como (C. Asmussen)

MOYGLARE STUD STAKES
1981 Woodstream (P. Eddery)

NATIONAL STAKES
1967 Sir Ivor (L. Ward)
1971 Roberto (J. Roe)
1972 Chamozzle (J. Roe)
1973 Cellini (L. Piggott)
1975 Sir Wimborne (L. Piggott)
1979 Monteverdi (R. Carroll)
1980 Storm Bird (T. Murphy)
1982 Glenstal (V. Rossiter)
1983 El Gran Senor (P. Eddery)
1984 Law Society (P. Eddery)
1985 Tate Gallery (C. Asmussen)
1987 Caerwent (C. Assmussen)
1988 Classic Fame (J. Reid)

BERESFORD STAKES
1947 Barfelt (G. Wells)
1962 Pontifex (T. P. Glennon)

1967 Hibernian (L. Ward)
1969 Nijinsky (L. Ward)
1970 Minsky (L. Ward)
1971 Boucher (J. Roe)
1972 Chamozzle (J. Roe)
1973 Saritamer (L. Piggott)
1979 Huguenot (T. Murphy)
1980 Euclid (G. McGrath)
1982 Danzatore (P. Eddery)
1983 Sadler's Wells (P. Eddery)
1984 Gold Crest (P. Eddery)
1988 Classic Fame (J. Reid)

BIRDCATCHER NURSERY STAKES
1962 Turbo Jet (T. P. Glennon)
1966 Theo (L. Ward)
1977 Pull The Latch (T. Carberry)
1981 Afghan (T. Murphy)
1982 Treasure Trove (P. Eddery)
1983 Western Symphony (C. Roche)
1988 Kyra (D. Gillespie)

IRISH LINCOLNSHIRE
1949 Hatton's Grace (M. Wing)
1950 Knock Hard (T. P. Burns)

IRISH CAMBRIDGESHIRE
1944 Dry Bob (M. Wing)
1957 Courts Appeal (J. Power)
1961 Travel Light (G. Bougoure)
1968 Hibernian (L. Ward)
1979 Habituate (D. Hogan)

IRISH CESAREWITCH
1944 Good Days (M. Wing)
1947 Cottage Rake (G. Wells)
1948 Hot Spring (M. Wing)
1949 Hatton's Grace (M. Molony)
1950 Hatton's Grace (M. Molony)

NAAS NOVEMBER HANDICAP
1946 Cottage Rake (J. Tyrrell)
1949 Wye Fly (H. Holmes)

LEOPARDSTOWN NOVEMBER HANDICAP
1959 Coologan (A. Briscoe)

UNDER NATIONAL HUNT RULES

THYESTES CHASE
1956 Sam Brownthorn (T. Taaffe)

LEOPARDSTOWN CHASE
1953 Lucky Dome (P. J. Doyle)

IRISH GRAND NATIONAL
1952 Alberoni (L. Stephens)

GALWAY PLATE
1952 Alberoni (L. Stephens)

GALWAY HURDLE
1951 Wye Fly (M. Molony)

Appendix 2
Big Race Successes Abroad

ENGLAND

ON THE FLAT

THE 2000 GUINEAS
1968   Sir Ivor (L. Piggott)
1970   Nijinsky (L. Piggott)
1983   Lomond (P. Eddery)
1984   El Gran Senor (P.
       Eddery)

THE 1000 GUINEAS
1966   Glad Rags (P. Cook)

THE DERBY
1962   Larkspur (N.
       Sellwood)
1968   Sir Ivor (L. Piggott)
1970   Nijinsky (L. Piggott)
1972   Roberto (L. Piggott)
1977   The Minstrel (L.
       Piggott)
1982   Golden Fleece (P.
       Eddery)

THE OAKS
1965   Long Look (J. Purtell)
1966   Valoris (L. Piggott)

THE ST LEGER
1957   Ballymoss (T. P. Burns)
1970   Nijinsky (L. Piggott)
1972   Boucher (L. Piggott)

CORONATION CUP
1958   Ballymoss (A.
       Breasley)
1973   Roberto (L. Piggott)

HARDWICKE STAKES
1977   Meneval (L. Piggott)

ECLIPSE STAKES
1966   Pieces Of Eight (L.
       Piggott)
1977   Artaius (L. Piggott)
1983   Solford (P. Eddery)
1984   Sadler's Wells (P.
       Eddery)

KING GEORGE VI AND QUEEN ELIZABETH STAKES
1958 Ballymoss (A. Breasley)
1970 Nijinsky (L. Piggott)
1977 The Minstrel (L. Piggott)

SUSSEX STAKES
1973 Thatch (L. Piggott)
1977 Artaius (L. Piggott)
1978 Jaazeiro (L. Piggott)
1981 King's Lake (P. Eddery)

WATERFORD CRYSTAL MILE
1975 Gay Fandango (P. Eddery)
1977 By My Guest (L. Piggott)

BENSON & HEDGES GOLD CUP
1972 Roberto (B. Baeza)
1983 Caerleon (P. Eddery)

CHAMPION STAKES
1966 Pieces Of Eight (L. Piggott)
1968 Sir Ivor (L. Piggott)

ST JAMES'S PALACE STAKES
1973 Thatch (L. Piggott)
1978 Jaazeiro (L. Piggott)

RIBBLESDALE STAKES
1975 Gallina (L. Piggott)

CORONATION STAKES
1974 Lisadell (L. Piggott)

GREAT VOLTIGEUR STAKES
1977 Alleged (L. Piggott)

KING'S STAND STAKES
1962 Cassarate (N. Sellwood)
1973 Abergwaun (L. Piggott)
1977 Godswalk (L. Piggott)
1978 Solinus (L. Piggott)
1987 Bluebird (C. Asmussen)

JULY CUP
1973 Thatch (L. Piggott)
1974 Saritamer (L. Piggott)
1978 Solinus (L. Piggott)
1979 Thatching (L. Piggott)

WILLIAM HILL SPRINT CHAMPIONSHIP
1978 Solinus (L. Piggott)

VERNONS SPRINT CUP
1972 Abergwaun (L. Piggott)

GEOFFREY FREER STAKES
1977 Valinsky (L. Piggott)

QUEEN'S VASE
1958 Even Money (A. Breasley)
1975 Blood Royal (L. Piggott)

ASCOT GOLD CUP
1958 Gladness (L. Piggott)

GOODWOOD CUP
1958 Gladness (L. Piggott)

QUEEN ANNE STAKES
1975 Imperial March (G. Dettori)

JERSEY STAKES
1956   Adare (W. R. Johnstone)
1975   Gay Fandango (L. Piggott)

CORK and ORRERY STAKES
1970   Welsh Saint (L. Piggott)
1974   Saritamer (L. Piggott)
1975   Swingtime (W. Carson)
1979   Thatching (L. Piggott)

DIADEM STAKES
1971   Abergwaun (L. Piggott)
1972   Home Guard (L. Piggott)
1974   Saritamer (L. Piggott)
1975   Swingtime (L. Piggott)

COVENTRY STAKES
1977   Solinus (L. Piggott)

QUEEN MARY STAKES
1964   Brassia (J. Purtell)

NORFOLK STAKES
1984   Magic Mirror (L. Piggott)

CHERRY HINTON STAKES
1977   Turkish Treasure (L. Piggott)

CHAMPAGNE STAKES
1981   Achieved (P. Eddery)

FLYING CHILDERS STAKES
1981   Peterhof (E. Hide)

MIDDLE PARK STAKES
1978   Junius (L. Piggott)

CHEVELEY PARK STAKES
1967   Lalibela (L. Piggott)
1981   Woodstream (P. Eddery)

DEWHURST STAKES
1969   Nijinsky (L. Piggott)
1973   Cellini (L. Piggott)
1976   The Minstrel (L. Piggott)
1977   Try My Best (L. Piggott)
1979   Monteverdi (L. Piggott)
1980   Storm Bird (P. Eddery)
1983   El Gran Senor (P. Eddery)

ROYAL LODGE STAKES
1975   Sir Wimborne (L. Piggott)

OBSERVER GOLD CUP
1973   Apalachee (L. Piggott)

WOKINGHAM HANDICAP
1975   Boone's Cabin (L. Piggott)

EBOR HANDICAP
1958   Gladness (L. Piggott)
1961   Die Hard (L. Piggott)

UNDER NATIONAL HUNT RULES

THE GRAND NATIONAL
1953   Early Mist (B.
        Marshall)
1954   Royal Tan (B. Marshall)
1955   Quare Times (P.
        Taaffe)

KING GEORGE VI CHASE
1948   Cottage Rake (A.
        Brabazon)

CHELTENHAM GOLD CUP
1948   Cottage Rake (A.
        Brabazon)
1949   Cottage Rake (A.
        Brabazon)
1950   Cottage Rake (A.
        Brabazon)
1953   Knock Hard (T.
        Molony)

CHAMPION HURDLE
1949   Hatton's Grace (A.
        Brabazon)
1950   Hatton's Grace (A.
        Brabazon)
1951   Hatton's Grace (T.
        Molony)

**GLOUCESTERSHIRE
HURDLE**
1952   Cockatoo (Mr A. S.
        O'Brien)
1954   Stroller (P. Taaffe)

1955   (Div I) – Vindore (Mr
        A. S. O'Brien)
        (Div II) – Illyric (T. P.
        Burns)
1956   (Div I) – Boy's Hurrah
        (Mr A. S. O'Brien)
        (Div II) – Pelargos (Mr
        A. S. O'Brien)
1957   (Div II) – Saffron
        Tartan (T. P. Burns)
1958   (Div I) – Admiral Stuart
        (T. P. Burns)
        (Div II) – Prudent King
        (T. P. Burns)
1959   (Div I) – York Fair (T.
        P. Burns)

SPA HURDLE
1954   Lucky Dome (T. P.
        Burns)

BIRDLIP HURDLE
1955   Ahaburn (T. P. Burns)

NATIONAL HUNT CHASE
1949   Castledermot (Lord
        Mildmay)
1954   Quare Times (Mr J. R.
        Cox)

**NATIONAL HUNT
HANDICAP CHASE**
1952   Royal Tan (Mr A. S.
        O'Brien)

FRANCE

ON THE FLAT

PRIX DU JOCKEY CLUB
1983   Caerleon (P. Eddery)

PRIX DE L'ARC DE TRIOMPHE
1958   Ballymoss (A. Breasley)

1977   Alleged (L. Piggott)
1978   Alleged (L. Piggott)

GRAND CRITERIUM
1967   Sir Ivor (L. Piggott)

USA

ON THE FLAT

WASHINGTON DC INTERNATIONAL STAKES
1968   Sir Ivor (L. Piggott)

Appendix 3
Year-by-Year Irish Record

	RACES	MONEY	POSITION
1943	1	£74	—
1944	10	£1206	—
1945	14	£1710	19th
1946	16	£2360	18th
1947	21	£4725	5th
1948	21	£3779	15th
1949	35	£7659	5th
1950	52	£9435	2nd
1951	42	£7279	4th
1952	26	£7113	3rd
1953	24	£12196	2nd
1954	17	£2996	20th
1955	15	£2669	17th
1956	29	£5295	9th
1957	40	£15571	2nd
1958	21	£4097	14th
1959	52	£23793	1st
1960	11	£4248	11th
1961	28	£8104	6th
1962	47	£27743	2nd
1963	27	£14417	3rd
1964	30	£24857	3rd
1965	36	£48643	2nd
1966	24	£35423	3rd

1967	27	£29088	3rd
1968	28	£26607	2nd
1969	44	£80533	1st
1970	30	£90928	1st
1971	49	£58474	2nd
1972	48	£65059	1st
1973	41	£62413	2nd
1974	30	£43552	5th
1975	38	£71497	2nd
1976	31	£73969	3rd
1977	33	£192820	1st
1978	47	£144976	1st
1979	43	£233224	1st
1980	45	£193930	1st
1981	40	£218000	1st
1982	49	£232486	1st
1983	28	£203411	2nd
1984	42	£769478	1st
1985	21	£415888	2nd
1986	21	£134219	9th
1987	43	£474552	1st
1988	33	£623017	1st
1989	27	£150112	7th
TOTAL	1477	£4,863,625	

LANDMARK YEARS: His winnings topped the half million pound mark in 1970; the million pound in 1977; the two million pound in 1982; the three million pound in 1984; the four million pound in 1987. In money terms, he was the champion trainer on 13 occasions, finished 2nd 11 times and 3rd 6 times. He twice won more races than any other trainer.

Appendix 4
Memorable Seasons In Britain

UNDER NATIONAL HUNT RULES

	RACES	MONEY	POSITION
1948–49	6	£10869	5th
1952–53	5	£15515	1st
1953–54	8	£14274	1st
1954–55	8	£12426	2nd

ON THE FLAT

	RACES	MONEY	POSITION
1958	9	£67543	3rd
1962	2	£36891	9th
1966	8	£123848	1st
1968	5	£99631	2nd
1970	5	£162286	2nd
1972	11	£154719	2nd
1973	8	£112098	4th
1975	15	£73549	9th
1977	18	£439124	1st
1978	8	£155405	10th
1983	5	£306682	8th

Bibliography

Francis, Dick. *Lester: The Official Biography* (Michael Joseph, 1986 hardcover and Pan Books, 1987 paperback).

Francis, Dick. *The Sport of Queens* (Michael Joseph, 1976).

Herbert, Ivor and O'Brien, Jacqueline. *Vincent O'Brien's Great Horses* (Pelham Books, 1984).

Holland, Anne. *Grand National: The Official Celebration of 150 Years* (Macdonald Queen Anne Press, 1988).

Lee, Alan. *Cheltenham Racecourse* (Pelham Books, 1985).

MacGowan, Kenneth. *The Rock of Cashel* (Kamac Publications, 1985).

Mortimer, Roger with Nelligan, Tim. *The Epsom Derby* (Michael Joseph, 1984).

O'Donnell, Augustine. *Saint Patrick's Rock* (The Cashel Press, 1979).

Slattery, Finbarr. *Horse Racing* (Killarney Race Committee, 1984).

Tanner, Michael. *The Champion Hurdle* (Pelham Books, 1989).

Watson, S. J. *Between the Flags* (Allen Figgis, 1969).

Welcome, John. *The Cheltenham Gold Cup* (Constable, 1957).

Wilson, Julian. *100 Great Horses* (Macdonald Queen Anne Press, 1987).

Wilson, Julian. *Lester Piggott: The Pictorial Biography* (Macdonald Queen Anne Press, 1985).

Wright, Howard. *The Encyclopaedia of Flat Racing* (Robert Hale, 1986).

Also *Ruff's Guide to the Turf; Timeform Publications* (including Timeform Black Book and Racehorses); *The Irish Racing Annual; Raceform Note-Book; The Racing Post, The Sporting Life, The Irish Field, The European Racehorse.*

Index

Abdullah, Kalid 263
Aga Khan 17
Alleged 165, 210, 236, 237,
    238–40, 246, 250–1, 252, 255
Alydar's Best 284
Arkle 95, 96, 155
Asmussen, Cash 14, 265–71
Assert 240, 243, 246, 258, 273,
    277, 278–80, 281
Astrometer 35

Baerlein, Richard 216
Baeze, Braulio 231
Balding, Toby 98
Ballymoss 4, 5–6, 7–8, 14, 85, 86,
    98, 177, 178, 179–88
Barclay, Sandy 218, 219
Be My Guest 246
Bell, Mrs Alice Headley 215
Bicester, Lord 121
Blue Sail 139–40
Boucher 228, 231
Bougoure, Garnie 196, 200,
    205–6, 207, 268
Brabazon, Aubrey 34, 37, 77,
    83, 85, 87, 88, 89–92, 94–5, 96,
    97, 98, 101, 114, 150, 167, 173,
    256
Breasley, Arthur 'Scobie' 3–9, 86,
    179, 180, 185, 206, 207
Brigadier Gerard 231

Burmann, F. W. 191, 199, 204,
    205
Burns, T. P. 5, 14–16, 25, 58, 77,
    78, 79, 80–1, 85, 95, 96, 106,
    129, 135, 137, 152, 177, 178,
    179–80, 183, 184
Byrne, Capt. Michael 261–2

Carson, Willie 228
Castledermot 99, 100, 141
'Chamour Affair' 168, 175,
    190–204, 205, 289
Cheltenham: Gold Cup &
    Gloucestershire Hurdle
    Winners 74–102; Champion
    Hurdle 111–14, 178–80
Classic Thoroughbreds 25–7, 249,
    266, 294, 295
Collins, Con 47
Coolmore Stud 16, 17, 244, 245,
    246, 251
Corry, Dan 99
Cosgrove, Maxie 93
Cottage Rake 38, 40, 42–3, 66–8,
    75, 80, 85, 87, 88–9, 111,
    116–17, 157, 167

Dancing Brave 263
Danzatore 247
Derby, Epsom 207–9, 220–35,
    236–8, 259–63

Dick, Dave 151, 152
Dickinson, Michael 84–5, 248–9
Doyle, P. J. 135, 138
Dreaper, Tom 80, 127, 128, 155, 156
Drybob 34
Dunne, Ben 142

Early Mist 119, 120, 122, 123, 124, 125, 127–33, 135, 136, 145, 151, 152, 153, 154, 156
Eddery, Pat 13–14, 28, 47, 86, 115, 242, 247, 259–65, 266, 279, 280
El Gran Senor 9, 16, 27, 86, 91, 210, 246, 259–62, 281
Engelhard, Charles 212, 222, 224, 225–7, 290

Farrelly, Dr Brendan 190
Featherstonhaugh, Bob 163
Flannery, Edward 48
Flannery, Frank 47–8, 58
Flour, Bob 237
Francis, Dick 88

Galbraith, John 227, 228, 229, 230, 231, 233
Gladness 177–8, 179, 180, 181, 183, 185, 186–8
Glennon, T. P. (Pat) 207
Godswalk 246
Golden Fleece 130, 210, 213–14, 215, 243, 244, 246, 249, 265, 277, 278, 280
Golden Miller 95–7
Golden Temple 267, 270
Good Days 34
Gordon, Jimmy 161, 163
Grand National (Aintree) 119–33, 141–58
Griffin, Bob 129–30, 204, 209, 223
Griffin, 'Mincemeat' Joe 119–26, 127, 139, 145, 147, 148, 149, 196
Griffin, Peggy 120, 121, 122
Guest, Raymond 207, 210, 215, 216–17, 218
Gunning, Louis 106

Haigh, Paul 131, 132
Hancock, 'Bull' 215, 234, 235
Harris, George 241–2
Hartigan, Hubert 163
Hatton's Grace 40, 63, 64, 74, 75, 78–9, 80, 85, 88, 99–100, 101, 102, 103, 104, 105, 106, 110, 111, 112–13, 114, 115, 116, 157, 161, 167
Head, Alec 5, 13, 68
Heffner, Robert 242
Hern, Dick 208, 223
Hill, William 75, 109, 216
Hills, Barry 230
Hogan, P. P. 31–2, 47, 94, 252, 255–8
Holmes, Bert 106
Horgan, John 26
Hutchinson, Ron 206, 207
Hyde, Tim 97

Inman, Hoss 239

Keeneland Sales 9, 16, 19, 20, 21, 238, 240, 241, 249
Kennedy, Eddie 135
Keogh, Moya & Harry 99, 100, 101, 103–4, 111, 112, 114, 116, 118, 123–4, 135, 137, 141, 142, 143
Kinane, Michael 270
Knock Hard 99, 101, 103, 104, 105, 106, 107, 110, 111, 114, 116, 117, 118, 133, 135, 136, 137, 138, 140

Larkspur 207–9, 216
Lavery, Judge 191
Law Society 255
Lomond 247
Lucky Dome 129, 132, 135, 136, 137
Lukas, D. Wayne 12, 21, 22, 28

MacGinty, Tom 264
McCalmont, Major Victor 196
McCormack, John 54

McDonald, Billy 238–9, 250–5, 258
McGrath, Joe 47, 196
McGrath, Mrs Paddy 226
McGrath, Seamus 206, 264
McGregor, Sidney 185, 186
McNabb, Nat 76, 101, 103, 104–5, 106, 107–13, 115, 117, 118, 141–2, 182, 183
McShain, John 98, 180–1, 184, 186, 189, 206, 210
Magnier, Clem 79
Magnier, John 9, 16–20, 26, 61, 70, 240, 241, 244, 245, 246, 251, 259, 286
Mahmoud 214, 215
Maktoum brothers 247
Manitoulon 228, 229
Marinsky 253
Marshall, Bryan 85, 121, 127–8, 129, 130–3, 135, 136, 137, 145–7, 151, 152, 155, 156
Minstrel, The 19–20, 185, 210, 236–7, 246, 254, 261
Mohammed, Sheikh 247–8, 284
Moloney, Brian 165
Molony, Martin 63, 64, 65–6, 82, 85, 90, 91, 92, 94, 95, 96, 97, 100, 102, 103, 106, 113, 114, 115–16, 256
Molony, Pierce 134, 139
Molony, Tim 117–18, 137, 153
Moore, Dan & Joan 101
Moore, George 206
Mulcahy, John 233–5
Murless, Noel 210, 211, 232
Myerscough, Philip 258

Nagle, David 23
Niarchos, Stavros 255, 267
Nicholson, 'Frenchie' 264
Nicholson, Hedley 180, 181
Nijinsky 19, 20, 85, 165, 209, 210, 212, 213, 214, 215, 219, 220–5, 226, 227, 228, 231, 255
Norris, Paddy 69, 83–4
Northern Dancer 19, 225, 247, 249

O'Brien, Charles 164, 165, 171, 175, 286, 292–3
O'Brien, Dan 24, 28, 30, 35–6, 38–40, 41, 43, 47, 48, 51, 52–61, 62–3, 130, 255, 256, 293, 296
O'Brien, David 44, 86, 91, 175, 240, 258, 259, 269, 272–85, 286, 288, 291, 296
O'Brien, Dermot 17–18, 24–5, 28, 35, 40, 41, 44, 47, 49, 50, 63, 66, 67–8, 69, 72, 74–5, 76, 77, 78, 79, 80, 82–3, 135–6, 137, 138, 139, 140–2, 146, 148, 158, 162, 163–4, 167–9, 173, 177, 185
O'Brien, Donal 30, 37, 40, 41, 53, 62, 70, 161, 162
O'Brien, Elizabeth (McClory) 175–6, 287, 288, 289, 290, 291, 292
O'Brien, Helena 39, 40
O'Brien, Jackie 28–33, 180
O'Brien, Jacqueline 9, 68, 85, 117, 123–4, 147, 158, 170–6, 189, 190–1, 192, 194, 195, 196, 240, 281, 286, 288, 289
O'Brien, Jane (Myerscough) 175, 176, 288, 289, 290
O'Brien, Kathleen 39–40, 41, 53–4, 55, 56, 58
O'Brien, Noel 40
O'Brien, Pauline (Fogarty) 40, 52, 53–6, 57–9
O'Brien, Phonsie 9, 31, 40, 54, 57, 65, 70, 72, 74, 79, 80, 81–2, 86, 103, 106, 115–16, 117, 135, 136, 139, 142, 143–4, 145, 146, 167–9, 173, 189, 199, 205, 222, 268, 288
O'Brien, Susan (Magnier) 72–3, 165, 175, 176, 286, 287–8
O'Brien, Vincent Dr: secrets of success, views on 3–9, 11–20, 236–49, 254–7, 262–3; childhood days 39–62; amateur jockey 24, 63–4; early days training 23, 28–38, 64–5; Cheltenham 74–119, 178, 180; Liverpool 119–33, 141–58;

licence revoked 134–41; Chamour affair 168, 175, 190–204, 205, 289; move to Ballydoyle 161–9; marriage to Jacqueline 170–6; begins training on the Flat 177–88; Classic races 205–85; Classic thoroughbreds 25–7, 249, 266, 294, 295; family man 286–93; final assessment 294–7
O'Callaghan, Maurice 162, 218
O'Grady, Willie 107
O'Hehir, Michael 150–1
O'Neill, Jonjo 47
O'Neill, Tony 46, 52
O'Sullevan, Peter 5, 6, 89, 296–7
O'Sullivan, Danny 49, 71, 162
O'Sullivan, Jimmy 49–50, 66, 71–2
Oxx, John Jun. 271
Oxx, John Sen. 207

Paget, Miss Dorothy 36, 90, 117
Persse, 'Atty' 131
Phillips, Michael 217, 264–5
Piggott, Lester 7, 8, 9, 10–12, 14, 28, 86, 115, 122, 179, 183, 185, 186, 206, 210, 211, 212–14, 215–16, 217, 219, 220–4, 228, 229, 230, 231, 233, 238, 245, 266
Piggott, Susan 10
Pincay, Lafitte 232
Pollet, Etienne 224
Powell, Brendan 47
Pratt, Tom 239
Prendergast, Paddy ('Darkie') 47, 86, 106, 139, 140, 183, 206, 207, 261, 297
Prince Regent 95–7, 155
Prix de l'Arc de Triomphe 213, 230–1, 236–40
Purtell, Jack 207

Quare Times 121, 130, 131, 149, 151–4, 155, 156, 157

Reid, John 270
Rheingold 230, 231

Richards, Sir Gordon 3, 4, 182, 207
Roberto 210, 227, 228–31, 232, 233
Roberts, Monty 238
Roche, Christy 86, 261, 269, 272–3, 277, 278, 279, 280, 281, 282
Rogers, Tim 244, 245
Royal Tan 99, 100, 119, 122, 123, 124, 125, 128, 131, 134, 135, 136, 139, 142, 143–8, 149, 151, 153, 154, 156–7, 196

St Martin, Yves 13, 208, 221, 265
Sadler's Wells 16, 246, 251
Sangster, Robert 9, 16, 21, 22–3, 26, 27, 47, 70, 85, 86, 236–40, 241, 242–9, 250, 251, 253, 255, 257, 278, 280, 284
Santa Claus 4
Saratogan 294–5
Scott, Brough 263, 297
Seattle Dancer 21–3, 87, 269, 271
Secreto 9, 86, 91, 259–62, 273, 280, 281–3
Sellwood, Neville 207, 208
Sir Ivor 210, 211, 212–13, 214, 215, 216, 217, 218, 219, 224, 228, 231
Sleator, Paddy 79
Smurfit, Dr Michael 26
Solford 35–7
Stack, Christy 68–9
Stack, Tommy 242
Stafford-King-Harman, Sir Cecil 196
Starkey, Greville 263
Stirling-Stuart, Major 'Cuddie' 93
Stoneham, Desmond 266, 279
Storm Bird 240–3
Stroller 178, 179
Swinburn, Walter 263

Taaffe, Pat 78, 85, 130, 131, 135, 138, 150, 151–3, 154–7
Taafe, Toss 152, 154, 157
Taylor, Charles 296
Taylor, E. P. 225

Teapot II 125, 150
Thatch 235
Thompson, Jack 207
Triptych 284
Try My Best 246
Turnell, Bob 82

Vaughan, Dr 'Otto' 93, 94
Vickerman, Frank 30, 31, 32–3,
  34, 35, 38, 42–3, 94, 97, 98, 180
Vigors, Tim 191, 244

Walwyn, Fulke 117, 142

Walwyn, Peter 264
Ward, Liam 85, 211, 215, 224
Weld, Dermot 14
White, Sir Gordon 252
Williamson, Bill 206, 227–8, 229,
  231
Windfields Farm 225, 296
Wing, Morny 114
Winter, Fred 117, 151, 152, 153,
  168, 179
Wylie, Judge W. E. 139, 140

York Fair 180